terra incognita

Terra Incognita as a series seeks to open a "thinking space" between the abandonment of politics often associated with postmodernism and the unreconstructed faith in politics which has characterized many modern emancipatory projects. Both of these positions function as grand narratives which circumscribe both theoretical and practical possibilities. In doing so, they have discouraged the thinking through of uncertainty.

Encompassing a range of theoretical and disciplinary approaches, the studies in *Terra Incognita* attempt to disrupt this opposition, expressing resistance, not only to "grand narratives," but to any abstractions or conceptual frames which enact closure. The series probes how Western societies reconfigure themselves in currents flowing within and beyond their borders. Of particular interest are the theatres of struggle involving relationships with indigenous peoples, equality-seeking movements and state-fragmenting nationalist movements.

Configuring Gender

EXPLORATIONS IN THEORY AND POLITICS

Barbara L. Marshall

Configuring Gender

EXPLORATIONS IN THEORY AND POLITICS

Barbara L. Marshall

broadview press

Canadian Cataloguing in Publication Data

Marshall, Barbara L., 1957-
    Configuring gender: explorations in theory and politics
Includes bibliographical references and index.
ISBN 1-55111-094-6
1. Sex role. 2. Sexism. I. Title.

HQ1075.M377   2000   305.3   C00-930045-7

Broadview Press Ltd. is an independent, international publishing house, incorporated in 1985.

North America:
P.O. Box 1243, Peterborough, Ontario, Canada K9H 7H5
3576 California Road, Orchard Park, NY, USA 14127
TEL: (705) 743-8990; FAX: (705) 743-8353; E-MAIL: customerservice@broadviewpress.com

United Kingdom:
Turpin Distribution Services Ltd., Blackhorse Rd., Letchworth, Hertfordshire SG6 3HN
TEL: (1462) 672555; FAX (1462) 480947; E-MAIL: turpin@rsc.org

Australia:
St. Clair Press, P.O. Box 287, Rozelle, NSW 2039
TEL: (02) 818 1942; FAX: (02) 418 1923

www.broadviewpress.com

Broadview Press gratefully acknowledges the support of the Book Publishing Development Program, Ministry of Canadian Heritage, Government of Canada.

PRINTED IN CANADA

Contents

Acknowledgements

Many, many people — family, friends, colleagues, students — have facilitated the completion of this book. While I cannot possibly name them all, a few must be singled out for special thanks:

• Claude Denis, dear friend and co-editor of the series, both suggested that I write this, and made sure that I did. That he set the bar impossibly high with his book didn't help. (Merci, mon ami!)

• Susan Knabe was not only an able research assistant, but a brilliant 'discussant' from whom I learned much.

• Students in my classes at Trent University have endured, with good humour and tough questions, some of the preliminary working out of these ideas. I would especially like to thank the students in my fourth-year seminar on gender who helped me 'test run' the manuscript.

• Deborah Parnis, Alan Law, Joan Sangster, Marg Hobbs, and Alena Heitlinger all read and commented on various bits and pieces, and sharpened my thoughts by doing so.

• For suggesting references, loaning me books, and/or providing me with unpublished or not-yet-published material, thanks to Suzie Young, Winnie Lem, Wendy Pearson, Greta Hofmann-Nemiroff, Linda Trimble, and Joanna Everitt.

• Staff at a number of libraries assisted me in locating materials. I would especially like to thank the interlibrary loans staff at the Trent University library and Andrea Trudel, formerly at the Canadian Women's Movement Archives at the University of Ottawa.

• The "Learnerds" provided me with good company, good questions, good laughs and lots of encouragement.

• The Friday beer gals gave some shape to my weeks, and reminded me to stop talking in my "professor voice" sometimes.

• Michael Harrison and everyone at Broadview tolerated the inevitable delays and made the publication process as pleasant as it could possibly be.

• Judy Pinto continued to keep me organized and made my life easier in many ways.

• Yiannis and Lucy continued to let me live with them despite the neglect of household duties and crabbiness that often accompanies writing.

• I would also like to acknowledge the wonderful community of feminist researchers and writers, both in Canada and abroad, some of whom I have met, but most of whom I haven't. That we disagree on many things does not dull, but rather hones our critical edge.

• Last, but certainly not least, I am grateful to the Social Sciences and Humanities Research Council of Canada, which provided me with the funds necessary to complete this work.

This book is dedicated to Lucy,
who couldn't wait until it was finished.

Introduction

From an advertisement for a computer game called "Gender Wars":

> *"Who says the sexes are equal? Years of difference have resulted in the ultimate gender war. It is not an issue of politics. It is not an issue of race. It is an issue of sex, so choose yours wisely. Annihilate all males... or females... you decide. The war between men and women has raged uncontrollably for over 2 centuries. Now, after a period of 'political correctness' and equality they've completely split up. In this top down shoot 'em up, you choose to take the side of either men or women. With your choice of 13 missions within each sector, you fight for victory in the war of the sexes."*

(www.gtgames.com/games/genderwars)

From an on-line review of this game:

> *"Pick a sex from a dazzling array of choices, either male or female."*

(www.charm.net/~wizards/computershow/reviews)

This little gem from cyberspace encapsulates some of the contradictory trends in the vernacular of gender. Is it just a more sophisticated word for sex, one that necessarily invokes 'political correctness'? How "dazzling" an array of choices can we take "either male or female" to be? Just what constitutes "common knowledge" about gender at the *fin-de-siècle* is puzzling. On the one hand, we're told that men and women are more equal than ever, and that it's time to call a truce in the "gender wars" (the updated term for the battle of the sexes). On the other hand, we're told that men and women inhabit two different cultures, speak two different languages, and perhaps even come from two different planets.

This book is about the concept of gender and its travels through academic and political contexts over the last few decades. 'Gender' has become a fairly standard concept in the social sciences as a marker of the social and cultural elaboration of sexual difference.[1] However, 'gender,' and its invariably complicated relationship to 'sex,' is not just a matter of academic concern, but has more general currency. Gender has not only been established as a central analytic concept in contemporary social analysis, but it has become part of our everyday vocabulary and part of the fabric of our everyday lives. Search any database using 'gender' as a keyword, and you will come up with thousands of references on a myriad of topics. Newspapers, magazines, television programs, and everyday conversations use the concept of gender, whether they name it as such or not. 'Gender' has become something of a portmanteau for anything relating to sexual difference.

One dictionary of sociology (Jary and Jary, 1991: 254) distinguishes between "common" and "sociological" usages of the term gender. The former, they suggest, refers simply to the distinction between males and females based on anatomical sex. We have all encountered this everyday usage, perhaps by checking a box labelled "M" or "F" on some bureaucratic form that asks for your gender. In the natural sciences, 'gender' is sometimes used as a simple euphemism for 'sex,' as witnessed by a recently published article in the *Canadian Journal of Physiology and Pharmacology* which seeks to shed light on the "Role of Gender and Vascular Endothelium in Rat Aorta Response to 17 Beta-Estradiol." The sociological usage of 'gender,' however, describes "a social division frequently based on, but not necessarily coincidental with, anatomical sex" (Jary and Jary, 1991: 254).[2] However, as ensuing chapters will demonstrate, the

---

1   This might be taken as a 'weak' or 'minimal' definition of gender.

2   That this distinction between the common and sociological usages of gender is now widely accepted by sociologists does not mean that it is consistently applied. A couple of years ago, my daughter Lucy got a kitten for her birthday. She really wanted a "girl kitten" and picked the cutest one of the litter, but it, on closer inspection, was equipped with male genitalia. Undaunted, she refused to succumb to the whims of biology, proclaimed the kitten to be a girl anyway, and christened the new member of the family 'Liz.' For Lucy, 'gendering' the kitten was an unproblematic act of simple declaration — of naming it so — and unlike the adults in the household, she consistently used 'she' and 'her' in

distinction between and the relationship between 'sex' and 'gender' are questions that are far from resolved.

Raymond Williams has noted in *Keywords* that problems of a term's meanings can only be explored through an analysis of the problems it is used to discuss (1983: 17). What I hope to demonstrate in this book is that how we talk about gender and what we take it to mean continue to be bound up with the substantive social issues with which we are engaging, and with the normative frameworks we bring to bear on those issues.[3] When I say "we" here, I do not just mean sociologists, or feminists, or any particular sorts of intellectuals who may claim authority to talk about such things. 'Gender' has taken up residence in the public consciousness and is one of the lenses through which we seek to understand ourselves, our everyday lives, and the public issues of the day. As Doyle McCarthy suggests: "that the social reality of gender — as a powerful collective category and a social fact that has entered our political lives, our professional discourse (scientific, medical, legal, etc.), and our everyday discursive lives — is undisputed. The collective awareness of the distinct sociocultural roles of men and women ... and so on, is a powerful contemporary social fact. Wherever one stands on the value of that fact, it is a fact all the same" (1996: 102–3).

A number of broad-scale social changes are implicated here — the rise of feminism as a social movement, the development of widespread public education and increased literacy, and the increasingly media-saturated character of modern life stand as some important and related

---

reference to Liz. Adults, including the veterinarian, found this cute and funny, and generally winked or rolled their eyes as they 'pretended' that the kitten was female. A few months later, I was sitting at the picnic table with a couple of colleagues who were visiting after a conference. The partner of one of my colleagues was expecting their first child, and another colleague inquired as to whether or not they knew the 'gender' of the baby yet. No one suggested, as in the case of Liz, that they might decide in advance what gender they wanted, and then declare it so! According to the dictionary distinction between 'common' and 'sociological' understandings of gender, my colleague the sociologist was slipping into the former, while my six-year-old daughter seemed to have a grasp on the sociological sense of the word.

3 It is precisely these normative frameworks, which often remain unexamined, that distinguish between feminist and non-feminist critiques of the term 'gender.'

instances. These, in turn, may be connected to other broad changes, such as those in economic structures, family forms, and political systems. All of these shifts have been, and continue to be, central to sociological analysis, as are the social origins of the concepts and ideas that organize the way we think about things. The concept of gender is crucial here. 'Natural' differences of sex once thought to be beyond the purview of the social have been de-naturalized and politicized, and academic concepts and explanatory frameworks (such as those of sociology and psychology) have become part of "common" knowledge. One of the things that distinguishes the social sciences as an intellectual endeavour is the way in which its analytical concepts become part of people's explanatory frames, and thus transform that which we study. Anthony Giddens calls this the "double hermeneutic": "the concepts and theories invented by social scientists ... circulate in and out of the social world they are coined to analyse ... (T)he concepts of the social sciences are not produced about an independently constituted subject-matter, which continues regardless of what these concepts are. The 'findings' of the social sciences very often enter constitutively into the world they describe" (1987: 19–20). The trajectory of 'gender' as a sociological concept serves as an excellent example of this double hermeneutic, reminding us of sociology's complex relationship to the social world we study.

My own academic career coincides neatly with that of the career of gender as a concept in sociology. I came to sociology and feminism at about the same time, and they have always been interwoven for me. Thanks to the intrepid feminist sociologists who preceded me and my peers, carving out gender as a legitimate area of sociological concern, I have had the opportunity to focus my academic career around the sociology of gender. Before women's studies programs were firmly established, sociology was one of the few programs that could provide a space for feminist work — this is due in no small part to the very sociological nature of 'gender' as the central concept in feminist analysis, and to the important role that feminist sociologists played in the development of women's studies. But it also relates to the very public nature of sociology as a discipline — the embeddedness of sociological analysis in its political and social milieu. 'Gender' has, in large part, been the mediating concept between the political interests of feminism and the intellectual interests of sociology.

This book might best be construed as part of an ongoing conversation between feminism and sociology (not that the two are entirely different species!) that I have been participating in for some years now. I have always thought of feminist theory as a robust form of critical social theory. As Craig Calhoun summarizes it, critical theory is not so much a "theoretical school" as an "interpenetrating body of work which demands and produces critique" in four important senses, all of which are defining characteristics of feminist theory:

a) a critical engagement with the theorist's contemporary social world, recognizing that the existing state of affairs does not exhaust all possibilities, and offering positive implications for social action

b) a critical account of the historical and cultural conditions on which the theorist's own activity depends

c) a continuous critical re-examination of the constitutive categories and conceptual frameworks of the theorist's understanding, including the historical construction of those frameworks

d) a critical confrontation with other works of social explanation that not only establishes their good and bad points, but shows the reasons behind their blind spots and misunderstandings and demonstrates the capacity to incorporate their insights on stronger foundations. (1995: 35)

What distinguishes *feminist* critical theory is, of course, its focus on gender in all four of these senses of critique. With respect to the first, feminist engagements with the contemporary social world emphasize the social construction of gender, identifying the many ways in which gender difference — usually manifested as inequality — is produced, experienced, regulated, and resisted, and suggest how prevailing modes of gender organization might be transformed. In the second sense, socio-historical shifts in the gender order that permit particular ways of thinking and theorizing about gender are of central concern. For example, the widespread entry of women into paid work, the adoption of 'official' policies of gender equality by most Western nations and the creation of spaces for feminist work in the academy are all concrete socio-historical changes that have transformed both the questions and the conditions of feminist social inquiry. In the third sense, feminist theorists continually reinvent their vocabulary — sex, gender, sex-roles, gender-roles, sex/gender system, patriarchy, gender-identity, gender order, gender trouble — as the limitations of previous conceptual apparatuses become apparent. In the fourth sense, feminists' engagement with other types of social explanation (such as Marxism or liberal theory or deconstruction) have centred on their "blind spots" with respect to gender. Framing all of these aspects of critique is the manner in which gender, as originally taken up by white, Western feminists, has been challenged as increasingly diverse voices enter the conversation.

But, it is *gender* as a focus (or as Seyla Benhabib [1989] puts it, "a problem horizon") that defines the feminist critical project. It is in the spirit of this critical project that I am undertaking a critical examination of 'gender' itself as a constitutive category, not only in feminist social theory but also in recent political debates. That the very term 'gender' has functioned as a lightning-rod for a number of different debates — both theoretical and political, both feminist and anti-feminist — is suggestive. I outline the key issues that have emerged from these debates, and argue that although gender has merit as analytic concept, it needs to be rethought in terms of its logic-in-use. It is now common to interrogate theory and politics from a 'gender perspective,' or through a 'gender lens.' However, if we accept that 'gender' is socially constructed, we must also engage in a reciprocal sort of interrogation, asking what such investigations can tell us about gender itself — as a social relationship and as an analytic category. Such an interrogation provides the overall framing for this book.

I begin, in Chapter One, with a review of the 'mainstreaming' of gender. Here I survey some of the descriptive, explanatory, and strategic uses of 'gender' and track the ways in which the sociological elaboration of gender has not been entirely successful in overcoming either the conflation of sex and gender or the conflation of gender and 'women.' In some ways, this is a tendency inherited from the tradition of classical sociological engagements with 'modernity,' but it is being reconstituted in novel ways in some contemporary work. I also look briefly at gender mainstreaming in public policy documents and general-interest books to demonstrate that the initial feminist optimism about gender as a de-essentializing and politically enabling concept has not always been borne out.

Chapter Two examines some theoretical critiques of the sex/gender distinction and of 'gender' as a core concept in feminism. Although academic postmodernism has contributed to a destabilization of overly dichotomous and generalizing conceptions of gender, an equally (if not more) important impetus has been the political failure of such understandings of gender to illuminate the complex material realities of sexuality, race, and class as they are constitutive of gender categories.

Chapter Three shifts the focus from 'gender' to 'women' as the latter have been represented in a specific political context: the relationship between feminism and the state in English Canada since the early 1970s. Here I wish to draw out the implications of politicizing gender and illustrate some of the complexities of constructing 'women' as a political constituency while simultaneously recognizing their diversity. Framed by a critique of liberal individualism, this analysis demonstrates that a tension between universal and particular is internal as well as external to feminism, and has implications for understanding 'identity politics' and the role of social movements more generally.

Chapter Four looks at the politicization of gender from a different perspective. Here, I am interested in the ways in which 'gender' has become a pejorative term in 'dissident feminist,' anti-feminist, and conservative politics. Criticized for either overemphasizing or underemphasizing sexual difference, 'gender' is singled out by critics of feminism as an affront to individualism. In doing so, they crystallize a number of unresolved questions regarding feminist understandings of gender as a critique of masculine modernity.

Chapter Five draws some of the issues raised in previous chapters into a larger context, examining the ways in which gender is continually reconstructed in global processes of economic and political change. The analysis here demonstrates that gender is integral to our shifting understanding of nations, states, and 'good citizens,' and that these, reciprocally, shape our understanding and experience of 'gender,' but not in any immediately predictable or determinable fashion. The contingency of constructing gender interests in differing contexts underscores the 'historicity' of gender.

In conclusion, I attempt to reassess the status of gender as both a theoretical and a political category. Taking the debates about 'gender' as exemplary of the broader legitimacy crisis of categorical identities, I suggest some strategies for reconfiguring our understanding of gender in a more contextualized and pragmatic way. Here I argue that far more attention needs to be paid to the relationship between abstract concepts and their concrete manifestations, and that feminists must be willing to work with gender conceptualized at different levels of abstraction.

Finally, a note to the reader. Every author has a reader in mind during the writing. I have envisioned my reader as a fellow-traveller, one who accepts the legitimacy and importance of feminist analysis, and is concerned with deepening and extending its insights. Specifically, I have written this with my senior students in sociology and women's studies in mind. These are fourth-year undergraduate students who have familiarity (usually through previous coursework) with the main contours of feminist theory and the key empirical manifestations of gender inequality in contemporary societies, and are interested in further critical inquiry into the various contexts and categories of feminist analysis. For the most part, they are interested in practical questions, so I have privileged these over detailed examination of philosophical and theoretical debates. I hope that more advanced readers — graduate students and colleagues — as well as readers in disciplines other than sociology and women's studies will also profit from some of the questions posed here. Such readers, should they need convincing that 'gender' is a concept urgently in need of examination, may want to begin by reading Chapter Four.

Alongside my assumptions about readers, I have written this with the assumption that it will not be the sole text for a course, nor read in isolation from other contemporary work dealing with similar themes. Thus, I have deliberately made this a short book. I make no attempt here to provide an encyclopedic review of theoretical and political debates, nor do I aspire to provide the definitive genealogy of gender as a concept. As such, I employ footnotes to provide pointers to useful literature for those who wish more background or details on a number of issues. In the end, I hope that the reader will treat this book not as a 'summing up' of the pitfalls and promises of gender analysis, but as an open-ended argument regarding the various uses to which such a concept can be put. I must stress the adjective 'open-ended' in the previous claim: to attempt closure, however temporary, on questions that continue to unfold on a daily basis is certainly futile.

ONE

Mainstreaming Gender

As its title suggests, this chapter will recount some of the ways in which the concept of gender has been 'mainstreamed' — in other words, the ways in which it has become a commonly accepted term and a standard point of reference in addressing an important dimension of social difference and inequality. The extent to which it has become a contested concept requires that we inquire into some of the various meanings with which it has been invested. It is impossible to understand certain of the current debates about gender without exploring some of its history, particularly in terms of its importance as an anchoring concept in feminist sociology.[1] I will begin with a brief review of the rather one-sided story that classical sociology had to tell about men and women, and then recount some of the ways that more recent sociology has revised that story. In doing so, I hope to convey some of the reasons why the sex/gender distinction was significant for feminists, why 'gender' has been such an important concept for feminist sociology, and why its incorporation into the academic mainstream has produced some rather mixed results. Of course, the concept of 'gender' has not only been adopted by academics

---

1 Although sociology is my initial frame of reference here, it is by no means the only discipline for which such a story could be told. As will become evident, 'gender' has been taken up as the basis of feminist work in an increasingly transdisciplinary way, and no discipline has been immune from debates about the nature and purpose of 'gender' as an analytic concept. See, for example Coole (1988) on political theory, Moore (1994) on anthropology, Scott (1988) on history and Unger (1998) on psychology.

— it has also become important in public policy and in popular litera-
tures. A brief review of these contexts will demonstrate that, despite the
potential of gender-based analysis to avoid essentialism and determinism
when addressing sexual difference, the language of 'gender' has been used
to express some rather essentialist and determinist notions. My purpose
in this chapter, then, is not to provide a complete or definitive account of
a semantic shift from 'sex' to 'gender,' but to look at what 'gender' is being used to say in different contexts so that we might better understand
the ensuing debates about its theoretical and political efficacy.[2]

Gender and Sociology: A Romance

ro-mance (n. *rō mans'*)
n.   1.   a novel or other prose narrative depicting heroic or mar-
            vellous deeds, pageantry, romantic exploits, etc. usu. in a
            historical or imaginary setting
       2.   a medieval narrative, orig. one in verse and in a Romance
            language, treating of heroic, fantastic or supernatural
            events, often in the form of allegory
       3.   a made-up story, usu. full of exaggeration or fanciful in-
            vention
       4.   a romantic spirit, sentiment or the like
       5.   romantic aura, setting, character or quality
       6.   a love affair
                              Random House Webster's College Dictionary

My account of the relationship between gender and sociology as a 'romance' reflects multiple aspects of this dictionary definition. Any narrative account of the trajectory of a disciplinary concept requires a good deal
of invention and imagination, as most of the concepts we work with are
'fanciful inventions.' Like other sorts of story-telling, sociology's construction of itself as a discipline contains great adventures and historical settings,
heroes and villains (not to mention helpless maidens), and like all good
stories, there's usually a moral. Sociological story-telling is often allegori-

---

2   Other useful examinations of 'gender,' although with different emphases and
     intents, include Delphy (1993), Flax (1986), Haraway (1991), Harding (1986),
     Hawkesworth (1997), Lorber (1994), Nicholson (1994) and Oakley (1997).

cal, in the sense of creating characters (such as men and women) who are intended to represent more abstract meanings and moral arrangements that the story is attempting to convey. No less so is it a romance in the more commonly used sense of the word as designating a sort of relationship. 'Gender' as an idea and as an analytic category did not, properly speaking, originate with sociology. Thus, sociology (as an institution) has had a 'relationship' with gender, and as with all relationships, both parties to it have been changed through the experience. Gender (like most concepts and categories we use in the course of our analytic adventures) spills over and forces a rethinking of the disciplinary frame. It has also blurred the boundaries between the intellectual and political, as it is 'gender' that has been at the heart of the intersections of feminism and sociology. This is not to suggest that all that is conducted under the name of the 'sociology of gender' can properly be thought of as feminist. As we shall see, some feminists argue that the critical force of 'gender' has been sacrificed by its incorporation into 'traditional' disciplines such as sociology. At the risk of pushing the analogy beyond its usefulness, the course of the romance has not always run smoothly, but the relationship endures. And, as with most relationships, there are different stories to be told by the different partners. I will first look at what has, by and large, passed as the 'official' disciplinary story, which begins with classical sociology.

The story of sociology as a 'modern' discipline that I learned as a student was a typical story, and, when it comes down to it, a very short one: out of the social and political ferment of the nineteenth century, Marx, Durkheim, and Weber came riding on their post-Enlightenment horses to bring us their respective visions of a common humanity on the cusp of a brave new world. Rarely acknowledged in the disciplinary history is the existence of vigorous women's movements that predate sociology and were often concerned with fundamentally similar issues.[3] Women

---

3 There is now a substantial body of literature which has underscored the importance of feminism in the eighteenth and nineteenth centuries, with respect to both its significance in social and political changes and its contributions to social analysis. This literature underscores the fact that sociology's *institutional* history is not its complete story. See, for example, Arni and Müller (1997), Gerhard (1999), Hoecker-Drysdale (1992), LeGates (1996), McDonald (1994), Spender (1982), Sydie (1987), Taylor (1983), Wobbe (1998). It is worth noting that

occupied a contradictory and ambivalent position in relation to the 'modern' as it has been sociologically interpreted, particularly in the sense of modernity as representing a gradual liberation of the individual from the bonds of tradition.[4] Women were cast as unable to fully transcend these bonds, and thus figured most frequently as a 'strategic absence'[5] in classical sociology. This has had profound consequences for how sociology developed its understandings of itself and of the 'modern' world — and these two understandings are intricately interrelated. As a discipline whose roots can be placed firmly in the Enlightenment privileging of mind over body, reason over superstition, and 'progress' over tradition, early sociology was remarkably resistant to a fully sociological understanding of women — and by extension, of men.

The late eighteenth and early nineteenth centuries saw a radical change in our understanding of the male/female distinction. As Thomas Laqueur argues in his historical investigations into the 'making of sex' (1990), the entrenchment of sexual dimorphism — the articulation of radical physiological differences between the sexes — had more to do with social and political currents of the time than any 'new' scientific discoveries. Sex, it seems, occupied a problematic position at the boundary of the natural and the social. As taken up by classical sociology, "the mind/body split rather than neutralizing sex difference had the opposite effect. There was

---

there are some signs that the discipline is recognizing the importance of early feminist thought. For example, Irving Zeitlin's *Ideology and the Development of Sociological Theory* (1994, 1997) has, in subsequent editions, added Mary Wollstonecraft, Harriet Martineau, and Harriet Taylor to the 'canon.' The "History of Sociology" section at the 1998 World Congress of Sociology had a session devoted to the work of Martineau. Also noteworthy is Charles Lemert's (1993) encyclopedic text *Social Theory: The Multicultural and Classic Readings*, which expands the traditional scope of social theory in important ways to include early work on sex, race, and colonialism.

4   For a more detailed account of classical sociology's treatment of women, and the implications of this for the manner in which the discipline has developed, see B. Marshall (1994).

5   By 'strategic absence,' I mean that what is often important in what a theory is saying can be found in what it is *not* saying. With respect to women, this means that we can glean much about a theory's conception of them by examining the their dis-locations or absences from important contexts.

a tendency to focus on the female, reproductive body in contrast to the masculine, rational mind ..." (Sydie, 1994: 118). Thus, 'manliness' could be understood as a bourgeois virtue to be achieved through active mastery over the natural — through the triumph of reason over passion, the hallmark of modernity (Jackson and Scott, 1997: 555). Women, on the other hand, were irretrievably embodied. They lay outside of the modern, connected to it through their relation to men. Subsequent feminist re-readings of the classics have highlighted the gendered nature of some of the characters portrayed. For Marx and Engels, women appeared as "wives and daughters" of the proletariat, the real historical actors (1872/ 1978: 488). Durkheim describes the old, unmarried woman, content with "a few devotional practices and a few animals to care for" (1897/1951: 215). For Weber, the 'gentler sphere' of emotion was for those who "couldn't bear the fate of the times like a man" (1919/1946: 155).

The gendered nature of modernity was not only apparent through the exclusion or marginalization of women in classical theory. For some theorists — notably, Durkheim and Simmel — gender differentiation was explicitly identified as integral to modernity. For Durkheim, it is a "morphological" difference — a categorical difference in classification — which marks the inequality of men and women. This morphological difference is the product of evolution. Men, once similar to women, evolved to become something different — social, mental, and moral human beings. In other words, they became modern. Given that women are inherently less social than men, they need less, and benefit less, from social regulation (1897/1951: 272). As Durkheim summarizes it, "the two sexes do not share equally in social life" (385). On his account, gender difference and inequality are the by-products of modernity.[6] Simmel[7] characterizes modernity in terms of the increasingly fragmented nature of 'sociation.' For him, "individuals necessarily move between a great number of social circles each of which only involves part of his personality" (Featherstone, 1991: 3). Women, unlike men, do not experience this fragmentation. They experience a greater 'unity of life' because their sex is

---

6 For an interesting reading of Durkheim, which places his work in the context of nineteenth-century French feminism, see Shope (1994).

7 On Simmel, see the collection edited by Guy Oakes (1984): also Felski (1995), Lichtblau (1989/90) and van Vucht Tijssen (1991).

always there — it is the thread tying all aspects of their existence to the body. Simmel at least explicitly identifies 'modernity' as masculine, even if it means he disallows a 'feminine' modernity. Simmel's account epitomizes the metaphysical exile of women from modernity that characterized classical sociological theory. That is, if the experience of modernity was encapsulated, for men, by their self-consciousness of differentiation and change, then women, quite simply, could not experience this.

Modernity was not just a metaphysical problem — it was also represented by a series of institutional reconfigurations. Most significant here were increasingly distinct boundaries between the public and private realms, with most sociological interest directed toward the former. This is well-illustrated by the overwhelming emphasis on capitalism, industrialization, secularization, and urbanization as the hallmarks of modernity. But the public/private distinction was (and continues to be) conflated with a masculine/feminine distinction, so that women were not seen to partipate in, or even experience, the effects of the institutional dimensions of modernity that were of such interest to sociology. Nor was it recognized that these institutional transformations were profoundly gendered, creating newly gendered characters (such as workers, citizens, and consumers). Sexual difference was absolute, located in the domestic/private, and hence located in women. Given that the starting point for classical sociology was to theorize the individual as social — that is as constituted only within society and social relations — it should have been able to embrace both public and private spheres as wholly social in their constitution, but it did not (Yeatman, 1986). The public/private dualism, instead, became expressed as a whole set of familiar dualisms — universal/particular, rationality/emotion, instrumental/expressive, economic/familiar. This set of dualisms was encapsulated through the distinct difference, understood as a dichotomy, between 'masculine' and 'feminine,' and was embodied by the sexual division of labour. Women's very subjectivity was construed as being of a fundamentally different order than men's and it certainly wasn't that of the 'modern' subject. As Denise Riley (1988) suggests, the "differing temporalities" of the category of "women," in relation to the emerging categories of "body," "soul," "society," and "the social" in post-Enlightenment may be read as a "history of an increasing sexualization, in which female persons become held to be virtually saturated with their sex" (8).

The introduction of 'gender' as a key concept in sociology and the subsequent growth of feminist scholarship that has taken up gender as its 'problem horizon' have gone a long way to revise the story told by earlier sociologists. If you look up gender in almost any contemporary guide to sociology, you will find some reference to its distinction from 'sex.' As Ann Oakley put it in the text which was to enshrine the distinction in sociology: "'Sex' is a biological term: 'gender' a psychological and cultural one" (1972: 158).[8] Here, she is drawing on the work of psychoanalyst Robert Stoller, whose book *Sex and Gender* (1968) has the following to say:

> Gender is the amount of masculinity or femininity found in a person, and obviously, while there are mixtures of both in many humans, the normal male has a preponderance of masculinity and the normal female a preponderance of femininity. (8–9)

Stoller developed this distinction between 'sex' and 'gender' from his work with (to use his framing) the *ab*normal. The sex/gender distinction was first introduced in the medical and psychoanalytic literature of the mid-1950s,[9] in the context of the treatment of individual pathologies — intersexuality and transsexualism. In this context, 'gender' was conceptualized as 'identity' — one's 'gender identity' was one's self-understanding, in a socio-psychological sense, as male or female. The medical/psychiatric problem of individuals for whom there was a lack of congruency between 'sex' and 'gender' (as identity) necessitated the distinguishing terms. As Bernice Hausman has argued convincingly:

> prior to the introduction of "gender" into twentieth-century discourse as a signifier of "social sex," "sex" was a signifier encoding both biological and social categories. "Gender" was no less operative in social relations, but it went unmarked as a separate aspect of being a sex. "Sex" came to refer solely to the

---

8 Jessie Bernard (1971) makes a similar distinction, also following Stoller, but Oakley is the most commonly cited sociological source.

9 Some date the use of 'gender' much earlier, such as Nellie Oudshoorn (1994), who suggests it was used by psychologists in the 1930s to describe psychological characteristics as distinct from physiological sex differences (cited in Oakley, 1997).

> biological realm when technology developed to the point that
> clinicians could routinely intervene at the level of (and there-
> fore change) physical signifiers of sex. (1995: 75)

As Hausman's argument suggests, just because 'gender' wasn't explicitly
identified, it doesn't mean that gender was not 'operative in social relations.' This is well-illustrated by the manner in which, historically, sociology's containment of women by their 'sex' has encoded all aspects of
their existence. A nascent conception of gender was subsumed within
sexual difference. A good part of the motivation for the feminist appro-
priation of the vocabulary of 'gender,' then, was to break this conflation
of the natural and the social. Feminist uses of the concept of gender, while
diverse, take their cue from Simone de Beauvoir's assertion that "one is
not born but becomes a woman" (1949/1961: 249). 'Gender,' as differentiated from biological sex, has been understood by feminists as socially
constructed, historically and culturally variable, and subject to reconstruction through conscious social and political action. That gender differences — understood as the differences *between* men and women — were
so clearly manifested as gender inequalities gave an urgency to the project
of their documentation as social constructions, not biological inevitabili-
ties. Such a perspective, though, was slow to emerge in the sociological
mainstream. Sociological interest in women, as it developed in mid-twen-
tieth-century sociology, still belied a distinct 'saturation' with their sex.
Contained, above all, in family sociology, women generally made appearances outside the family only as interesting social problems — for example, as the post-war "working mother." Yet a disciplinary vocabulary started
to develop which at least permitted the incorporation of women into the
realm of the social. Above all, the term "sex role"[10] became common,
including early usages by Parsons (1942) and Komarovsky (1946), and

---

10   The concept of 'role' was already well-established in the discipline. Connell (1987:
     47) suggests that formulations of the concept go back to at least the 1930s, and
     while different formulations vary in detail, most contain the key assumptions of
     (a) an analytic distinction between the individual person and the social posi-
     tion, and (b) actions or behaviours assigned to the position, which are deter-
     mined by specific social norms or expectations, and enforced through social
     sanctions.

by the late 1960s a considerable literature on "sex differences," "sex role socialization," and "sex stratification" had emerged.

By the mid-1970s, conceptual labels such as 'gender' and 'gender roles' were beginning to appear in the sociological literature, and were coexisting alongside the earlier terminology. A review article published in the *Annual Review of Sociology* in 1975, "Sex Roles in Transition: A Ten-Year Perspective," notes that: "The topic of gender roles is of relatively recent interest and has a somewhat confusing status. Different writers use the term differently, and it is necessary to distinguish among sex, sex identity, sex role, gender, gender identity, and gender role" (Lipmen-Blumen and Tickamyer, 1975: 302). The authors try to sort out these sometimes overlapping meanings by re-asserting Stoller's association of 'gender' with identity and self-identification, while talking about 'sex roles' as 'socially prescribed.' Thus, they suggest that to "understand the nature of gender roles, it is useful to view them as mediating factors between gender identity and sex role. Via gender roles, which develop out of gender identity, males and females are funnelled into what is socially defined as sex-appropriate behaviour" (ibid.: 303).[11] Unlike the identity-grounding nature of 'gender,' as it was understood in the psychological literature, the concept of 'sex role' is clearly intended to shift the focus to the social, with the individual invoked as the performer of a role:

> The study of sex roles concerns roles within all structured settings, the norms and rules governing role performance in these settings, the correlates of role location and performance, the special situation of deviant roles and those who occupy them, and the mechanics of role change. (ibid.)

Considerable emphasis, then, is given to 'sex role socialization,' and sexual inequality (to use the preferred terminology here) is discussed in terms of 'limitations of role choices,' 'marital roles,' and 'occupational roles.' Although the feminist movement is given credit for influencing

---

11 The presumption of heterosexuality as part and parcel of both 'gender' and 'sex roles' is evident, both in the author's inclusion of homosexuality in the category of 'intersexual disorders,' and in the application of 'gender' to encompass the traits which may be "identified as basic to a woman's identification as a *sexual female*" (Lipmen-Blumen and Tickamyer, 1975: 303; emphasis added).

and giving impetus to sociological investigations, the vocabulary of sociology predominated: sex becomes a 'differentiating variable,' a 'stratification variable,' a variable in 'social mobility,' a factor in 'status inconsistency.'

Feminist critiques of this framing were quick to appear. The terminology of 'sex roles,' in particular, was taken to task by feminists who were critical of the manner in which the concepts of 'role' and 'sex' were deployed (Eichler, 1985: 621). First, 'role theory' as such was tainted for many feminists by its functionalist heritage, and particularly for its association with the theory of Talcott Parsons (Stacey and Thorne, 1985: 307). Parsons treated the post-war domestic division of labour (in the white, American, middle-class nuclear family) as a natural consequence of 'role differentiation,' with men specializing in the 'instrumental' role and women specializing in the 'expressive' role, to which they were predisposed by their biological role in child-bearing.[12] The functional complementarity of male and female roles implied here suggests the critique that the concept of 'role' obscures questions of power and inequality. Critics frequently note that sociologists would never talk about 'class roles' or 'race roles.' Problematic, as well, was the implication, contained in the terminology of 'sex roles,' that social behaviours ('roles') are an unproblematic reflection of biology ('sex'). As Eichler (1980: 12) notes, 'sex roles' was likely the only widely used concept combining a biological variable with a culturally determined pattern in this way.[13] Finally, the entire conceptual apparatus of 'sex roles,' 'sex role stereotyping,' and 'sex role socialization' was seen as reifying a dynamic aspect of individual-society relationships. As Lopata and Thorne (1978: 720) argued, such terms were "often written and talked about as if they exist concretely rather

---

12 "In our opinion, the fundamental explanation of the fact that the bearing and early rearing of children established a strong presumptive primacy of the relation of mother to the small child and this in turn establishes a presumption that the man who is exempted from these biological functions should specialize in the alternative instrumental direction" (Parsons and Bales, 1955: 23).

13 To make her point here, she notes that there is no such term as 'race roles,' indicating that in this case "we do not explain different behavior patterns on the basis of race itself but rather in terms of a power differential which coincides with racial distinctions" (1980: 13).

than being analytic constructs." However, the shift from 'sex roles' to 'gender'[14] did not entirely solve these problems.

Feminist sociology insisted on gender as a fundamental dimension of social life and as a central analytic category within the discipline, without which the key interests of the discipline (such as work, politics, family, education, religion, and 'culture') could not be adequately understood. Gender was *everywhere* — in differentiated subjects and unequal allocations of social and economic resources. An important task in feminist sociology's insistence on the acknowledgement of the gendered dimensions of social life was to draw attention to aspects of the social that had been overlooked by mainstream sociology. Pathbreaking works such as Ann Oakley's *The Sociology of Housework* (1974) and Meg Luxton's *More Than a Labour of Love* (1980) insisted that domestic work, primarily done by women, was real work, and worthy of sociological attention. Pat and Hugh Armstrong's *The Double Ghetto* (1978) documented the gendered division of labour, both inside and outside the paid labour force. The list

---

14 While this shift was evident in feminist sociology, there continue to be contradictory trends in the organization of disciplinary knowledge as a whole. Sociological Abstracts is the main (although not only) resource for tracking the discipline over time. "Gender/genders" was introduced as an indexing term in 1972, but discontinued in 1985. "Gender differences" was used only from 1984 to 1985, "gender inequality" only for the year 1985. In 1989, Sociological Abstracts published a *Thesaurus of Sociological Indexing Terms* (Booth and Blair, 1989). If you look up "gender," you are directed instead to "sex," where you'll find the following note: "Use limited to *analyses of gender*. Do not confuse with Sexual Intercourse or Sexual Differences" (221; emphasis added). The entry on "sexual differences" will tell you that this term is used "in analyses in which a social problem or phenomenon is explained as a consequence or correlate of the differences between males and females. *These differences may be biological or stem from sex-role socialization*" (221; emphasis added). This would seem to be a rather pertinent distinction for sociologists, not to mention limiting in its exclusion of other possible explanations for 'difference' which are not neatly reducible to 'sex-role socialization.' The abstracts themselves are organized in sections that designate major fields of study. In 1973, a section called 'Feminist Studies' was introduced, which in 1986 became 'Feminist/gender studies.' This section continues to have two subfields: feminist/gender studies and sociology of gender and gender relations. What classifies an article or a book as one or the other is unclear from reviewing the abstracts.

of topics put onto the sociological agenda is a long one, but it is possible to single out a few: different experiences of (and returns from) education and employment; domestic violence; sexual assault, the portrayal of women in the media; the uneven impact of various social policies on women and men; the experience of separation and divorce, women's access (or lack thereof) to health services, child care, and other social services; and the treatment of women offenders in the criminal justice system. Feminist sociology has been concerned not simply with documenting gender difference, but with understanding how gender difference is constructed as social inequality. Feminist usages of gender, then, have always been bound up with exposing its relationship to power and status.

One of the central concepts used by feminists to explain the manifest differences in men's and women's social statuses was 'patriarchy.' While the term 'patriarchy' was in wide circulation in feminist work, debates about it among feminists were frequent, and reflected different conceptualizations of the roots of women's oppression by radical and socialist feminists (Franklin, 1996: xiv, see also Acker, 1989; Beechey, 1979; Fox, 1988; B. Marshall, 1994; Pollert, 1996; Rowbotham, 1981). Criticized by some for being too abstract, ahistorical, over-generalizing, and simplistic, its utility has been defended by others because of its political import in *problematizing* gender inequality. In its most sophisticated sociological theorization, patriarchy is defined by Walby as "a system of social structures and practices in which men dominate, oppress and exploit women" (1990: 20), and she identifies six key structures which constitute it: paid employment, household production, culture, sexuality, violence, and the state. In Walby's most recent book (1997), she uses 'forms of patriarchy' and 'gender regimes' as parallel terms, and focuses on the shifts from 'private patriarchy' or 'more domestic gender regimes' (characterized by the subordination of women by individual men in the home) to 'public patriarchy' or 'more public gender regimes' (characterized by the subordination of women within the paid workplace and the state). She argues that this strategy permits a complex understanding of how age, class, ethnicity, and region interact to produce varying degrees of gender inequality within different forms of patriarchy or gender regimes. For example:

> older women will be more likely than younger women to be
> involved in a more domestic gender regime. Women whose

> own occupations place them in higher socio-economic groups
> are more likely to be in a more public form, Women of Paki-
> stani and Bangladeshi descent are more likely to be in a do-
> mestic form, and Black Caribbean women more likely to be
> in a more public form than white women. (Walby, 1997: 6)

Thus, Walby's shift in terminology, which centres 'gender,' reflects the shift in feminist analysis to understand patriarchy more "adjectivally" (Bradley, 1996: 93) — a shift also advocated by others (e.g., Connell, 1990; B. Marshall, 1994), who have favoured conceptions of gendered structures framed in the more relational sense of 'gender orders' or 'gender regimes,' with 'patriarchal' understood as a useful way of describing particular and concrete manifestations of gender relations.[15] As Walby recognizes, analyses of the relationship between forms of gender regimes and degrees of gender inequality rest on empirical questions, and cannot "be determined in a priori fashion" (1997: 6).

In addition to the work of bringing women's lives and experiences into the purview of the social, and documenting gender inequality and gendered social processes, feminist sociologists insisted that adequate theories and methodologies for the discipline had to take gender into account in more than a peripheral way. As one review of disciplinary history puts it, there was a shift from a "sociology of women" to the "gendering of knowledge" (Franklin, 1996). Dorothy Smith, in a recent retrospective, recounts her alienation with trying to "write sociology" in the early 1970s:

> It caused me acute anxiety. I used to drink a glass or so of
> brandy to get going. Looking back, I see that as the mark of
> the profound alienation of my located subjectivity and the

---

15 The terminological shift from patriarchy to gender regimes in Walby's most recent work does not, however, signal a conceptual shift for her. She maintains that patriarchy, if adequately theorized, remains a useful concept for understanding large-scale gender inequality. The terminological shift was intended to facilitate more productive debates about the nature and consequences of various forms of patriarchy/gender regimes in a scholarly environment which tends to treat 'patriarchy' as a red flag, signalling some sort of ahistorical essentialism. Thus, while Walby's terminological shift does not represent a distinct conceptual shift for her, it does need to be understood as related to the more general conceptual shifts in feminist theorizing. My thanks to Sylvia Walby for clarifying this for me in personal communication.

mode in which I had to write. I had no ground from which
to write into the objectified male-grounded textual ordering
of sociology. It was a difference between myself and male colleagues. (1992: 133)

In a series of publications, Smith developed a justly influential feminist
sociology of knowledge, based on her insight that to take a woman's perspective constitutes a "radical critique" of sociology (1974).[16] It is not
enough, she argued, to turn "women's issues" into "sociological issues,"
limiting our efforts to adding into the sociological frame that which has
been excluded. The problem lay, not just in the subject matter of the
discipline, but in the way sociology is *thought*. Its theories, methods, concepts and practices are all rooted in "the male social universe," and the
fact that some women participate in this universe does not change that.
This is the source of the "radical disjuncture," the "profound alienation,"
that the feminist sociologist experienced. Political philosopher Mary
O'Brien (1981) coined the term "malestream thought," which gained wide
circulation among feminists to describe the (masculine) gendered character of the taken-for-granted knowledges of traditional disciplines. The
more that feminists examined the standards of knowledge and the practices of sociology, the more those standards and practices were charged
with being flawed by a deep androcentrism. Not all feminists agreed on
the appropriate epistemological path.[17] Some, such as Eichler (1988),
advocated a modified empiricism, which would produce better, more
objective knowledge by removing masculine bias. Others, such as Stanley
and Wise (1990), followed Smith more closely in advocating a distinctive standpoint for women, one which rejects the standard of 'objectivity'
as itself a masculine ideal. All, however, sought to take a critique of gender to the heart of sociological practice, and in the process to transform

---

16 It is difficult to describe how profound this insight was at the time. My own
encounter with Smith's work as an undergraduate sociology student in the 1970s
was one that truly changed my relationship to the discipline. The original 1974
article was revised and republished as the first chapter in Smith (1990), and
stands the test of time well.

17 I address some of these epistemological questions in B. Marshall (1994). See
also Fonow and Cook (1991) and Hawkesworth (1989).

both the discipline and the social world that provided its context. To assess its success in these terms results in a rather mixed review.

Although the import of feminist sociology in producing a rich and varied 'sociology of gender' cannot be overstated, there continue to be signs that sociology, as an institution, remains selectively "gender blind (but gendered)" (Franklin, 1996: xiv). Most of the major sociology journals in Canada, the U.S., and Britain have published trend reports on the extent to which feminist insights have been incorporated into the mainstream of the discipline (see, for example, Alway, 1995; Eichler, 1985; Maynard, 1990; Oakley, 1989; Roseneil, 1995; Stacey and Thorne, 1985), which, taken as a whole, indicate that while we've come a long way, much distance remains to be travelled. On the one hand, gender is quite firmly established as a legitimate focus of sociological investigation, as witnessed by the course offerings of most sociology departments, the conference programs of most of the professional associations, and the great increase in published work. On the other hand, there are concerns that the sociology of gender has been marginalized by its development as a subsection of the discipline, rather than transforming the conceptual core. As Abbott (1991: 189) has argued, the integration of feminist work on gender has been most advanced in some subareas which are now "almost becoming identified as 'female areas' (for example, 'family' and 'health')." Relatively little impact has been made, she notes, in reconceptualizing, in a more fundamental way, theory, class and mobility studies, and political sociology — all higher status, male-dominated areas (ibid.). This is due, in no small part, to the lingering hold of the public/private dualism as grounding the analysis of gender. Despite the extent to which feminist sociologists have insisted upon the need to analyze the gendered dimensions of all aspects of social life, this dualism remains a rather tenacious tendency, and leads to the paradoxical situation of mainstream sociology ostensibly recognizing that gender is important, but refusing to recognize the extent to which its core assumptions need to be rethought to accommodate this insight. A couple of examples will illustrate this.

In 1986, *Current Sociology*, the official journal of the International Sociological Association, published a 152-page trend report on Anglo-Canadian sociology (Brym, 1986). In this otherwise comprehensive review of the development of sociology in English Canada, work on economic development and underdevelopment, social movements, voting patterns, and the class and ethnic dimensions of stratification, the only mention of gender is in one three-page section dealing with class. Although Brym is unequivocal in recognizing its significance there, reviewing research that demonstrates gender to be the most powerful predictor of status and wage attainment, he issues no call to reorient class analysis to more fully understand this phenomenon. Instead, he proceeds directly to a lengthy section on ethnic stratification in which gender appears to have no relevance.[18]

Ten years later, in 1996, Kenneth Thompson's *Key Quotations in Sociology* includes an entry for gender which instructs us to "see also FAMILY" — not work, class, culture, education, or any other number of sites which might figure gender as centrally important, but only FAMILY. In other respects as well, this book is curious for its construction of the relationship between feminism and sociology. The book is divided into two sections, "key concepts and topics" and "key sociological thinkers": not one woman figures in the latter section. In the "key concepts" section, there are four headings (other than 'gender' itself) under which gender appears (very fleetingly): ageing, citizenship, education, and health. In the section on 'gender' as a key concept, included among the ten people cited is Samuel Johnson, with his 1763 observation that "a woman's preaching is like a dog's walking on his hinder legs. It is not done well, but you are surprised to find it done at all."[19] Perhaps Jeffrey Alexander, on the back cover of the book, is being more accurate than he suspects in lauding Thompson for managing "to tell the story of sociology in a compact, fresh and compelling manner, and also to describe society itself."

---

18   The volume of feminist sociological work published by 1986 was quite considerable — see, for example, Eichler's (1985) 'state of the art' review. Brym's trend report was expanded and published as a monograph (Brym, 1989) under a different title (*From Culture to Power*), with a lengthy appendix authored by feminist sociologist Bonnie Fox addressing the feminist challenge to political economy. Although the appendix is certainly a valuable addition, it replicates the pattern of recognizing the importance of gender while leaving the core analysis unaltered.

19   Now, I appreciate a bit of levity as much as the next sociologist, but no such facetious entry is included under any other heading (imagine invoking Uncle Tom in the entry on race!).

Distressing, as well, is at least one recent American reassessment of sociology as a discipline which connects the increased attention given to gender in theory and research to both an undesirable politicization of sociology and its loss in centrality as an institutionalized discipline (Horowitz, 1993).[20] Irving Horowitz[21] argues that sociology has become a 'set of ideologies' and 'Balkanized' under the sway of 'special interest groups' — the radical left, feminists, sexual minorities, ethnic and racial groups. For him, it is not enough that these 'special interests' have developed their own journals, but "(E)ven some highly reputable older journals, such as *Social Science Quarterly*, regularly turn over their pages to the mantra[22] of ethnicity, race and gender" (Horowitz, 1993: 17).

So there are a number of different ways that the story of gender and sociology can be told[23] and the impact of feminist sociology assessed.

---

20 A similar argument has been made in the field of Canadian history. See, for example, the interview with Michael Bliss and Jack Granatstein in the Toronto *Globe and Mail*, Feb. 6, 1992, and the response by Kealey, Pearson, and Sangster (1992).

21 That Horowitz is making such a charge is surprising, given his reputation as an astute political sociologist and biographer of one of American sociology's greatest radicals, C. Wright Mills. Ava Baron, in a review of the feminist impact on historical sociology, refers to another sociological luminary, Charles Tilly, as singling out feminists as "symbols of intellectual disorder and disciplinary decay" (Baron, 1998: 19). As she summarizes his critique, Tilly "focuses on the troublesome and nettlesome feminists who threaten to lead otherwise 'rational men' into the abyss" (of poststructuralism) (ibid.). This is rather reminiscent of Machiavelli's charge (Sylvester, 1994: 5) that "women tempt men to mix private affairs and public matters in ways that reduce rationality"!

22 The use of the term 'mantra' is telling here. A mantra is (outside of its religious connotation as an incantation) generally regarded as an empty phrase or slogan. To use it to refer to concepts such as ethnicity, race, and gender, in this context, evacuates those concepts of their social meanings and consequences. Emberley (1996) and Fekete (1994) also use the term in this way.

23 There is evidence that there are considerable national variations in feminist success in sociology. Some accounts suggest that Canadian sociology has been a more hospitable home for feminists than has been the case in some other countries (Porter, 1995) or other disciplines in this country (Vickers, 1996). However, here too, there are calls for a 'fuller' transformation (Christiansen-Ruffman, 1998; Eichler, 1992).

On one account, we've come a long way, but we're still waiting for the revolution; on another, the revolution's gone too far; on yet another, well, gender's important but we'd best leave that to the women to talk about amongst themselves. Whichever of the narrative accounts one prefers — that is, wherever one stands on the value and consequences of the phenomenon — there is no doubt that 'gender' has entered into sociology's conceptual toolkit.

So, what do sociologists talk about when they talk about 'gender'? As Denis (1993: 258) suggests (in quite a different substantive context), the place to look for expressions of disciplinary understandings of key concepts is not in "advanced theoretical probings published in specialized journals." Rather, "the place to look for sociological understandings that are at once basic and have a wide currency is in introductory manuals." Introductory textbooks, while they vary in style, organization and emphasis, are all designed to convey a *sense* of the discipline and what is important to it. In a review of six recent introductory texts,[24] there is no doubt that 'gender' has hit the mainstream in the discipline's presentation of self. All the texts except one had a chapter devoted exclusively to 'gender' (or 'sex and gender,' or 'gender inequality,' or 'gender relations'). The one text that didn't (Schaefer et al., 1996) included a chapter on "stratification by gender and age." In no text was 'gender' confined to this one chapter — references to gender were also included in most other chapters, especially those on socialization, family, education and work, and in one (Hale, 1995), feminist perspectives stressing the gendered aspects of the topic at hand were included in every chapter. Some of the texts even attempted to problematize the standard sex/gender distinction[25] (especially Anderson, 1996, Hale,

---

24 The books reviewed were Anderson (1996), Brym (ed.) (1998), Hale (1995), Henslin and Nelson (1996), Kendall, Murray, and Linden (1997), and Schaefer et al. (1996). All are Canadian, or Canadian editions. Authors of the single-authored texts (Anderson and Hale) and at least one of the authors in the others are women. Brym differs from the others in that it is an edited collection, with each chapter written by an "expert" in the field, but at least 5 of the 21 chapters are written by women.

25 This was done most thoroughly in the two texts which included separate chapters on sex and sexuality, in addition to the chapters on gender (Anderson, 1996, and Valverde, in Brym, 1998).

1995, and Valverde, in Brym, 1998) which was most commonly presented in a manner almost identical to Oakley's 1972 definition cited at the beginning of this chapter. For example:

> *Sex* refers to the biological and anatomical differences between females and males ... *Gender* refers to the culturally and socially constructed differences between females and males found in the meanings, beliefs and practices associated with "femininity" and "masculinity." (Kendall et al., 1997: 359–60)

Other concepts that were defined fairly consistently across texts included gender role ("a set of expectations governing social behaviour that is specific to one sex," Anderson, 1996: 472), gender identity ("the self-concept of a person as being male or female," Schaeffer et al., 1996: 382), gender socialization ("the process by which children are taught and internalize behaviour deemed appropriate for their particular sex," Hale, 1995: 516), and gender inequalities ("hierarchical asymmetries between men and women with respect to the distribution of power, material well-being, and prestige," Boyd, in Brym, 1998: 188). Thus, the 'gender story' presented in introductory texts goes something like this:

> Human beings are anatomically differentiated into males and females (okay, it's not always this clear-cut, but let's set that aside). What's really of interest for sociologists is how those anatomical differences are given social significance. So, we use the concept 'gender' to talk about the social aspects of being male and female. One of the most important parts of an individual's social self is their gender identity. They learn this, as they learn the other important aspects of being a member of society, through socialization. Societal expectations, and especially stereotypes of what males and females should be like, delineate fairly gender-specific behaviours, attitudes, and activities, that we call gender-roles. The problem, though, is that gender roles and gender differences aren't symmetrical. They constitute persistent inequalities, with far more of the valued social resources (material goods, political power, prestige, individual independence) accruing to men-as-a-group than to women-as-a-group. All kinds of social processes and institutions contribute to the maintenance and reinforcement of these inequalities, including language, family structures, educational systems, religious beliefs and institutions, mass media and

popular culture, science and medicine, the structure of the
economy, and government policies. Feminism is an important social movement that has struggled for the elimination
of gender inequality.

There is no question that the re-telling of this story in introductory texts
constitutes a great advance over the picture of the discipline that was
painted just a few years ago.[26] What is unclear, though, is whether the
mainstreaming of 'gender' has accomplished much of a substantial shift
in disciplinary understanding, as 'gender' still seems to point primarily to
places where women are present in the text (and vice versa). That is, when
sociologists talk about 'gender,' they are, for the most part, talking about
'women.' Thus, with few exceptions, social phenomena as diverse as bureaucracies, motorcycle gangs, and language can be discussed without reference to gender, *unless* women are anchoring the reference. In its sharpest
form, this is represented by the index of one text (Schaefer et al.,1996),
which at the end of the entry on 'gender' instructs us to "see also, women."
There is no entry for men in the text's index. The fact that sociologists
are including women in discussions of a wide range of issues is a good
thing, and one that no feminist would argue against, but it does not quite
fulfill the potential of gender as an *analytic*, as opposed to a descriptive,
concept. Is women's saturation with their 'gender' a great advance over
their saturation with their 'sex'?

The manner in which 'gender' has travelled into mainstream sociology appears to be characterized by the two dominant modes of theorizing gender that Connell identified as faulty more than a decade ago (1985,
1987): role theory and categorical theory. In general, the substitution of

---

26 Ferree and Hall (1996) did an extensive analysis of the treatment of gender,
race, and class in discussions of stratification in American introductory texts
published between 1982 and 1988. They found that gender was almost exclusively discussed at the micro-level, with gender conceptualized as a 'trait' significant in socialization. In this context, gender socialization was analyzed solely in
terms of the acquisition of traits that impede achievement for women. They
noted, for example, that while girls are frequently depicted acquiring the trap-
pings of traditional femininity, "boys are *never* shown learning to ogle women
or learning the masculine version of heterosexuality (at fraternity parties, for
example)" (938). By contrast, race was treated as a 'meso,' or group level, concept, and class as a macro, or structural, concept.

'gender' for 'sex' in role theory (i.e., from 'sex role' to 'gender role') does little to address its fundamental weaknesses: its underlying functionalism, its inability to grasp the *dynamics* of change,[27] its underemphasis on power, its tendency to reify 'roles,' and its focus on individual behaviours rather than social institutions. However, if "role theory tends to dissolve into individualism, categoricalism resolutely stays with the big picture and paints it with a broad brush" (Connell, 1987: 54). Categorical theories are characterized by (a) the association of interests with specific categories (e.g., 'men' and 'women'), (b) a primary analytic focus on the "category as a unit, rather than on the processes by which the category is constituted, or on its elements or constituents," and (c) a conception of the social order as comprising "a few major categories — usually two — related to each other by power and conflict of interest" (ibid.). Neither sort of theory is adequate to an analysis that goes much beyond treating 'gender' as a variable.

The 'romance' of gender and sociology, then, is a complex story. Despite the introduction of gender as a means to get at the social construction of difference and power in a way that the elision of sex and gender did not permit, some legacies of the classical tradition persist. For one thing, the introduction of 'gender' into the sociological vocabulary seems to have done little to loosen its containment by the feminine. Perhaps more importantly, the ubiquitous usage of gender in a categorical sense has the effect of rendering it static and unproblematically linked to biological referents, which are precisely the problems that feminists identified in early sociology. As Carver (1998: 18) summarizes a similar review of political theory, 'gender' tends to be "loosely synonymous with 'sex' and lazily synonymous with 'women.'" Importantly, this is not just a problem of academic terminology, but is replicated in the manner in which the turn to gender has been taken up by policy makers and popular social commentary.

---

27 As Connell notes, the problem is not that role theory doesn't recognize change, but the manner in which change is understood. Implicit is an understanding of change as something which "happens" to roles from outside, or results from the "real self" that resists the constraint of some role. "The problem is rather that role theory cannot grasp social change as history, that is, as transformation generated in the interplay of social practice and social structure" (1985: 263).

Gender Outside the Academy

"Gender" has not been in the exclusive purview of the academy, and it is much to the credit of both feminist academics and feminist activists (not mutually exclusive categories!) that 'gender,' 'gender equality,' 'gender analysis,' 'gender perspective,' and so on have become part of the discourse of public policy, both in Canada and in the international context.

Canada's federal government[28] has officially endorsed "gender-based analysis" in policy development, implementation, and analysis. A series of documents were produced in response to Canada's commitment, as a member country of the United Nations, to formulate a national plan for the advancement of the status of women: first, a broad statement of the objective and principles of gender-based analysis and a generic guide to using gender-based analysis in policy-making (Status of Women Canada, 1995, 1996), and later, a shorter and more focussed set of documents for policy analysts and managers within the bureaucracy of Human Resources Development Canada (HRDC, 1997a, 1997b). As explained in the policy guides, gender-based analysis is intended to ensure that social and economic differences between women and men are taken into account at all stages of the policy process. There was some slippage, however, in the conceptual foundations between the original statement from Status of Women and its later reformulation in HRDC. The Status of Women backgrounder, while defining gender clearly in the context of the customary sex/gender distinction, was exceptional in stressing the relational aspect of gender:

> *Sex* identifies the biological differences between women and men.
>
> *Gender* is the culturally specific set of characteristics that identifies the social behaviour of women and men and the *relationship* between them. Gender, therefore, refers not simply to women or men, but to the relationship between them, and the way it is socially constructed. Because it is a relational

---

28 Among governments and international organizations endorsing gender-based analysis are the governments of New Zealand and Norway, the United Nations, the World Bank, and the International Labour Organization (HRDC, 1997a: iii).

term, gender must include women *and* men. Like the concepts of class, race and ethnicity, gender is an analytical tool
for understanding social processes. (Status of Women Canada,
1996: 3; emphasis in the original)

The relational emphasis and the stress on gender as an analytical perspective is flattened out in the translation to the HRDC guide, where a simple role perspective is presented:

Sex refers to the universal, biological differences between
women and men ...
 Gender roles are learned behaviours that condition which
activities, tasks and responsibilities are perceived as male and
female. Gender roles are not constant, but changeable over
time, and have wide variations within and between cultures.
(HRDC, 1997a: 1; emphasis in the original)

The original Status of Women document on gender-based analysis is also
explicit in terms of its political implications, emphasizing the positive
role that policy interventions can have in creating social change, and placing gender-based analysis in the context of "building an equal and more
just society" (1995: 77). Gender-based analysis is presented in purely pragmatic terms to HRDC, emphasizing its benefits in terms of more informed decision making, meeting international commitments to equality
(given Canada's responsibility as signatory to a number of international
conventions on promoting gender equality), reducing the likelihood that
policies and programs will be subject to challenges under the Charter of
Rights and Freedoms, minimizing 'potential embarrassment' for the government should its policies be criticized as having a negative impact on
women, and even in terms of expanding its marketable skill set of policy
analysts and managers. In its responses to "frequently asked questions,"
HRDC, while emphasizing the desirable goal of 'gender equality,' disassociates gender-based analysis from feminism, advocacy, or "the promotion of any view, such as a lobby group's view" (1997a: 20).[29] Observing

---

29 While not mentioning 'feminism,' they do recognize that "Women and men in
 Canada have fought for many decades for legal, social and economic equality,"
 and that "Every advance we enjoy today is due to dedicated people who worked
 very hard for it" (HRDC, 1997a: 20–21).

this 'translation' of gender into administrative terms makes it difficult to ignore the feminist critiques of the dominance of 'gender' as an analytic category as "missing the point about male dominance" (Braidotti, 1994). On the other hand, it is equally difficult to ignore the argument that, despite its faults, the gender-as-role theory and categorical analysis have provided the grounds on which the most progress has been made in the sphere of concrete policy changes. As Connell puts it: "the two most politically effective accounts of gender accounts that we know to be wrong" (1996: 158).

The United Nations, in the adoption of the Forward-Looking Strategies document which emerged from the Nairobi conference in 1985, also shifted its focus from 'women' to 'gender' (Stienstra, 1996: 15). In 1995, the production of the Platform for Action of the UN Fourth World Conference on Women in Beijing represented a comprehensive adoption of the "language of gender, and, specifically, of gender mainstreaming" (Baden and Goetz, 1997: 5).[30] Paragraph 38 of the Beijing Declaration unequivocally asserts "that a gender perspective is reflected in all our policies and programmes" (United Nations, 1995c).

The concept of 'gender mainstreaming' in the UN has its roots in development work over the last few decades, and particularly in the shift from Women in Development (WID) to Gender and Development (GAD) as a paradigm for integrating research and practice. WID approaches, which developed in the early 1970s, sought to integrate women into development initiatives. As Rathberger (1990) notes, this approach worked within the general assumptions of modernization theory, which saw 'development' as "a process of slow but steady linear progress" (491). It was recognized that women's experience of development was different

---

30 The 'mainstreaming' of gender at the Beijing conference also became the focus of the conservative critique, as will be explored in Chapter 4. The centrality of 'gender' to the UN framework as well as the volatility of the concept in this context may be gauged by the obsession in some of the conservative analyses with counting the number of times that 'gender' appears in the Platform for Action. However, of four sources which mention this, all come up with different numbers: Woodard (1995) says 216 times, Cook (1995) says 163 times, Garcia-Robles (1995) says 60 times, and Joseph (1995) says 300 times. I declined to undertake my own word count, but can confirm from my reading of the Platform for Action that the term is used with some regularity.

from men's — for example, they were less likely to benefit from new agricultural technologies — and this justified a focus on 'women' in research and development practice. Such a focus, however, was "focussed only on how women could better be integrated into ongoing development initiatives" (491), rather than at the more fundamental transformation of gendered social structures. The GAD paradigm developed in the 1980s, more influenced by socialist feminism than by the liberal underpinnings of WID, and sought a more comprehensive analysis of women's situation via the concept of 'gender': "GAD is not concerned with women *per se* but with the social construction of gender and the assignment of specific roles, responsibilities and expectations to women and to men" (Rathberger, 1990: 494; see also K. Young, 1997).

The shift from 'women' to 'gender relations' as the central analytic category in feminist development work resonated with the shift in feminist social science more generally, but as Rathberger (1990: 495) suggests, it is a shift whose radical impulse is less easily translated into practice. The shift to 'gender' has also been charged with diffusing the radical impulse of earlier approaches, particularly in relation to the 'mainstreaming' of gender:

> As gender has become a more mainstream and therefore more respectable and fundable field of research, new players are entering the field, who bear no allegiance to feminist research and may not even be familiar with its basic texts, concepts and methodologies. Economists, statisticians and econometricians ... responding to the growth in demand from major development bureaucracies for research and analysis to inform their new 'gender-aware' policy directions, have taken up research into gender issues. This recent body of research has tended to look at gender as an interesting statistical variable ... While such research may be of great interest and can provide invaluable insights and empirical evidence, it can under-specify the power relations maintaining gender inequalities, and in the process de-links the investigation of gender issues from a feminist transformatory project. (Baden and Goetz, 1997: 7)

Thus, in examining both the academic and policy contexts, feminists have seen gender-consciousness reconstituted in not-necessarily-feminist ways. This reconstitution can be seen most clearly, though, in popular tracts on gender. Those that appear to have captured the popular imagination are those that see gender differences as being rather static and immutable — whether "socially constructed" or not. Such explanations do not need to reassert biological explanations that explicitly attempt to collapse gender back into sex. My concern here is to look at how explanations relying on cultural or social sources of difference become just as rigid and essentialized as those that point to 'nature.' Media darling Camille Paglia goes so far as to suggest that those of us teaching about gender should "break out of the ghetto of academic publishing" and "consider assigning the kind of general-release books whose sales in the many millions indicate that they have struck a chord with the mass audience." To this end, she suggests that books like Deborah Tannen's *You Just Don't Understand* (1990), John Gray's *Men are From Mars, Women are From Venus* (1992), and comedian Tim Allen's *Don't Stand Too Close to a Naked Man* (1994) "draw upon the wisdom of actual experience to present a picture of sexual relations far more persuasive than anything current academic theorists have produced" (Paglia, 1997: B4). I shall take up Paglia's suggestion, and look at two of these.

Deborah Tannen, who holds a doctorate in linguistics and teaches at a prestigious American university, analyzes the different conversational styles of men and women, with the intent of helping them to better understand and communicate with each other, and thus improve their relationships. Her basic premise is that "boys and girls grow up in what are essentially different cultures" (1990: 18) — that is, that processes of gender socialization are so effective, males and females might as well be considered "foreign" to one another. Thus, she adapts the principles of "cross-cultural" communication to male-female conversations. Filled with folksy anecdotes and case studies, it is an enjoyable and friendly book, which guides the reader through all the different communicative strategies that differentiate men and women — their different "genderlects." In the end, it aspires to be a translation guide, and in the final chapter even invokes the worst-case scenario of an American tourist who ends up in a Turkish prison because she failed to grasp the subtleties of cross-cultural communication — clearly meant as a metaphor for the potential consequences of not taking the very real differences of genderlects seriously. Tannen is clear in her belief in gender equality, as well in her recognition that gender difference is often manifested as asymmetry. She is not a biological determinist who would have us believe that 'nature' has set out these intractable differences. It is, for her, a *cultural* differ- ence in the extreme — not just a gendered culture that differentiates between males and females, but two distinct cultures — and recogni- tion of this is, for Tannen, the best route to personal and relational hap- piness. As she puts it: "Recognizing gender differences frees individuals from the burden of individual pathology" (17) and "Once people real- ize that their partners have different conversational styles, they are in- clined to accept differences without blaming themselves, their partners, or their relationships" (297).

If being from different cultures isn't enough to explain the seem- ingly fixed and absolute differences of gender, then you might want to consider the thesis that men and women come from different planets. John Gray's immensely popular *Men are From Mars, Women are From Venus*, which has spawned a number of sequels, a board game, a CD- ROM, audio cassettes, and a seminar industry, has a project similar to Tannen's but takes the "cross-cultural" metaphor to a new level.[31] Once upon a time, the allegory goes, Martians and Venusians saw each other and fell in love. They accepted the fact that they were different, and built happy relationships taking this into account. Then, they travelled together to Earth where a strange thing happened: they forgot they were from different planets, and their relationships have been in trouble ever since. The secret to repairing those relationships is, as it is for Tannen, to accept gender differences and learn to communicate across cultures (Gray even provides a Mars/Venus phrase book to help in "translation"). He, too, sees recognizing the explanatory power of gender differences as freeing for the individual. As he elaborates in an interview:[32] "People today, more than ever before, are hungry for ways to understand our differences in a positive way, to answer the question we have about the

---

31 According to Gray's home page (http://goodbiz.com/johngray), the first Mars/ Venus book has sold 6 million copies in the U.S. and been translated into 38 languages. John Gray has a B.A. and M.A. in "Creative Intelligence" from the Mahorishi European Research Institute, and a Ph.D.in Psychology and Human Sexuality from Columbia Pacific University, which, according to its web page (http://www.cpuniv.udu), provides a "non-resident" independent study program.

32 Interview with John Gray at http://goodbiz.com/johngray/jginterv.html.

opposite sex: Are some of the problems a gender thing or are they specific to this relationship?"

In a sense, Paglia is correct to suggest that these sorts of popular tracts present a "persuasive" account, which resonates with many people's experience (as do jokes about women's obsession with shoe sales or the invisible umbilical cord attaching men to TV remote controls). That these sorts of accounts overgeneralize and reify differences is not the only problem — more vexing is that positing gender as a fixed and absolute binary difference, and according it explanatory power as such, hardly constitutes analysis.[33] Even if those differences are recognized to be socially or culturally derived, such a strategy serves only to re-naturalize that binary. In such accounts, 'gender' becomes a simple replacement for 'sex' as the descriptor of pre-constituted categories. "Only human beings," says the unabashedly conservative Barbara Amiel, "would be so potty as to try to deny gender-specific behaviour" (1995: 13). Only human beings? I'll leave it to the reader to ponder the implications of that statement.

Gender Mainstreaming: A Mixed Legacy

The mainstreaming of gender into social analysis has certainly produced some mixed results. Initially deployed as a means of breaking the conflation of the natural and the social, and as a way of bringing women into the realm of the social, gender as a sociological concept has sharply exposed the masculinity of modernity. Yet feminist sociology uses gender not simply to describe differences between men and women, but to expose its links to power and inequality. The intent is to problematize gender as a social relationship, and to transform not only sociology as an academic discipline, but the social world as well. However, categorical and essentialized conceptions of gender have not always functioned in an emancipatory way, and may act to shore up, rather than disrupt, the opposition between masculinity and femininity.

---

33   Frith and Kitzinger (1997) provide an interesting account of how this sort of understanding of gender underpins 'miscommunication' as an explanation for sexual assault.

Despite the initial emancipatory impulse in distinguishing gender from sex in a move to de-essentialize the former — to see it as variable, malleable, and relational — gender itself has become essentialized in its usage in various contexts. In some contexts, it merely identifies the point at which 'women' become relevant to the analysis, leaving the rest untouched. In others, it becomes just another word for 'sex.' As Terrence Carver (1998: 22) summarizes it, such usage "constantly reinscribes the supposedly obvious and supposedly well-understood categories male and female, men and women, back into political ideas, just when these ideas are starting to be really problematic, politically interesting and interestingly complex." Or, as Paola Melchiori, an Italian feminist, suggests, "Even 'gender,' which was meant to escape nature traps, is … becoming as rigid as nature in its exploratory capacity" (1998: 97).

Yet some attempts have been made to develop more sophisticated sociological theorizations of gender, which try to move beyond these limitations, and which can more adequately account for the complexity of gender in social life. R.W. Connell's work (1987, 1995), for example, argues that gender is a way of structuring social practice "that constantly refers to bodies and what bodies do" (1995: 71), and gender relations thus understood "form one of the major structures of all documented societies." The practice of gender is found at all units of analysis — the individual, discourse/ideology/culture, and social institutions — and is structured around (a) relations of power, (b) relations of production, and (c) relations of emotion, attachment and sexual desire ("cathexis"). Judith Lorber (1994, 1996) attempts to develop a 'new paradigm' for understanding gender, one which takes as its starting point a conception of gender as a social institution "that establishes patterns of expectations for individuals, orders the social processes of everyday life, is built into the major social organizations of society, such as the economy, ideology, the family, and politics, and is also an entity in and of itself" (1994: 1). The extent to which these more complex understandings of gender will be taken up by mainstream sociology, and used to develop its analytic strength, remains to be seen. Certainly, it is an undertaking that I endorse, as will become evident in later chapters. In the next chapter I want to turn to another question — that of whether such efforts to theorize gender can withstand the more general assault on the very concept from *within* feminism.

TWO

Destabilizing Gender

Q. "Gender" means
    (a) anything;
    (b) everything;
    (c) nothing;
    (d) not sex;
    (e) women;
    (f) men too;
    (g) something superficial so you can change it at will;
    (h) all of the above.
           — from "A Po-mo Quiz," in Bell and Klein (1996)

"Gender? oh, I know your sort: wimmin? Yes, well ..."
           — Liz Stanley (1997)

Almost since its entry into academic circulation, the sex-gender distinction, and the growing preference for 'gender' as the category of interest, has been the subject of debate in feminist literature across a range of disciplines. Nonetheless, the relative success of feminist sociology has been measured by the extent to which gender, as an orienting concept, has been taken to heart by mainstream sociology, and how extensively a focus on gender has transformed or 'revolutionized' the theory, methods, and subject area of the discipline.[1] This perspective tends to assume general agreement on "what gender is, how to study it, and why it is

---

1 As suggested in the previous chapter, the case of sociology is not unique. Feminist 'success' in many other disciplines is generally measured in the same way.

important.... In other words, gender is treated as an established concept in a discipline which need only take it more seriously as a central category of analysis" (Ingraham, 1994: 213). A number of recent debates and commentaries suggest that a more rigorous examination of the status of gender as both a conceptual anchor and as a link to political concerns is overdue. As Rosa Braidotti argues: "I think that the notion of 'gender' is at a crisis point in feminist theory and practice, that it is undergoing intense criticism from all sides both for its theoretical inadequacy and for its politically amorphous and unfocused nature" (1994: 36). It is not just a matter of terminology, but how the concept of 'gender' is understood that is at the heart of most of the debates.

The Trouble with Gender: Feminist Debates

The debates about gender within feminism have raised questions about both the ways in which gender is used and the very distinction between sex and gender upon which the concept is based. The questions raised are not simple questions of the truth or falsity about the sex/gender distinction, or the 'real' meaning of 'gender,' which can be answered through the accumulation and evaluation of 'evidence.' Rather, they are questions about its continuing utility, and the implications of how we conceptualize 'gender' for advancing the various political interests of feminism. The political efficacy of gender-analysis for advancing the interests of *women*, then, must be seen as one of the backdrops to these debates. They are also animated by feminist encounters with a set of academic and theoretical debates about postmodernism and poststructuralism.

While in the previous chapter, the idea of 'modernity' provided a backdrop for tracking the emergence of gender as a focus in sociology, the debates here about what gender means and whether or not it is a useful concept for contemporary feminism need to be understood within the context of 'postmodernity' as an increasingly influential idea in the social sciences and humanities. Rita Felski (1989b: 36) provides a useful description of the "postmodern problematic," which encapsulates some of its key features. These include:

a)   "the proliferation of information technologies and the gradual shift towards postindustrial (although not postcapitalist) society"

b) "an increasing skepticism towards metanarratives" (such as liberalism and Marxism)

c) the "re-emergence of feminism and other social movements which have foregrounded difference and exposed the patriarchal, heterosexist and ethnocentric nature of dominant Western ideals"

d) the "mass dissemination of signs and images"

e) "a shift in philosophical and social theory towards linguistic paradigms accompanied by a sustained critique of foundationalist thought"

Thus, the "postmodern problematic" points to a nexus of both social and philosophical/theoretical shifts. Closely associated with the latter are the theories and methods of 'poststructuralism,' which are concerned with language, discourse, and representation.[2] With respect to the sex/gender distinction and the ways in which gender is used, the sorts of questions that are raised, and the impetus for raising them, are influenced by differing attitudes toward the postmodern turn. To elaborate, I will outline four of the key lines of critique that may be discerned in the feminist literature.[3] Those more sympathetic to the postmodern turn are more likely to criticize gender as based on a faulty distinction between nature and culture, and as an over-determining narrative in itself — one which flattens out important differences. Thus, those more critical of the postmodern turn fear that the way that 'gender' has been taken up depoliticizes and/or erases the material bases of women's oppression.

---

2 Although I believe that postmodernism and poststructuralism should be distinguished, this task is made difficult by their frequent conflation in the literature (often via the hybridized term 'postmodernism/poststructuralism'). Agger (1991) and Huyssen (1990) provide some helpful distinctions. Because my concern here is to focus on the ways that postmodern and poststructuralist themes have been taken up and/or rejected, I will use the terms used by the authors that I am discussing.

3 Collapsing these rather complex debates into four categories is, of course, quite arbitrary, and these four lines of debate are neither mutually exclusive nor exhaustive.

(1) The basic distinction between sex and gender has been criticized for reinforcing a nature/culture dualism and for reifying sexual dimorphism. The purpose of the distinction as it was incorporated into second-wave feminism was to differentiate between sex as a biological 'fact' and gender as socially constructed, and hence socially alterable. This was the premise of much of the sociological work on gender socialization that sought to document the various ways in which sexually differentiated bodies become 'gendered,' as well as anthropological work that sought to document the great variety of gendered roles that may be attached to those bodies cross-culturally. Nicholson has described this manner of understanding the sex-gender distinction in terms of a "coatrack" metaphor: "Here the body is viewed as a type of rack upon which differing cultural artifacts ... are thrown or superimposed" (1994: 81). Delphy (1993) suggests a metaphor of container and contents, where 'sex' was the container, and 'gender' the contents.

The distinction between biological sex and social gender, however, was never straightforward. As early as 1980, Margrit Eichler suggested that "the distinction does not work," and that "the difficulty lies in the actual link between biological and social aspects of sex rather than in a lack of terms which describe the two aspects" (p.12). Increasingly, feminists realized that the social organization of sexual difference ('gender') went "all the way down" (Nicholson, 1994: 83). Buttressed by the interrogation of sexual dimorphism through analyses of intersexuality, hermaphroditism, 'third genders,' and genealogies of the body (Fausto-Sterling, 1993; Foucault, 1980a; Herdt, 1994; Jordanova, 1989; Laqueur, 1990), the assumption of two biological sexes that provided the material base for a gendered superstructure seemed to fall away. As John Hood-Williams has summarized the import of this critique: "Gender is always already implicated within the attempts to define sex — whether as difference or similarity" (1996: 13).

(2) A number of critiques suggest that the concept of 'gender' is too universalizing and too overdetermining, implicating it as shot through with racism, classism, and heterosexism. To invoke gender, it is argued, is to necessarily invoke some kind of essentialism, constructing a homogenous category called 'women' (and, conversely, another called 'men'). Thus, Spelman argues that gender, conceptualized in this way, calls into being "one who is all and only woman, who by some miracle

of abstraction has no particular identity in terms of race, class, ethnicity, sexual orientation, language, religion, nationality" (1988: 187). Where attention to 'gender difference' once meant the mapping out of differences between 'women' and 'men,' more recent work has turned the question of difference inward, to see gender categories themselves as infinitely differentiated. Not only is a failure to see gender itself as infinitely varied in its manifestations problematic, but the privileging of gender as the analytic focus leads to what Friedman (1995: 14–15) calls "categorical hegemony" — a tendency to subsume all other "systems of alterity" which hinders the understanding of how various hierarchies work together, and makes it impossible to understand how individuals can occupy contradictory subject positions. Recognition of the internal differentiation of gender categories has become a *sine qua non* of contemporary feminist analysis, but how to move beyond the mere (and obligatory) recognition of this in the introduction to a book or article about gender continues to be a problem for many scholars. Gender is seen to 'intersect with,' 'interact with,' be 'configured by,' be 'articulated with' other categories of difference, but "when tractor and trailer are articulated they remain tractor and trailer" (Cealey and Hood-Williams, 1998, para 2.9).

(3) Some feminists have argued that the turn to gender has meant a depoliticizing turn away from 'women.' Debates about 'women's studies' versus 'gender studies' and 'women's history' versus 'gender history' have become common as academic programs, researchers, and publishers grapple with new labels. An explicit focus on 'women' as a category whose members share something — some 'Otherness' — has provided a crucial political link to the politics of women's movements. Thus, some fear that a shift to 'gender' will sever this political link. We saw, in Chapter One, how this has indeed been the case in some translations of gender theory into gender policies. In the mainstream of the social sciences as well, there is no doubt that some usages of 'gender' have had this effect, where it has often become an academically sanitized substitute for 'women.' As Joan Scott has argued, this sort of use of gender "is meant to denote the scholarly seriousness of a work, for 'gender' has a more neutral and objective sound than does 'women.' ... [It] seems to fit within the scientific terminology of social science and thus disassociates itself from the (supposedly strident) politics of feminism" (1988: 31). Stanley and Wise (1990: 45)

see "the study of gender as a de-politicized version of feminism, akin to studying 'race relations' rather than racism and colonialism." Related arguments charge the conceptual shift to 'gender' with positing an unwarranted symmetry between the categories 'women' and 'men,' and with directing academic attention (and scarce resources) to the latter. Richardson and Robinson (1994), for example, suggest that the increasing use of the term 'gender studies' over 'women's studies' "decreases the amount of 'space' for women in education in the context of what is still often a male-dominated curriculum and institution" (17). They are particularly critical of mainstream publishers who have subsumed women's studies lists under gender studies lists, which are giving increased prominence to books on men and masculinity. As they summarize it, the move "away from discussing women's oppression in terms of the (problematic) category of 'woman' to use gender as an interrogating and organizing category and/ or by focussing on men/masculinity" represents "a deradicalization of women's studies, taking the heat off patriarchy" (ibid.: 25; see also Robinson and Richardson, 1996). The shift to 'gender' may also be used as a very *deliberate* disassociation from feminism, as is the case with the periodical *Feminist Issues*, which was reborn as *Gender Issues* in 1998. The 1992 editorial statement of *Feminist Issues* declared its dedication to "feminist social and political analysis," "providing the theoretical framework that is crucial to dissecting and exposing the ideology and social institutions within which women live and have lived historically" and its intent to "contribute to strengthening and developing feminist theoretical analysis and the women's movement." The new *Gender Issues* explicitly distances itself from any political motivations. It should come as no surprise that some feminists hear alarm bells go off when they see 'gender' instead of 'women' or 'feminist.'

(4) The emphasis on gender as *socially constructed* has, for some, signalled a shift from the material to the discursive: one which cedes too much to discourse and culture at the expense of a more materially grounded analysis. Critiques of this shift "from things to words" (Barrett, 1992) do not take issue with the assertion that gender *is* socially constructed, but want to stem a complete "descent into discourse" (Palmer, 1990), by insisting on a continual referral to the concrete and material differences of sex upon which the social edifice of 'gender' is constructed. Generally invoking either a reproductive or an economic substructure (or

both), these critiques fear that 'gender' as the analytic beacon will shed light only on its epiphenomenal forms. In one version of this critique, Jill Vickers (1994) argues for an approach that makes central the link between social power and reproductive sex. The social constructionist emphasis on gender, she suggests, "makes us evasive about the biology of sexual reproduction for fear of being accused of being biological determinists" (183). In another version, Sylvia Walby (1992) charges that the shift from 'structure' to 'discourse' denies feminists the tools to grasp and explain the persistent, and macro-social, inequalities between men and women. Similarly, Diana Coole (1994), while sympathetic to the emphasis on culture and the discursive construction of gender, laments the inability of such approaches to deal with the "pervasive and substantial" material inequalities between men and women. The critiques of 'gender' here are linked, not so much by an antipathy to the term or idea of gender, but by a deep scepticism of the supposed extreme to which 'social construction' has been taken in some theoretical accounts of gender. As one critic puts it:

> Gender analysis moved beyond the material and cultural representation of sex (biological differences) to a totally abstract representation of sexual and all other kinds of differences between women and men created by society. Thus, material experiences become abstract representations drawn almost exclusively from textual analysis; personal identities and all human agency become obsolete, and disembodied subjects are constructed by discourses. (Hoff, 1996: 407)

Two recurring and related themes underlie the feminist debates about gender — the inscription of 'difference' and 'diversity' as the *leitmotif* of both feminist politics and feminist theory, and the increased influence of postmodernism and poststructuralism in the academy. Unlike some accounts that locate both of these developments in the same grand sweep of intellectual fashion, I want to begin by arguing that the former is more directly related to shifts in the political constituency of feminism, as previously marginalized women have carved out spaces from which to speak, and the latter is related to a more generalized 'crisis of knowledge,' that has relentlessly scrutinized all the 'grand narratives' that have (mis)informed Western intellectual systems. Thus, 'difference' and 'diversity' are not questions that postmodern theory put on the agenda, but questions that have led to a widespread questioning of the 'categorical hegemony' of existing theoretical accounts of gender.[4] The manner in which postmodernism has called into question the impossible unity implied by gender as an analytical category is termed "gender scepticism" by Susan Bordo:

> Where once the prime objects of academic feminist critique were the phallocentric narratives of our male dominated disciplines, now feminist criticism has turned to its own narratives, finding them reductionist, totalizing, inadequately nuanced, valorizing of gender difference, unconsciously racist, and elitist. (1990: 135)

Feminist responses to postmodernism and poststructuralism have often been hostile. Postmodernism has been characterized as "little more than old-fashioned pluralism rewritten in a French accent" (Murray, 1997:37), "a happy polytheism of language games"[5] (Benhabib, 1990: 123); and "ahistorical and misogynist, as well as politically paralyzing" (Hoff, 1994: 446). As outlined above, some of the strongest critiques of the postmodern turn in feminist theory have linked it directly to the emergence of 'gender' (as opposed to 'women') as the preferred category of analysis (Hoff, 1994; Modleski, 1991; Sangster, 1995). Here it is argued that 'gender' supplants 'women,' erasing their materiality, and thus dissolves the political grounds for a 'women's movement.' This sort of argument is most closely associated with radical and socialist feminist analyses that stress the importance of retaining a woman-centred focus, and specifically one that is attendant to both differences between women *and* persistent differences between women and men. Writing in *Socialist Review*, Barbara Epstein (1995) identifies academic feminism as primarily responsible for the theoretical hegemony of poststructuralism, and what she sees as an attendant depoliticization of theory.

---

4 If I seem critical here of some postmodernists/poststructuralists taking credit for forcing feminists to think more carefully about how they invoke 'gender,' I am. As will become clearer a bit further on, I am equally critical of feminists who see the whole concept of 'gender' as a clever poststructuralist way of ignoring women.

5 My favourite metaphor of this genre comes from Lorrie Moore's novel *Anagrams*, where she invokes the image of "language playing so ardently with itself that it goes blind" (1986: 56).

But there has been another sort of response to the poststructuralist/
feminist alliance — one more closely connected to cultural conservative
projects. On this account, poststructuralism (again, generally conflated
with postmodernism) is seen as part and parcel of an intellectual takeover
of 'special interests' in the academy, which has replaced systematic and
cumulative knowledge acquisition with the "mantra" of "race, gender and
ethnicity" (Emberley, 1996; Fekete, 1994; Horowitz, 1993). Thus, Gross
and Levitt (1994) can group together feminism, anti-colonialism, envi-
ronmentalism, queer theory, postmodernism, and other forms of "cultural constructivism" in their scathing critique of "the academic left," a
potent force that has undermined the legitimation of natural science as
the most privileged form of knowledge. Feminism is charged with want-
ing, not just "full judicial equality for women," but "a complete over-
throw of traditional gender categories, with all their conscious and
unconscious postulates" (3). As I will explore in Chapter Four, this
phantasmic creation of 'gender' as an authoritarian category has been taken
up as a political resource in a variety of anti-feminist projects. That the
conceptual language of 'gender' is seen to be complicit in both the radical
and conservative critiques of the postmodern turn would seem to put it
squarely at the heart of debates about modernity vs. postmodernity.

The rethinking of 'gender' as a category invokes some other weighty
theoretical debates. One of these debates which has become particularly
contentious within feminism is that around essentialism versus nominalism in our understanding of the ways in which we 'become gendered.'[6]
Essentialism suggests that there is some common bedrock, or 'essence,'
to 'woman' (and by corollary 'man') which makes it possible to talk about
'women' and 'men' as intelligible, and in some sense unified, gender categories. Nominalism, on the other hand, asserts that 'women' and 'men'
exist only in and through the manner in which they are named thus (hence
the *nom* in nominalism). This is, of course, a bald and somewhat overstated juxtaposition of the two poles of the debate, and almost no one
will admit to a full-fledged endorsement of either extreme. Yet this opposition continues to fuel some rather spirited debates about the utility of
'gender.' The charge of 'essentialism,' especially, has become something

---

6 I discuss the tension between essentialism and nominalism in the debates about
gendered subjectivity in more detail in Marshall (1994), especially chapter 4.

of a theoretical insult, and something few feminists would admit to.[7] But I do not think that we need to move from the assertion that the category 'gender' has no essence to the argument that to invoke 'gender' invariably implies an essence. After all, we continually invoke categories that have no such assumption.[8]

For now, I want simply to raise the question of how theory can be given so much credit for either political paralysis (the radical critique) or political chaos (the conservative critique). Surely the apparent disillusionment with the grand narratives of modernity, scepticism regarding "modernity's claim that society's political self-making can and will bring about funda-

---

7 Martin (1994) provides a useful overview of how 'essentialism' has become the *j'accuse* of many contemporary feminist debates, and some of the pitfalls of this tack. See also Alcoff (1988).

8 To use a silly example, I think we would all agree that there is no 'essence' to the "Class of '78" at your high school. While it would be possible for someone to treat that category as if there was some fixed, shared essence (perhaps based on the cognitive changes wrought by a particular algebra teacher) it would not be necessary to do so to still have some intelligible sense of the invoking of that category. It may be understood as a group of individuals who shared some (but certainly not all) experiences, is defined in relation to/from other groups (the class of '68, those who went to a different school, those who didn't go to high school) and is internally both differentiated and stratified (female, male, popular, nerdy, athletic, scholarly, poor, wealthy, and so on). To stretch the analogy even further than is perhaps warranted, some 'members' of the category may feel a particularly strong identity-connection (the ones who organize the reunions and write the newsletter) while for others there may be little or no sense of commonality (the ones who haven't even kept their mailing addresses updated), and this is something that may change over time or in relation to other events (divorcing the class president?). Thus, we do not need to believe in any common essence to a category for it to have intelligible meaning, even in a sense which recognizes that it is mutually constitutive with other categories, as is always the case when we talk about 'gender.' This example bears some similarity to attempts by Connell (1987) and Young (1994) to adapt Sartre's concept of 'series' to describe gender categories. A number of theorists have also drawn on Wittgenstein's notion of 'language games' and 'family resemblances' to flesh out this sense of gender. However, the point I wish to get across here is intuitive enough that I shall, for the time being, eschew theoretical elaboration. I will return to Young's development of the concept of 'seriality' in the conclusions.

mental human emancipation" (Denis, 1997: 14), and recognition that calling political 'agents' into being — whether on the basis of gender, class, race, citizenship status, or whatever — will always be a rather precarious and contingent matter, is more a result of reflections on practice than something accomplished by theoretical fiat. This is particularly the case for feminism, which like other explicitly political endeavours, is concerned to a greater degree with the utility of theory to illuminate the 'dailiness'[9] of women's lives, in all their infinite variety, and to inform projects of social intervention, than it is to the working out of philosophical puzzles. So, I shall agree with Rita Felski's assessment that "poststructuralist theory is neither necessary for nor antithetical to political struggles" (1997b: 69).

It is in the rethinking of gender in relation to other categories of analysis that some of the most interesting questions have been raised about the implications of the 'postmodern turn' in feminism. In reflections on how other markers of difference inflect, and are inflected by, gender, the affinities to and antipathies toward the deconstruction of gender become clearer. I will look at some of the axes of difference that have generated the most sustained attention, beginning with the extremely problematic relationship between gender, sex, and sexuality. This relationship lies at the heart of the very idea of 'gender.' I will then look briefly at the intersections of gender with two other analytic categories — race and class — that have generated a good deal of debate within feminism. My purpose here is to illustrate that the relationships between gender and other categories of difference, and how we conceptualize those relationships, have both theoretical and political dimensions. That is, these relationships were not just 'troubled up' by the theoretical interventions of postmodernism, but have a history which belies any simple narrative of a theoretical shift from the material to the discursive, or from modern to postmodern. This is not to suggest, however, that there is nothing new or novel to be gleaned from the more recent theoretical debates — as Barrett and Phillips (1992) suggest, to assess the latter as nothing more than the "recycling of old debates in new terms" is as unproductive as to hail them as the final transcendence of old problems. As they put it: "(T)he concepts and categories through which we appropriate, analyse, and construct the world have a history within which we are ourselves implicated" (7–8).

---

9 This term is Aptheker's (1989).

Gender and Sexuality

One of the most difficult aspects of 'gender' to untangle is its articulation with sex and sexuality. This is apparent from its earliest incarnations in the work of John Money and his colleagues in the 1950s. Given Money's founding role in introducing 'gender' into the vocabulary of the social sciences, I want to consider in some detail his recent (1995) critique of its career as a concept. Money provides a "lexical history" of gender, beginning with his doctoral dissertation on hermaphroditism, where he struggled with finding a term to express "libidinal orientation, sexual outlook, and sexual behaviour as masculine and feminine in both its general and its specifically erotic aspects" (1995: 20). As he describes it: "After several burnings of the midnight oil I arrived at the term, gender role, conceptualized jointly as private in imagery and ideation, and public in manifestation and expression" (ibid.: 21). Against his original intent that 'gender role' would be understood as a "unitary phenomenon ... both interior and exterior" (23), this conception "failed to hold its own in competition with the dichotomizing power of the academic zeitgeist in which the sociocultural is territorially separate from the psychological and psychobiological" (23). Thus, 'gender role' (the exterior) became separated from 'gender identity' (the interior). What Money derides as the 'neutering' of gender was further advanced by the canonization of the sex/gender distinction in the social science literature, after the publication of Stoller (1968). On his account:

> The new usage of gender in the social sciences not only divorced gender from biology, but also from the biology of procreation. Moralistically and politically, there was a hidden bonus in this divorce, for it allowed gender to be divorced also from the lustful carnality of the sex organs. Aphoristically, gender was located in the head, and sex in the pelvis.
> (Money, 1995: 27)

Second-wave feminism, he suggests, was divided between those who did or did not acknowledge sexuality. For those who did not, acceptance of this neutered conception of 'gender' as the basis for platforms for equal rights meant that "people might as well have been Ken and Barbie dolls ... with nothing between their legs" (73). But Money reserves his greatest scorn for the explicit "sexualization of oppression" in the work of 1970s' feminists like Susan Brownmiller and Andrea Dworkin, who generalized masculine sexuality as the key source of female oppression. This was, for Money, the thin edge of the wedge that has fuelled the "deviousness" of feminists' separation of "lust-free gender" from "lust-filled sexuality": "Their enemy was men, and their target was men's lust. It could hardly have been men's gender, since gender equality of career rights was the source of the struggle" (129). Thus feminist campaigns against sexual harassment in the workplace are portrayed as part of the "devious campaign against men ... attacking male flirtation, sexuality and eroticism, in its normal as well as its pathological expression" (132).[10] Money's analysis here is a wide-ranging attack on "social constructionism," which he depicts as the bastard postmodern child of the separation of sex (biological, genital, lustful) and gender (cultural, cerebral, lust- free), and on feminism, which he claims has made a crucial error (resulting in either sterile non-sexual politics, or the demonization of male lust) in accepting this separation. The cartoon-like versions of both feminism and postmodernism portrayed here aside, Money's attempt to reassert a biological basis for gender is interesting in its illustration of the underlying assumptions about the relationship between gender and heterosexuality. He culls the scientific literature to develop a "multivariate and sequential" theory of psycho-sexual development whereby chromosomes, hormones, neurological pathways, and environmental influences interact to produce the "adult gendermap": "a developmental representation or template synchronously in the mind and brain depicting the details of one's gender identity/role" (96). The gendermap, including all sorts of images and practices, is coded masculine, feminine, or androgynous. The gendermap includes or overlaps (Money uses both terms) something called the "lovemap": another template in the brain which contains sexuoerotic imagery and practices. It is the gendermap that "codes" the lovemap as "masculine, feminine or bisexual" (96). Successful relationships depend on the compatibility of the "maps." Here, the most important criteria for compatibility seem to be career/family orientation and erotosexual orientation. "Erotosexual" mismatching occurs in both same or mixed sex cou-

---

10 This caricature of a sex-phobic feminism is also drawn (albeit from a different set of sources) by "post"feminist critics such as Fekete (1994), Paglia (1992, 1994), and Roiphe (1993).

ples, and it is frequently the case that "neither of the two partners is exclusively homosexual nor exclusively heterosexual in sexuoerotic orientation, but that both are somewhat bisexual, although not to the same degree" (118). Here the lines between gender and sexuality become the most blurred, as when Money discusses the case of the homosexual man whose ideal lover would be a man who is "ostensibly straight" or the heterosexual woman who is "fascinated by the filial attentiveness and uncoercive sexuoeroticism of a predominantly gay man" (119). How are we to code these signifiers ("ostensibly straight," "uncoercive sexuoeroticism") outside of cultural markers of *gender*? To use Money's own example of Barbie and Ken dolls epitomizing gender without sex, it is precisely the non-genital markers that make them "ostensibly straight" *in certain contexts.*[11]

The lingering heterosexism that underlies conceptions of 'gender' should come as no surprise, then, given its origins. Nor is the gendered expression of sexuality (and the sexualization of gender) a novel concept — this is a gender-lesson we usually learn in the playground, and one which sexual science has not ignored. Hot on the heels of homosexuality's removal from the *DSM-III* (the American Psychiatric Association's *Diagnostic and Statistical Manual*) was the introduction of a new diagnosis: "Gender Identity Disorder of Childhood" (Sedgwick, 1993). As Sedgwick notes, the diagnosis was nominally gender-neutral, but in actuality treated boys and girls quite differently, with girls being diagnosed only in the rare cases where they asserted that they *were* male (e.g., claiming that they had or could grow a penis). Males, on the other hand, could be diagnosed for a range of behaviours, including "preoccupation with female stereotypical activities as manifested by a preference for either cross-dressing or simulating female attire, or by a compelling desire to participate in the games and pastimes of girls" (*DSM-III*, cited by Sedgwick). The related research interest lay in using gender-nonconformity in childhood as a predictor of adult homosexuality, primarily for boys. Reviewing some of this research, Elspeth Probyn (1996) challenges the overall framing of these studies, with their construction of certain gendered behaviours as 'normal,' and the subsequent correlation of these with 'normal' heterosexuality. The flipside, of course, is the correlation of gender *non*conformity (read *ab*normal) with

---

11   For a different take on Barbie, see Rand (1995).

sexual nonconformity — homosexuality — and a replaying of the folk belief that homosexuality is synonymous with defective gender. Thus, the origins of a denaturalized sexuality are sought in a "naturalized and homogenous conception of gender" (ibid.: 107).[12]

Gender is so thoroughly 'heterosexualized,' and heterosexuality so thoroughly gendered, that disentangling sex, gender, and sexuality might seem an impossible task (and a futile one, according to some perspectives). That heterosexuality is important in the production and reproduction of gender inequalities has long been recognized (see for example, Rich, 1980). As Judith Butler summarizes it, 'gender' can achieve stability and coherence only in the context of a "heterosexual matrix": "a hegemonic discursive/epistemic model of gender intelligibility that assumes that for bodies to cohere and make sense there must be a stable sex expressed through a stable gender ... that is oppositionally and hierarchically defined through the compulsory practice of heterosexuality" (Butler, 1990: 151n6). The extent to which feminist conceptions of 'gender' are to be implicated in shoring up a "heterosexual imaginary" (Ingraham, 1994) places sexuality, alongside race and class, at the centre of debates about difference, raising questions about just what else a primary focus on 'gender' obscures. These debates, particularly in their "queer" manifestations, have also raised some important ontological questions that go to the heart of the sex/sexuality/gender matrix. Although there are some continuities with earlier sociological accounts of the 'social construction' of sexualities, the "queer" in queer theory[13] signals an important shift in sensibilities. Parallelling the critiques of gender categories as essentializing,

---

12 Probyn's concern here is to move from the critique of this sort of research to a critique of how similar assumptions underlie certain gay and lesbian recollections of childhood. More detailed consideration of this argument is beyond the scope of the present work, but it contributes eloquently to a critique of the type of logic which individualizes the past in the service of uncovering the truth of the present 'self,' and in which "there is only one line of movement, one that goes from the present to the past in order to justify the present" (1996: 116–117).

13 Queer theory is largely a development of the last decade, and can be located in some key early texts, including Butler (1990), de Lauretis (1991), Fuss (1991), and Sedgwick (1990). The collection edited by Seidman (1996) provides a useful set of readings that establish the relevance of queer theory for sociology.

universalizing, and shoring up the binary that enacts them, queer theory has taken the categorization of sexual identities — lesbian, gay, heterosexual, homosexual — and contested the manner in which they have been accorded stability in earlier theoretical formulations. Queer theory emphasizes *in*coherency and *in*stability in configurations of sex, gender, and sexual desire. Phenomena such as intersexuality, transgendering, and cross-dressing are taken as exemplifying the limits of stable identity categories, and are seen to radically 'trouble up' the binaries of man/woman and hetero/homo. So what has the impact been on conceptions of 'gender'? Within sociology, it seems, not much. In Steven Seidman's introduction to a symposium on queer theory and sociology in the journal *Sociological Theory*,[14] he asserts that "queer theory and sociology have barely recognized one another" (1994: 174). A number of contributors attribute at least part of this lack of recognition to the fact that queer theory's academic location has been in the humanities rather than the social sciences, but there are other reasons as well. Chrys Ingraham argues convincingly that feminist sociology's theories of gender have reproduced the naturalizing of sexuality, and have left "heterosexuality as the unsaid on which gender depends" (1994: 209). This is accomplished through a "bracketing off" of heterosexuality as a central principle of social organization, and one which is integrally linked to the material conditions of patriarchal, capitalist social orders. Echoing the arguments of Judith Butler, Ingraham asks whether gender would exist at all without institutionalized heterosexuality, and argues that the starting point of feminist sociology should not be 'gender,' but '*hetero*gender' (ibid.: 216). Taking seriously the destabilizing of sex, sexuality and gender as conceptual anchors would, as Judith Lorber suggests, require a thorough rethinking of disciplinary conventions, and the building of "new complex cross-cutting constructs into research designs" (1996: 151). But much of both the sociological and feminist resistance to queer theory is linked explicitly to its association with postmodern/poststructuralist cultural theories and the emphasis on the performative.[15] In particular, some feminist critiques see queer

---

14   The articles in this symposium are included in Seidman's edited volume, *Queer Theory/Sociology* (1996).

15   Hennessy (1995) and Seidman (1995) have attempted to provide a more materialist grounding in response.

theory as epitomizing what's wrong with postmodernism/poststruc-turalism, finding it inherently androcentric, valorizing of gay male culture, and undermining feminist politics (Jeffreys, 1994, 1996; Wilkinson and Kitzinger, 1996).

The ontological quagmires of sex/sexuality/gender suggested by queer theory are not just interesting theoretical questions. When the British Columbia Human Rights Commission recommended the inclusion of "gender identity" as a prohibited ground of discrimination in the provincial Human Rights Code, a debate was generated within the feminist community about the implications for women's organizations. *Kinesis*, a Vancouver-published (but nationally distributed) feminist monthly carried an article in its March 1998 issue consisting of a conversation among four women who had grave concerns about the recommendation. Arguing that there is a continuing need for women-only space, they see the potential integration of transgendered persons (specifically male-to-female transsexuals) into previously women-only spaces as part of "the backlash against the women's movement and feminism" (Woo et al., 1998: 15). Placing the transgendered movement on the same continuum as the false memory syndrome lobby and father's rights groups, they view it as yet another attempt by men (even though they are now technically women) to undermine the women's movement. As one of the women summarizes it:

> The M-to-F makes the transition into a position of less privi-lege, but brings with him the comfort of having had that privi-lege and power. And the denial about why women are resisting is typically male. It proves to me that they can get surgically altered and become "women." But it shows they have been socialized as men to demand the space from us instead of cre-ating space for themselves. (ibid.: 16)[16]

The authors also single out queer theory and postmodernism (of which the former is seen to be a part) for deconstructing "terms we still need in order to define what is happening" — terms such as women, men, les-

---

16 This, too, illustrates the 'essentializing' of gender, even as it is understood as socially constructed, although with a very different political sensibility than that demonstrated by the Mars/Venus type of thinking discussed in Chapter One.

bian, gay. "Queer theory destroys and collapses valid differences. How is that truly challenging social structures and injustice?" (ibid.: 15). The original article elicited some spirited debate on the "letters to the editor" page over the ensuing months, and the majority were highly critical of the underlying essentialism. As a couple of contributions noted, concep-tualizing M-to-F transgenders as "still men" means, as its corollary, that F-to-M transgenders must still be women, and included in women-only spaces. The conflation of sex/gender/sexuality was noted, and the issue taken as a clear illustration of the "inherent difficulties in identity politics and binary thinking about gender" (Cecill, 1998: 20). Although this ar-ticle and the letters of response cannot be taken as representing the entire range of views within the feminist community, they do illustrate that the somewhat rarified debates about the ontology of gender in the academy have been taken up in the context of practical consequences in move-ment politics. The complex relationship of genders and sexualities surely problematizes conceptions of gender at their most basic level.

Gender and Race

Anna Julia Cooper, writing in 1892, recounts a train journey, and upon seeing at a station stop "two dingy rooms with FOR LADIES swinging over one and FOR COLOURED PEOPLE swinging over the other," her bemusement in "wondering under which head I come ..." (Cooper, 1993: 196). Cooper's poignant reflections encapsulate the dilemma of categorical analyses when more than one category is relevant (as is al-ways the case). It also points (as do many other accounts) to the fact that questions regarding the ways in which gender and race conjoin long pre-exist the deconstructive sensitivity of the late twentieth-century acad-emy.

It is difficult to compare 'gender' and 'race' as analytical categories for several reasons. As Haraway (1991: 241) points out, in comparison to the distinction between biological sex and cultural gender, there is no linguistic marker to distinguish the biological and cultural dimensions of race, even though "the nature/culture and biology/society binarisms per-vade Western race discourse."

In some usage, though, 'race' and 'ethnicity' are becoming coupled in a way similar to the 'sex'/'gender' pairing. Anthias (1990), for example, suggests that 'race' is often used to suggest an 'origin story' rooted in biological immutability, while 'ethnicity' identifies "particular cultures as ways of life" (20). As she cautions, though, 'ethnicity' is no less prone to being essentialized (as we have also seen with gender) and can provide just as much justification as 'race' for racism.[17]

Because of the well-established language of sex/gender to distinguish the biological/cultural and the lack of such a clear corollary for race, attempts to integrate race and gender frequently (and correctly) problematize concepts of 'race' while accepting gender as a relatively unproblematic social representation of a sex-category. It is commonplace to put "race" (or "ethnicity") in quotation marks, with an accompanying footnote to suggest that this is because of the term's contested nature.[18] The meaning of gender, on the other hand, is supposedly apparent by its very usage. This holding of gender as stable (and at the centre of the analysis) has resulted in 'race' becoming a qualifier of gender in much feminist work.[19] To begin with gender, and then to layer race onto it, is a problematic strategy. It pulls the margins toward the centre. The result may be something like what happened to that venerable icon of Western womanhood, "Betty Crocker." In September 1995, General Mills announced its intention to update Betty Crocker's image. Unveiled in the spring of 1996, the new Betty Crocker was a computer

---

17 Noteworthy is that, in both cases, it is the supposedly biological referent (sex, race) that provides the language of protest (sexism, racism).

18 Stasiulis (1990) is a notable exception, explicitly eschewing this convention of placing race in quotation marks, while supporting the intent behind doing so (i.e., to emphasize the social construction of race). As she argues, "it remains that race, like gender, has biological referents and is most commonly associated with physiognomically based difference such as skin colour. Moreover, the emphasis that is placed on the social nature of constitution of races is also applicable to gender, ethnicity and class, all of which have specific and intermeshed material and ideological modes of reproduction" (Stasiulis, 1990: 295n.1).

19 But, as with 'gender' pointing to and problematizing women in the way it has been taken up, so too does 'race' point to and problematize 'non-whites.' For a trenchant critique of feminism in this respect, see du Cille (1994), who argues that many feminists "see whiteness as so natural, normative and unproblematic that racial identity is a property only of the nonwhite" (607).

composite of 75 women of different ages and ethnicities, resulting in an ambiguously multiculturalized image. As one report described her: "Her blue eyes have morphed brown and slightly almond shaped. She is tanner than ever, although she would still require a pretty strong sunblock whenever she makes it out of the kitchen. And her light brown hair remains straight, silky and auburn-streaked, recoiffed into a becoming anchor-woman do" (L. Smith, 1996). This is hardly the model for a revised conception of the gendered subject for feminism. It does little to recognize the manner in which gender is constructed *through* race, and vice versa. It barely modifies previously problematic conceptions of 'gender' and 'race' as stable referents, and does not capture the complexity of their experience. This has its theoretical corollary in bell hook's charge that when white feminists have attended to the concerns of women of colour, they have done so by "hearing only what was said about race and racism" (1990: 21), not what was being said about gender itself.

Again, the race/gender configuration is not just theoretically contentious. Analysts such as Kim Crenshaw (1991, 1995) in the U.S. and Nitya Iyer (1997) in Canada have demonstrated that, in legal discourse, and often in feminist interventions, race discrimination and sex discrimination are treated as discrete and separate categories. Iyer's analysis of some 300 Canadian human rights cases, where race or sex discrimination was claimed, demonstrates that the complex ways in which race and gender interact with each other and with other grounds of discrimination, cannot be accommodated by the legal frames of reference. The framework used to adjudicate human rights complaints takes the dominant group (white, male) as the centre, and treats divergence from this norm as taking a number of divergent paths, one of which may be the alleged grounds for discrimination. As a result, "antidiscrimination doctrine appears almost entirely oblivious to the fact that a complainant alleging race discrimination also has a gender, or that someone alleging sex discrimination also has a race" (Iyer, 1997: 252).[20] These divergences from the norm are also taken to be individual in their location and effect,

---

20 However, Iyer argues that the human rights adjudicators, at the hearings, do see the individual as both 'raced' and 'sexed.' Even though this may not be explicitly recognized, it may influence the outcome of the adjudication process.

as in all of the cases analyzed, "the problem was conceptualized as the respondent's reaction to a characteristic of the complainant and not as the product of a relationship shaped by a set of hidden norms and perspectives" (ibid.: 259).

Clearly, the implications of the intersections of gender and race go far beyond the usual caveats about being more sensitive to difference, and avoiding undue abstraction.

Gender and Class

Much has been said about the manner in which gender has destabilized conventional conceptions of class. In the 'story' of the development of sociology recounted in the previous chapter, the analysis of capitalism was a major preoccupation, and provided the grounding for the most influential sociological theories of modernity.[21] 'Class' continues to be one of the cornerstone concepts of sociological theory and research. However, a long-standing set of debates has problematized the ways in which class is understood, both theoretically and empirically. Without recounting these lengthy and voluminous debates,[22] it is possible to say, with some confidence, that it is now widely acknowledged that 'class' is (and always has been) 'gendered' and 'raced.' Where the fracturing of gender by class is taken up in a sustained way, it is most likely to be by those working in the tradition of political economy, gesturing more toward the material conditions associated with labour markets and distribution mechanisms that disadvantage women and racially ethnic minorities,[23]

---

21 One of the best accounts of the relationship between capitalism, modernity, and social theory is Sayer (1991). See also Giddens (1971).

22 I have done this elsewhere (Marshall, 1994, especially chapter 2), and there are many good accounts. Bradley (1996) provides an excellent introduction and an extensive bibliography. Hansen and Philipson (1990) have anthologized a wide and very useful selection of socialist-feminist work.

23 Some of the most interesting work in Canada, for example, has looked at the contradictory position of immigrant domestic workers, demonstrating that among women, differences of class, race, and nationality are extremely important. Arat-Koç (1989), for example, argues that a "crisis of the domestic sphere," occasioned by the entry of large numbers of well-off women into paid labour,

rather than by those who focus on the construction of difference through discourse. But, as Bannerji (1995) argues:

> (If) "difference" implies more than classificatory diversity, and encodes social and moral-cultural relations and forms of ruling, and establishes identities by measuring the distance between the ruler and the ruled, all the while constructing knowledge through power — then let us try to imagine "class" or class politics without these forms and contents. (30)

The false opposition (as Bannerji puts it) between questions of "identity" (as questions of gender and race have often been cast) and those of "class" needs to be rejected. Why, then, does class seem to have been eclipsed in some recent feminist theory? Part of the reason must be sought in the postmodern reassessment of the important of class as a basis for identity. While it still gets mentioned, often in a list of 'significant differences,' it is difficult to keep class in view without some conception of capitalism as a system that still has some currency as a mode of social organization. Capitalism, on the postmodern account, has become disorganized and fragmented, and hence class no longer acts as a coherent social division.[24] Sylvia Walby (1992), in a critique of postmodernism, argues that inattention to gender and ethnicity in such accounts results in an over-fragmentation of these categories, which misses the manner in which gender, ethnicity, and class are reconfigured and continue to structure social divisions. The postmodern turn, then, is seen as a turn away from structures that produce and reproduce difference (such as capitalism or patriarchy) toward the production of difference through identities, culturally and discursively produced.

The opposition of material versus cultural in the construction of gender, sexuality, race/ethnicity, and class is increasingly recognized as an unproductive one. Thus, Nancy Fraser (1997) calls for a melding of

---

prompted the state to develop mechanisms for (largely visible minority) immigrant women to enter Canada as a special class of labour to fill the void. Other types of "paid domestic work" (Arat-Koç and Giles, 1994) in the service industries also reflect, from this perspective, "gender and racial/ethnic dimensions of the industrial solution to the reproduction of labour power" (ibid.: 1).

24 For a recent discussion of some of these debates, see Bottero (1998).

socialist economics with deconstructive cultural politics as the most promising strategy for moving beyond this opposition. She frames the dilemma as one of 'recognition' versus 'redistribution' and calls for a strategy that integrates the two. As she recognizes, such a strategy involves a more sustained rethinking of dominant cultural constructions of identities and collectivities. "The task, then, is to figure out how to finesse the redistribution-recognition dilemma when we situate the problem in this larger field of multiple intersecting struggles against multiple, intersecting injustices" (Fraser, 1997: 32). Recognition that class identities are always constructed through gender, sexuality, and race, that gender identities are always constructed through race, class, and sexuality, and so on, is a good place to start. What remains is the necessity to transcend the "bland intersectionality" (Stasiulis, 1990) of many existing accounts, which takes us back to some of the questions raised earlier about how theoretical categories such as 'gender' are deployed, and if and how they should be destabilized.

Feminism and Postmodernism Revisited

We can see that contemporary feminism has not been immune to the more generalized crisis of knowledge prompted by the growing influence of postmodernism and poststructuralism in the human sciences, and that feminists have contributed some of the most interesting interventions. Feminism's emphasis on gender as the single most important category of analysis has certainly been called into question by the postmodern critique. Despite some feminist scepticism about its usage, a defence of gender is central to the feminist critiques of postmodernism. Deconstruct gender, they fear, and we've deconstructed any political possibilities that feminism might have. After all, past experience has demonstrated time and again that, in either theory or politics, where gender has not been insisted upon as a category of analysis, gender-blindness is the result. At the same time, the categorical hegemony of gender has been subjected to a trenchant critique for its occlusion of other forms of difference, and this has, for some, provided a compelling reason for nudging feminism toward a more postmodern form of analysis.

Nancy Fraser and Linda Nicholson, in their widely cited "Social Criticism without Philosophy: An Encounter between Feminism and Postmodernism,"[25] argue that feminism and postmodernism, while wary of one another, are actually concerned with a "common nexus of problems" (1990: 19), and have much to offer one another. Feminism, they suggest, offers a needed corrective to the androcentrism and political naiveté of postmodernism, while the latter may help expose the lingering essentialism of the former. In the development of their argument, however, the strongest critique of essentialism in feminist theory emerges, not from the tools provided by theorists of the postmodern, but from feminist politics which "generated a new set of pressures which have worked against metanarratives":

> as the class, sexual, racial and ethnic awareness of the movement has altered, so has the preferred conception of theory. It has become clear that quasi-metanarratives hamper rather than promote sisterhood, since they elide differences among women and among the forms of sexism to which different women are differentially subject.... (S)uch theories hinder alliance with other progressive movements, since they tend to occlude axes of domination other than gender. (1990: 33)

Thus, if there is a compelling argument for feminists to rethink the way that they have conceptualized 'gender' as an analytic category, it has far more to do with the political motivations of feminist theory than aspirations to philosophical virtuosity.

Yet some feminists are struck with an overwhelming sense of déjà vu: as one critique suggests, some of the supposedly cutting edge insights read like Europeans 'discovering' the 'new world,' in that they seem to have perceived "a new and uninhabited space where, in fact, feminists have long been at work" (Mascia-Lees, Sharpe, and Cohen, 1989: 14). After all, feminists' rejection of identity as an unproblematic reflection of some natural essence long predated the poststructuralist deconstruction of the subject.[26] Similarly, a long history of feminist deconstructions of traditional academic disciplines exemplifies a pro-

---

25 This essay was first published in 1988, and has been reprinted in numerous anthologies. Citations here are to the version included in Nicholson's 1990 collection, *Feminism/Postmodernism*.

26 As Valverde (1990: 234) reminds us, Foucault was 'still in diapers' when de Beauvoir asserted that "one is not born a woman, one becomes a woman."

found critique of disciplinary categories and the power/knowledge nexus they embody. Within sociology, more than twenty years of feminist work has deconstructed academic discourse with an aim to illuminating its socially constructed and partial nature, through various sorts of textual analyses.[27] Many of the recent debates seem to be treading on well-worn feminist ground, and have, in the process, tended to set up abstract oppositions — such as modern/postmodern, material/discursive, and essentialist/nominalist — which do not accurately reflect the complexity of feminist theory or politics.

'Gender,' in its travels as an analytic category, illustrates some of the issues at stake here, and provides an instructive case for destabilizing some of the theoretical oppositions. The possibilities here are illuminated by Kathy Ferguson's (1993) interrogation of another set of oppositions — what she calls interpretation and genealogy as metanarratives in feminist theory. Interpretation, or the articulation of women's experience and voice, rests on an 'ontology of discovery' — the assumption that there is some order and meaning to gender categories that can be uncovered — while genealogy, or the deconstruction of those very categories, rests on a counter-ontology — the assumption that there is no order to be discovered. Each strategy reveals some (incomplete) understanding, and each represents a challenge to un-gendered conceptions of knowledge. As Ferguson notes, it is possible to become 'enframed' in either framework, "seeing only the battles each practice names as worthy and missing the ways in which contending interpretations or rival deconstructions cooperate on a metatheoretical level to articulate some possibilities and silence others" (1993: 7). Yet what can be seen in feminist analyses is a fluidity between interpretation and genealogy which belies their opposition. As Ferguson demonstrates, feminist interpretation must employ genealogical strategies in order to critique dominant interpretations and to create a space for feminist understandings. By the same token, genealogy depends on interpretation "to provide something to deconstruct, and one can follow the genealogical position to a return to interpretation (i.e., interpretation is all there is)" (29). As she summarizes it:

---

27 See, for example, Bernard, 1973; Cook and Fonow, 1990; Farganis, 1986; Millman and Kanter, 1975; Smith, 1974.

> Interpretation produces the stories we tell about ourselves, and
> genealogy insists on interrogating those stories, on producing
> stories about the stories. This interrogation could go on for-
> ever: stories about stories about stories about …; the infinite
> regress of metatheory. But that evasive manoeuver need not
> dominate the field. One can insist on (unstable) bridges be-
> tween interpretation and genealogy, ironically constructed,
> with a commitment to continue combined with a recogni-
> tion of limits. (29–35)

This is precisely the strategy that I wish to take in my rethinking of (and,
ultimately, my defence of) gender as a category of analysis: the incorporation of both interpretive and genealogical moments within a strategy of
critique. Just as one need not become a full-fledged positivist to identify
certain objective and oppressive conditions of women's lives, one need
not embrace the metatheoretics of postmodernism to find deconstructive
strategies useful. Such a tack also avoids the tendency, displayed ironi-
cally by many of those who reject such modernist arrogance, of positing
a linear conception of theoretical development with postmodernism its
apogee. The holding-in-tension of the interpretive and genealogical moments in feminist research and theory has its corollary in the multi-vocal
theory and coalition politics which have increasingly come to define feminism, recognizing that "privilege and oppression are often not absolute
categories but, rather, shift in relation to different axes of power and powerlessness" (Friedman, 1995: 7).

Some of the debates about the nature of gender reviewed in this
chapter might leave the impression that such theoretical questions are
of strictly academic interest. After all, most of us manage to navigate
our way through our daily lives with little problem in identifying who a
'woman' or a 'man' is, and whatever our opinion of those categories, or
how tightly held our notions of what they are like and why, it seems
perfectly obvious that they exist. These sometimes esoteric theoretical
debates, however, have a good deal of political relevance. How we think
about the individual, and her/his relationship to other individuals and
to social structures, is fundamental to the way that we think about things
like rights and laws, and even what we consider to be a legitimate topic
of public concern. These are the issues that provide the backdrop for
feminist politics.

For feminism, some critical political questions are contained in the complex relationship between 'gender' and 'women.' While accepting that there are contradictory and contested meanings associated with any manifestation of gender as a male/female distinction, feminism remains committed to an approach "which analyses how this distinction reproduces inequalities between men and women at every institutional level. It therefore authorizes the marking out of certain categories — namely women — as relatively disadvantaged" (Kandiyoti, 1998: 145). In other words, even as feminists accept (in varying degrees) a certain gender-scepticism at a conceptual level, the political interests of feminism require that it "deal with the world as if it were actually constituted by the categories presented as self evident" (ibid.: 146). The next chapter turns to the terrain of feminist politics to explore some of these complexities.

THREE

Politicizing Gender

> In the 60's, women rebelled against constraints of domesticity and fought the good fight for political equality and financial independence. The postfeminists of the mid-80's ... are less concerned with waving a feminist banner than with focussing on personal needs and wants.
> — Bronwyn Drainie, 1986[1]

> Let's junk the slogans: the war's over.
> — Danielle Crittenden, 1990[2]

> Only by the jostlings of equality can we form a just opinion of ourselves.
> — Mary Wollstonecraft, 1792

Political interests do not emerge unproblematically from any human essence, objective social position, or transcendental coming-to-consciousness. Recent history is surely full of lessons of this sort. It is no secret that members of the proletariat frequently vote for conservative politicians, not socialists, or that women can sometimes be the fiercest critics of feminism. Consider the following comment by former Progressive Conservative MP Dorothy Dobbie: "I am not in any way, shape or form, a feminist. My first job was in a battery factory, where I was paid less than the man next to me, operating the same machine. I quit — but it didn't sour me

---

1 *Chatelaine Magazine*, September 1986.

2 *Chatelaine Magazine*, August 1990.

or turn me into a radical feminist. I simply learnt that God helps those who help themselves" (cited in Gray, 1989: 19). For Dobbie, and many others, the appropriate focus of political action should be that which fosters individual success rather than the achievement of collective gains. Given this, it should come as no surprise that feminism has regularly been declared dead, nor that it refuses to lie down. As the quote from Mary Wollstonecraft above suggests, more recent attempts to declare feminism passé fail to grasp the continuing significance of several centuries of the "jostlings of equality."

My focus in this chapter will be on gender as a political category. While our most immediate experience of gender may be at the level of individual difference, gender is also "a primary way of signifying relations of power" (Scott, 1988: 42). The theoretical and political dimensions of gender are intricately interrelated. This interrelationship is underscored by the importance of the political interests of feminism in understanding some of the theoretical history of 'gender.' That is, both the promotion of gender as a useful concept and the critiques of gender for its conceptual inadequacies have been given impetus by assessments of how it has functioned to advance the interests of 'women.' Thus, the arena of feminist political activity provides a useful context for exploring the problematic relationship between 'gender' and 'women.'

While the appearance of 'gender' in the guise of 'women' here may seem contradictory in light of my earlier critique of the elision of gender and women in some sorts of analyses, the claiming of a gendered identity ('woman') as a political resource in feminism is prompted by the exclusionary nature of the presumably gender-neutral (but masculine) arena of politics. The constitution of 'women' as political constituency poses a significant challenge to liberal individualism, which remains the dominant framing of politics in societies such as ours. My first task will be to review some of the assumptions of conventional ways of thinking about politics, and to suggest how feminism calls them into question. I will then sketch out a framework, drawing on a conception of feminism as a 'public sphere,' through which we can understand the manner in which gender is given salience as a political concept through the construction of gendered identities and interests. Throughout this chapter, I will illustrate some of the complexities of taking 'women's interests' as a manifestation of gendered politics through an analysis of the relationship between English-Canadian feminism and the Canadian state since the early 1970s. In the relationship between gender, feminism and the state, none of these emerges as an unproblematic entity.

Challenging the 'Grammar of Liberalism'[3]

The 'de-naturalization' of gender — that is, the identification of gender difference and inequality as not an inevitable reflection of individual sexual difference — grounds the continuing politicization of gender, and it has transformed a range of issues, previously considered 'private,' into demands for political change. That is, it transformed (and continues to transform) the "universe of political discourse" (Jenson, 1987: 65) — that which sets the parameters of political action by limiting who is considered to be a legitimate political actor, what issues are considered to be legitimate matters for public debate, and what political remedies are considered to be feasible or appropriate. Its most important effect, though, is to "inhibit or encourage the formation of new collective identities and/or the reinforcement of old ones" (ibid.). The struggle to form collective identities immediately comes up against the dominant political framing of individuals, and thus feminist struggles to transform the universe of political discourse pose quite a challenge to conventional conceptions of 'politics.'

Tom Darby and Peter Emberley (1996) have recently articulated a defense of liberal constitutionalism, which sets out in clear terms (although for purposes very different from mine) what is at stake in such a challenge. According to their tracing of its history, liberal constitutionalism developed for good reasons — having learned our lessons from past strife, political power was invested in law, before which all persons were equal

---

3 I am borrowing this phrase from Stacey Young (1997), who has taken it from Benedict Anderson's (1983) conception of nationalism as a 'grammar' — a fundamental structuring of the way in which we think about our place in the world. In this sense, it is "much more fundamental even than perspective, as it is the medium through which we formulate, express, promote, or alter perspectives" (Young, 1997: 1). At the core of this grammar is a strict separation of public and private.

as 'legal personalities.'[4] "The elaborate artifice of the constitutional state, in which the concrete particulars of individual and communal life were restricted to 'legal personalities' was the result of a prudent calculation of the disruptive consequences of permitting appeals to religious, ethnic or cultural differences within a constitutional structure" (238). At our current historical juncture, however, the "very principles" underlying liberal constitutionalism are being challenged. They suggest, correctly, that some hard questions are being asked (and the manner in which they phrase them should give some indication that their answer to each is a resounding 'no'):

> Should the redressing of 'historical wrongs' be permitted to run roughshod over equality of opportunity? Should all representative political institutions correspond exactly to the statistical profiles of the population at large? *Should the experiences of gender, race, sexual orientation, and cultural difference be permitted to re-arrange our[5] notions of the family, marriage, political decision-making or education?* (239; emphasis added)

They argue that the extent to which these questions have even been asked represents a fundamental confusion about the relationship between "nature and convention,"[6] and that the (presumably 'natural') relationship of nature to convention has been distorted through the "emphasis on language" (243), where "the meaning of words has little or nothing to do with natural or historical referents and everything to do with power. In this condition, words are used to advance political agendas" (244). It is

---

4   That this is a remarkable erasure of the historical and ongoing struggles of various groups (women, slaves, the landless, aboriginals, immigrants) to be included as 'legal personalities' goes without saying. But let's stick with their logic for the time being.

5   One can only wonder who the "our" in this sentence represents, given that every person has "experience of gender, race, sexual orientation, and cultural difference."

6   As they define these terms: "By conventional we mean what is based on agreement or force, what is artificial, arbitrary and temporary. The natural is something that is permanent and that endures over time.... Our laws and policies may be conventional, but they ought to accord with what is natural, that is, with what is not of our own making but which can guide our making" (239).

no surprise, then, that they take the displacement of 'sex' by 'gender' as a signal example of the "abandonment of nature" (245). What Darby and Emberley cast as a 'misunderstanding of political order' on the part of those who would question the historical understanding of the relationship between nature and convention, is, on the contrary, a very sound understanding. The natural *is* conventional, and, as feminists have long suggested, the personal *is* political. Thus, what Darby and Emberley cast as a dangerous threat to the great achievement of modern nation-states, that "(T)he very principles underlying representation, legislative deliberation, and the primacy of individual rights — the principles of legislative constitutionalism — are all being challenged" (238), might be taken as a productive starting point for a rethinking of politics by modernity's Others.[7] The 'grammar of liberalism' that underlies Darby and Emberley's defence is still one that engages feminism, but as I will attempt to show, the practice of feminist politics has demonstrated the need to encompass as well more complex understandings of the relationship between the 'natural' and the 'conventional.' These point to the need to take seriously the discursive, meaning-producing aspects of oppositional movements — here, we can see that 'gender' is not just taken as a political point of departure, but is actively created *through* politics. As Nancy Fraser notes, "groups of women have politicized and reinterpreted various needs, have instituted new vocabularies and forms of address, and so, have become 'women' in a different, though not uncontested or univocal, sense" (1989: 172).

Some interesting political questions have emerged from the tension between feminism conceived of as speaking for collective rights for 'women,' and the liberal democratic framework of individual rights. The rhetoric of individual equality rests upon some theory of formal justice — an 'ethic' of rights that takes as its subject some abstract, universal 'individual.' This ethic both theoretically and practically excludes the bearers of certain particularities from the universalistic discourse of equality. This is what I will refer to as the universalism/particularism dilemma, and it underlies many of the debates about the revitalization of democracy in which feminists have been vigorously engaged. These debates are

---

7 Women, of course, do not exhaust this category. For an original and insightful critique of Canadian modernity read against the aspirations of Canada's First Nations, see Denis (1997).

also animated by the tensions within feminism about the possibility of speaking of 'women' collectively. Just as feminists have criticized the abstract 'individual' of liberalism for its exclusionary nature, so too have different groups of women criticized the abstract 'woman' of feminism. Thus the universalism/particularism dilemma exists within feminism, as well as in feminist critiques of liberal democratic theory and practice.

A useful concept for exploring some of these questions, as they pertain to the politicization of gender, is that of the 'public sphere.' Some concept of a public sphere has always been central to social and political theory, representing the arena of citizenship, where the particular needs of concrete persons and principles of universality are reconciled. In its classical sense, as described by Habermas (1989)[8] in his study of the eighteenth-century 'bourgeois' public, this public sphere was envisioned as an arena of public discussion, open to all, enabling the individual to engage in informed debate about issues of the "common good" — in other words, to act as a citizen. Theoretically, this public sphere was open to all, but practically it was dominated by the male, educated, property-owning class. Thus, 'gender' ostensibly had no place in the public sphere, while in practice it permeated it. What, then, is the analytic potential of a concept like the 'public sphere' when an explicit politicization of gender is introduced? Rita Felski (1989a, 1989b) suggests that it holds the potential for confronting the tension between universal and particular (despite the fact that Habermas never followed this line of analysis). Thus, she articulates a feminist counter-public, which "does not claim a representative universality but demarcates a gender-specific space" and, at the same time, directs its politics outwards, "challenging existing structures of authority through political activity and theoretical critique" (1989a: 233–234). Such a conception has the potential to recognize the problematic construction of gendered interests, which are continually enmeshed with other oppositional interests, such as race, class, and sexuality, while avoiding

---

8   Extended discussions of Habermas' theory of the public sphere, including some feminist critiques and assessment of its application in media studies may be found in Calhoun (1992), Fraser (1997), Marshall (1994, 1995), and McLaughlin (1993). More recently, Habermas has continued his dialogue with democratic theory, begun in his early work on the public sphere, in his development of a theory of 'deliberative democracy' in *Between Facts and Norms* (1996).

the conclusion that no such interests can be invoked. Thus, what is critically important here in addressing the universalism/particularism dilemma is the conception of the feminist counter-public as comprising simultaneously internal and external political moments. Internally, it seeks to confirm the specificity of the different ways that women are 'women,' and seeks to create solidarity across diversities, and externally, it seeks to press claims on behalf of 'women' and challenge prevailing power relations. Although it is clear that some groups (such as educated, able-bodied, economically privileged, white women) have more access to agenda-setting in this feminist public sphere than others, it nonetheless demarcates a space for debate, within which concrete experiences of different groups may be articulated. Such a conception allows us to grasp feminist politicizations of gender as "a process of meaning *production* which actively generates diverse accounts of female identity, and which is linked to the political interests and struggles of an oppositional *community*" (Felski, 1989b: 46; emphasis added). Feminist counter-publics do not reside in any particular institution or organization, but can be thought of as a "series of political and cultural strategies" (Felski, 1989a: 235), or in more general terms, as political projects.[9]

'Politics' as such, is not limited to matters involving the state or its institutions.[10] Theoretically, interest in Foucault's concept of "governmentality" (1991) has, for some analysts, eclipsed the centrality of the 'state' as the locus of power. We must escape, he says, "from the limited field of juridical sovereignty and State institutions, and instead base our analysis of power on the study of the techniques and tactics of domination" (1980b: 102). Echoing some of the theoretical turns mapped in the last chapter, and in relation to changing political contexts, there has been a shift within feminist theory from "a focus on social structure (the state) to one on political discourse and culture (citizenship)" (Curthoys,

---

9 Within these political projects, different feminisms may share goals, but disagree on how to best achieve them, or they may share recognition of problems, but disagree on solutions. Historically, for example, there are long-standing differences within varieties of feminism on the rationale for and/or desirability of suffrage, birth control, and protective legislation.

10 For example, there is warrant for considering the popular media as a key, extra-governmental arena of political activity.

1993: 34). This is not to say that the 'state' does not remain an important site of struggle. Even in its post-modern decentring, the nation-state continues to be a significant social and political force and, as the arbiter of 'rights,' one to which claims for both redistribution and recognition, to use Fraser's (1997) terms, are made.[11] One of the key features of the terrain of politics today, she argues, is a shift in the "grammar of political claims-making" from redistribution to recognition. Although class-centred political movements stressed redistribution of resources and economic equality in their understanding of 'justice,' identity-based movements — of which feminist and multicultural movements are taken to be exemplars — reframe claims-making in terms of cultural recognition. But to see them solely in terms of an identity-interest is to obscure what Fraser calls their 'bi-valent' character, or the manner in which their claims for recognition and redistribution are intertwined. Setting up redistribution and recognition as either/or choices, is, as Fraser argues, replicating a false opposition between the material and the cultural.[12] Furthermore, the manner in which

---

11   The couplet "redistribution and recognition" is Fraser's intervention into a longstanding debate within versions of feminist and democratic theories that have counterposed the recognition of difference to social equality. This has often been phrased as a dilemma, given that claims based on group difference may be seen as antithetical to, or undermining, claims to general equality. As Fraser suggests, the simultaneous pressing of claims for recognition and redistribution is conflictual, but not unresolvable, given that any project of social justice must call for both "economic redistribution and multicultural recognition" (1997: 14). Ute Gerhard defuses the dilemma by reminding us that, far from being antithetical, 'equality' and 'difference' are related at the most fundamental level:

> Basically, in the logic of the concept of equality as a principle of law, equality doesn't mean 'sameness' or 'identity' because 'equality' is a term of relativity.... It expresses a relationship between two objects, people or things, and determines in what respect they are to be seen as equal.... Logically, equality requires that the two objects being compared be different, otherwise there would be no need for equality. (Gerhard, 1995: 43)

12   Consider an issue like pay equity, which might be seen to epitomize the material — how much more material can you get than money? As a number of analyses have shown, though, the debates about, and implementation of, pay equity programs have been about a lot more than money. Pat Amstrong (1997), for

struggles for recognition have been cast, exemplified by the use of "identity politics" as a "derogatory synonym for feminism, anti-racism and anti-heterosexism," implies that "the inherent thrust of such politics is a particularistic self-assertion that rejects the universalism of 'common dreams' and has nothing to do with justice" (Fraser, 1997: 5). This, as we shall see, is a pervasive interpretation of the politicization of gender. Feminism, as an oppositional public, has never emptied claims for recognition of the redistributive implications,[13] nor of their broader implications for 'justice' writ large. Struggles with the political state over recognition in the citizenship arena are at the same time struggles with the welfare state over redistribution, and both speak loudly to the 'common good.' By debunking liberalism's claim to 'reasonableness' and 'objectivity' represented through the state, oppositional movements, such as feminism, insist on the political relevance of those 'concrete particulars' that have traditionally been relegated to the sidelines.

Gender Politics:
Feminism and the State in English Canada

The contemporary feminist movement in Canada has developed in close relation to the post-World War II welfare state, which saw state involvement in both the economy and the domestic sphere as legitimate. As Brodie (1995: 39) summarizes it, "The welfare state was grounded on new impositional claims about the proper role of the state and the rights of citizens." The relationship between 'women,' as a social collectivity and as a political constituency, and the state has always been contradictory. Feminism has engaged with the state and its institutions on a number of fronts, which embody the interrelationship between demands for redistribution and claims for the recognition of gender. These include the

---

example, recounts the interpretive struggles around what constitutes an "employer," a "job class," and so on, and the struggles over how women's work itself is to be understood and evaluated. Similarly, Janine Brodie's (1997b) analysis of the discursive shifts in Canadian abortion politics underscores the extent to which different idioms of 'rights' play a crucial part in constructing the conditions under which women can control their fertility.

13 Bread *and* roses, anyone?

range of state activities that are implicated in both the production and regulation of gender, "the diversity of women's points of entry into the power relations of states" (Weir, 1987: 95), according to their race, nationality, class, sexual orientation, and physical ability, and the extent to which the state has been instrumental in shaping the character of the feminist movement. The agenda for a conference on "Women and the State" held in 1987[14] sets out some of the issues and contradictions:

> The state is powerful; its activities profoundly affect Canadian women's lives. In our struggles as feminists we inevitably come up against the state in terms of our demands for legislation to ensure sexual equality, our call for better funding for women's organizations, our struggles for the provision of social services and our insistence on equal access to educational and employment opportunities. But in these struggles we often see feminist demands shaped and distorted by state policy, legislation and funding programs. (OISE, 1987)

The conference agenda identified the issues that continue to shape current debates: (a) women's experiences with the state, as state workers, as recipients of transfer payments, as users of state services, as immigrants, as regulated by the state in matters of work and sexuality; (b) specific sites of struggle around pay equity, immigrant women, daycare, lesbian rights, reproductive rights, mental health issues, welfare rights, sexual abuse, housing, criminal justice, and domestic workers; (c) state responses to women's struggles, in the form of hearings, commissions, legislation, and funding; and (d) strategies for change, including coalition building, cross-class and race alliances among women, popular education, electoral politics, and alliances with other movements. It was explicitly recognized that "the state is not simply repressive," that "the state is neither completely autonomous nor ... simply an instrument of capitalism, patriarchy or imperialism," and that the "state is not a monolith" (ibid.). The recognition of this complexity in women's relationship to the state needs to be placed in the context of their recognition as political subjects.

---

14 This conference, held at the Ontario Institute for Studies in Education in February of 1987, is the subject of a useful commentary by Weir (1987). My references are to the original conference documents, held at the Canadian Women's Movement archives.

Looking at the relationship between feminism and the state over the last few decades suggests that this has not been a straightforward or linear process of progressive political inroads. Three critical events that provide a backdrop to some of the discussion to follow bear brief mention here: the Royal Commission on the Status of Women, which reported in 1970; the specific inclusion of gender equality in the 1982 Charter of Rights and Freedoms; and the negotiations leading up to the referendum on the constitution in 1992. They are all significant as points of political mobilization around gender, through which women became differently constituted as a political constituency, and they also illuminate that 'gender' has never stood alone in the demands for recognition or distribution.

Canada's Royal Commission on the Status of Women (hereafter, RCSW) was a watershed in feminist-state interaction.[15] Struck in response to intense lobbying,[16] it held hearings over a two-year period, in all regions of the country and from all sorts of groups and individuals. The final report contained 167 recommendations on a wide range of issues. Whatever the assessment of the success or failure of the RCSW in obtaining substantive gains, it was instrumental in constituting women as a political constituency, politicizing many existing women's groups and making them more explicitly feminist, and spurring federal and provincial governments to create mechanisms for the representation of women's interests in state bureaucracies. Interest in monitoring implementation of the report's recommendations provided an impetus for institutionalizing some of the political momentum among women through various organizations, most significantly the National Action Committee on the Status of Women (NAC). Three key state institutions were developed to represent women's political interests: the Women's Program within the Secretary of State, Status of Women Canada, and the Canadian Advisory Council on the Status of Women.[17] The RCSW's idiom of universalism

---

15 Marjorie Cohen, for example, names the RCSW as "the most significant single event in establishing a sense of a women's movement in Canada" (1993: 4).

16 See Monique Begin's (1992) important account of the relationship between English-Canadian and Québecois feminists during this process.

17 The most detailed account here is Sue Findlay's (1987). Jenson and Phillips (1996), drawing on Findlay, term this institutional configuration the "women's state," and track its 'quiet dismantling' in the mid-1990s. This will be taken up in Chapter Five.

muted some of the complex questions, emerging even then, of representation and identity (Arscott, 1995a, 1995b) — questions which have,
more recently, come to the forefront. Subsequent debates within feminism, and within the broader political arena about the representation of
'women' and 'women's issues' in political discourse have engendered reflections on representation more generally and have resulted in sustained
attention to processes of identity formation in increasingly diverse political communities.

The Charter of Rights and Freedoms, as part of the repatriation of
the Canadian constitution,[18] provided another key site for mobilization.
After the federal government cancelled a planned Women's Constitutional
Conference, and the president of the Canadian Advisory Council on the
Status of Women resigned in protest, a massive grassroots mobilization
ensued to ensure that women's equality rights were entrenched in the
Charter. Two sections of the Charter were of particular concern: Section
15, which guarantees "equal protection and equal benefit of the law without discrimination," and specifically includes race, national or ethnic origin, colour, religion, sex, age, or mental or physical disability as prohibited
grounds of discrimination, and which protects affirmative action programs
against charges of reverse discrimination; and Section 28, which guarantees all rights and freedoms in the Charter "equally to male and female
persons." Of particular importance, and the focus of much of the feminist mobilization, was assurance that women's equality rights would not
be subject to the override provision (section 33 — the 'notwithstanding
clause') — that is, that neither the federal nor provincial governments
could pass an act that would specifically nullify those rights.[19] It is important to recognize here that not all Canadian women's groups were sup-
portive or active here. In particular, Québecois feminists "opted for a more
cautious stance," looking instead to the already entrenched Québec Char-

---

18 Until the enactment of the Canada Act in 1982, Canada's constitutional document was the British North America Act (1867), an act of the British Parlia-
ment.

19 The most detailed account of this is Penney Kome's *The Taking of Twenty-Eight:
Women Challenge the Constitution* (1983), although Kome's account does not
deal with the lack of mobilization among Québecois women. See also Vickers
(1993).

ter of Rights (de Sève, 1992: 134), and being reluctant to endorse a Charter introduced as part of the patriation of the constitution which did not have the assent of Québec. Many aboriginal women also doubted the priority of securing the rights of individual women over their collective national rights as First Nations.[20] Nonetheless, with the Charter, sex and, by extension, gender become specific grounds on which full citizenship may be argued, and, along with other grounds introduced by the Charter, ushers 'Charter Canadians'[21] onto the political scene. This signifies a distinct "citizenship regime" that addresses both citizens as individuals *and* that "recognized and represented particular *categories* of citizens" (Jenson and Phillips, 1996: 112), and thus opens up the question of 'rights' to be interpreted in a more complex way. Recognizing that "(R)ights on paper mean nothing unless the courts correctly interpret their scope and application" (Razack, 1991: 36), feminist groups actively monitored the interpretation of the Charter, and the Women's Legal Education and Action Fund (LEAF) was founded in 1985.[22] In addition to education and lobbying, LEAF sponsors and intervenes in individual legal challenges that have the potential to advance collective gains in terms of gender equality. Gender becomes salient, then, in both constitutional and judicial terms.

From 1982 to 1987, negotiations to bring Québec into the constitutional fold (recalling here that Québec was not signatory to the 1982 repatriation) dominated political debate. The Meech Lake Accord (1987), recognizing Québec as a 'distinct society,' went through a lengthy ratification process, to meet its final defeat in the Manitoba legislature, when Elijah Harper said "no" in 1990, moving aboriginal self-government to the top of the constitutional agenda. The Charlottetown Accord, which tried to address the aspirations of both Québec and the First Nations,[23] was defeated in a referendum in 1992. NAC opposed the Accord on a

---

20 For an excellent account of some of these issues, see Vickers (1993).

21 "Charter Canadians" is a term coined by political scientist Alan Cairns, who uses it to describe those groups granted "constitutional identity" by the Charter: specifically, women, aboriginals, official language minorities, ethnic minorities, and "the various social categories listed in S.15" (Cairns, 1988: S121).

22 For an excellent history and analysis of LEAF, see Razack (1991).

23 Among other issues, such as Senate reform, amending procedures, and federal-provincial divisions of power.

number of grounds, including concerns about an implied 'ranking' of equality rights in the Canada Clause, lack of equity in Senate reform, unclear protection for aboriginal women's equality rights, the potential undermining of national social programs, and the extent to which the Accord satisfied the demands of Québec.

The foregoing issues and debates frame the questions that I am particularly interested to explore here, which focus on how English-Canadian[24] feminism has conceptualized the 'political' nature of gender — especially in terms of its understanding of the state, the realm of legitimate 'women's issues,' and the possibility of adequately representing 'women's interests.' In reviewing the politicization of gender in post-RCSW English-Canadian feminism I am relying on a range of sources, including academic accounts (of which there are a number of excellent studies[25]), conference reports and organizational publications,[26] and the textual record contained in the magazines and newspapers of the feminist press.[27] The latter are particularly important. The feminist press pro-

---

24   Most federally-oriented feminist organizations are based in English Canada, and while some of these (such as NAC) aspire to cross linguistic and cultural divisions, they are more likely to engage the federal state on issues such as the constitution, national social programs, and international trade issues than their counterparts in Québec. Feminism in Québec has a different and complex relationship to questions of nationalism, as well as to social policy issues, where they are more likely to look to Québec City than Ottawa. I do not mean to imply here that Québec feminism is only, or primarily, about nationalism. As Micheline de Sève correctly reminds us, the federal orientation of English-Canadian feminism is in itself a form of nationalism: "Nationalism, as a collective instrument to forge cultural links, is no more exterior to feminism in Québec than federalism is in the rest of Canada" (1992: 115). For other discussions, see Bashevkin (1996), Burt (1986), Lamoureux (1987), and Vickers (1993).

25   See, for example, Adamson, Briskin, and McPhail, 1988; Backhouse and Flaherty, 1992; Brodie, 1995; Carty, 1994; Pierson et al., 1993; Vickers, Rankin, and Appelle, 1993; Wine and Ristock, 1991.

26   The Canadian Women's Movement Archives, housed at the University of Ottawa, and the repository of organizational records, publications, conference reports, and other documentation for thousands of organizations, is an amazing research resource.

27   Publications reviewed include *Branching Out, Breaking the Silence, Broadside, Herizons, Kinesis, Upstream,* and *The Womanist.* I focused on non-academic,

vides a visible record of "feminist movement," and in particular, an important record of how the organized, majoritarian women's movement (to use Jill Vicker's term) has communicated with its 'community.' To quote Esther Shannon, former editor of *Kinesis*, "Feminist newspapers provide the most immediate and personal record of where the women's movement came from, where it is today and how its politics are evolving" (1994: 18). They also represent a key site through which academic debates "filter ... to the women's movement through people's multiple roles and locations" (Ng, 1993: 197).

There has been a distinctive shift in the attitudes toward the state from the immediate post-RCSW period,[28] when many feminist organizations had a clear focus on state-initiated change. The National Action Committee on the Status of Women, still the most visible representation of organized feminism, was created as a coalition of women's groups to monitor implementation of the RCSW's recommendations.[29] Likewise, Canada's longest-publishing feminist newspaper, *Kinesis*, originated as the newsletter of the Vancouver Status of Women Council, which was organized to, among other things, promote action on the Report of the RCSW. Both had a state-focused orientation, emphasizing lobbying, in the immediate post-RCSW years. NAC's relationship with the federal government was shaped through lobbying and their interactions with the newly created 'women's state': Status of Women Canada, the Advisory Council on the Status of Women, and the Women's Program of the Secretary of State, and they generally accepted the RCSW's report "as a blueprint for change" (Vickers et al., 1993: 90). By the late 1970s, the expanded and increasingly diverse constituency of NAC

---

generalist publications — those which intended to reach and represent a broadly defined 'feminist community.' Of these publications, only *Herizons* and *Kinesis* are still publishing.

28 This is not to suggest, however, that all feminists, nor indeed all feminist periodicals, enthusiastically embraced a focus on state action in the wake of the RCSW. See, for example, the critical review of the RCSW in the early Vancouver periodical *The Pedestal* ("Pie in the Sky," January 1971), reprinted in Pierson et al. (1993: 35-37).

29 On the history and continuing significance of NAC, see the excellent study by Vickers et al. (1993).

forced attention to internal structures of representation, and a shift to-ward a less reactive policy-reviewing stance — to a more proactive policy-*making* stance — began.

In the early years, *Kinesis* had regular features such as a monthly focus on a particular recommendation of the RCSW, a 'letter lobby,' which targeted particular issues and the appropriate minister to write letters to, profiles of 'women at the top' (i.e., feminist bureaucrats, or 'femocrats' in more current lingo). These state-oriented features were gone by the end of the 1970s, and by the early 1980s feminist politics seemed to have moved a long way from the initial glow of the RCSW. For example, in its farewell editorial in 1980, the *Upstream* collective identified an overemphasis on state-initiated change as contributing to its downfall: "The implicit suggestion in that kind of reporting is that the federal government or other institutions will give us our liberation....We feel now that we should have carried more articles on the political differences that exist within the movement's movement, and on the process that different women go through to reach the viewpoints that they hold."[30]

In subsequent years, increasing attention has been paid to the differ-ent levels of 'the state' — municipal, provincial, federal, and increasingly global political bodies are recognized as having distinct, and not always unitary, effects. State involvement in the production and regulation of gendered identities and statuses is dispersed over a range of institutional sites — such as social assistance, employment, education, health, immi-gration, rights protection bodies, international trade, and the military. But there has been increasing recognition that different levels of 'state' do not necessarily work in concert; they are, in fact, often contradictory, and they act on behalf of no unified interest. The concerns about the devolu-

---

30 Certainly the dependence of most organized feminist groups on state funding has been a contentious issue. As I have explored elsewhere (Marshall, 1995), exigencies of state funding have fuelled the tension between what Briskin (1991) calls 'disengagement' and 'mainstreaming' as feminist strategies, and have be-come significant instruments of control and containment of feminist activism. As Pollack (1993: 3) summarizes it, "groups are being forced to compete with each other, are unable to do effective long-term planning, and feel increased pressure to tailor their projects and activities to fit government criteria, thus threatening their ability to define issues from a grassroots perspective."

tion of power in proposed constitutional amendments were, in large part, centred on the potential conflicts between federal and provincial government initiatives with respect to women (see, for example, Brown, 1992; Burke, 1992). These different manifestations of 'the state' were also apparent in analyses of the greater faith of Québecois women in the provincial state than the federal (Burke, 1992; Busque, 1991; Hénaut, 1991), in the concerns of First Nations women about aboriginal self-government versus the protection of the Charter of Rights (Day, Nicholson, and Rebick, 1991; Hill, 1992; Hill and Jaffer, 1992; Huang, 1992a), and in analyses of the potential conflicts between legislative and judicial interpretations of the Charter (Buist, 1987).

Feminists have long spoken to a broad range of issues. Over the last two decades, however, feminist analyses have been brought to bear on such issues as international trade agreements, and the process of 'nation-building' through the repatriation of the constitution and the subsequent attempts to amend it via the Meech Lake and Charlottetown accords. These interventions have considerably expanded the limits of what have traditionally been considered 'women's issues.' Two key issues surface here. The first is a critique of the outright exclusion of women from the process of 'nation building,' which has raised important questions about what is the community that the state represents. In references to the Meech Lake Accord, we were continually reminded of the '11 white men' who were around the table (Buist, 1987; Cole, 1987; Day, 1992; Day et al., 1991; Pollack, 1990). In the continuing constitutional discussions surrounding the Charlottetown Accord, the question of who legitimately 'belongs' to the political community was raised particularly loudly. Prime Minister Brian Mulroney branded opponents[31] of the Charlottetown Accord "enemies of Canada."[32] The mainstream media and some eminent political scientists persisted in referring to women as a 'special interest' group, or as 'Charter Canadi-

---

31 While NAC took an official stance of opposition to the Accord, not all feminists agreed. Particularly important were party politics, with feminists such as Audrey McLaughlin supporting her party's endorsement of the Accord. Paradoxically, NAC found itself in the 'no' camp with the right-wing Reform Party, which opposed the Accord for entirely different reasons.

32 *Globe and Mail*, August 22, 1992.

ans,' implying that they expressed only a narrow self-interest rather than intervening with the greater good in mind.[33] The juxtaposition of "enemies" versus defenders of Canada and "Charter" versus "ordinary" Canadians, reasserts the familiar framing of 'us' and 'them': the primacy of the universal, however mistakenly conceived, against the politicization of particularities. Feminists relentlessly reminded the politicians, and each other, that the process of building a democratic nation cannot proceed through undemocratic and unrepresentative processes. As Sunera Thobani summarized it in the wake of the 'no' vote on the accord, "the women's movement is going to keep pressing for more democratic representation and processes at every level in Canadian society" (cited in Jaffer, 1992: 3). The second issue here is the focus of feminist analyses on practical, tangible consequences as opposed to abstract imaginings about 'Canada' as a nation.[34] The emphasis, instead, of feminist interventions into such national projects as the Free Trade Agreement, the Multinational Agreement on Investment, and constitutional projects has been on its material effects — again, inextricably linking issues of recognition and redistribution. Analysts such as Sylvia Bashevkin (1989) argues that this does not represent a move away from feminism's traditional concerns with issues of women's legal rights and social conditions, but an integration of these concerns with broader economic and political questions. Or, as Sandra Burt puts it, bringing gender concerns to mainstream political concerns explodes the 'artificially constructed' category of 'women's issues' (Burt, 1995: 371).

---

33 As Linda Trimble notes, this reflects a grossly inaccurate understanding of feminist interventions in the constitutional debate. Not only were the issues raised by feminists significantly addressed to the "greater good," but women hardly spoke as one voice. The 'Charter Canadians' conception of feminist action here entirely erases the gendered dimensions of national, linguistic, and regional politics, and vice versa. It also speaks to a larger issue, which will be taken up in the next chapter, regarding the assumed inability of those deemed 'particular' to transcend the limits of their particularity. As she puts it: "When women speak they are heard as women, and therefore as persons with partial views limited to their gendered experiences. When men speak, they are heard as impartial, ungendered citizens who legitimately express the public good" (1998: 150).

34 In my review of more than twenty years of feminist periodicals, I have not come across one 'Canada Day' edition!

This is not to say that feminist analysts were not interested in the concept of Canada as a nation, but that a fundamentally different version of 'nationhood' emerged from grappling with the consequences for differently situated women. As Barbara Cameron put it in an article in *The Womanist* (1991: 40): "The way forward for us is to commit ourselves to creating a new voluntary relationship of equality among Québec, English Canada, and the First Nations, and while we are doing this, we have to devote ourselves to fighting for the rights of women and minorities within these societies.... We want a total feminist vision on the table ... during constitutional discussions. We want to make the political elites respond to our agenda this time — we have been responding to theirs long enough." Yet to speak of 'our' vs. 'their' agenda raises the problematic question of who 'we' are.[35]

By the early 1980s, the critique of oppression was taking an increasingly inward look, focussing on how the mainstream women's movement marginalized many women, in particular women of colour, poor women and lesbians. A still-evolving series of debates, sometimes crystallizing around key events[36] has led to a growing awareness that the continuing critical 'edge' of feminism depends on its taking up struggles that do not necessarily privilege gender. That earlier phases of the women's movement did not, or were not able to, take up this challenge has in at least one case been linked to its lack of efficacy: the farewell editorial of *Breaking the Silence* in 1989 regretted that "*Breaking the Silence* does not have the resources, knowledge or experience to discuss the issues that are now on the cutting edge. Perhaps it is because today's burning issues are not middle-class, educated, white feminist issues and that's what our collective largely is." Phil Masters, a long- standing member of the *Broadside* collective when it ceased publishing in 1989, expressed a similar sentiment in her hopes that something would come along to fill the gap left by that paper's demise: "[T]he group who takes up the challenge should not consist solely of white, middle-class women, but must include women of colour and Third World women, women who have the important questions

---

35 I particularly like Susan Jackel's twist on the old Lone Ranger joke — "Who's this 'we,' white woman?" (1991: 43).

36 Such as International Women's Day events, the split at the Women's Press in Toronto, and the forced resignation of June Callwood from Nellie's.

for the present movement" (cited in Wine, 1989: 8) The sense that the evolution of feminism as a revolutionary movement depends on its taking up anti-racism was echoed by Sunera Thobani in *Kinesis* (1991: 7): "The revolutionary element in feminism right now is the women of colour and I think that if white feminists don't become anti-racist, then it will become a bankrupt movement."

This is closely related to a shift in feminist thinking about 'representation' itself.[37] The earliest question raised about representation was fairly direct: where are the women? This centring of gender as an unproblematic category was the overriding framework of analysis inherited from the RCSW, and frames much feminist political analysis in the early to mid-1970s. For example, readers of *Kinesis* were encouraged to vote for female candidates in elections and to lobby for more and better representation of women in official structures. Yet, even then, it was not a simple question. A flurry of letters to *Kinesis* in 1974 both praised and criticized the paper's decision to endorse candidates on the basis of gender. And while there was predictable dismay over a male (Marc Lalonde) having ministerial responsibility for the Status of Women, more complex questions were already being raised about what representing the interests

---

37 The shift in editorial statements of feminist publications is illustrative here. In 1974 the editorial statement of *Kinesis* declared that it was "dedicated to a philosophy consistent with the women's movement" as if this was self-evident. In 1994 *Kinesis* strives "to be a non-sectarian feminist voice for women and to work actively for social change, specifically combatting sexism, racism, classism, homophobia, ableism and imperialism." Similar shifts can be found in the editorial statements of other publications, indicating the overriding move toward diversity and recognition of multiple and intersecting grounds of oppression as defining any sense of feminism. Another example might be found in editorial representation. In 1984, the editorial collective of *Breaking the Silence*, in the context of a survey of feminist organizations, answered, in response to the question "Do you have people from different backgrounds in your group?": "As a newsletter we have the advantage of being able to print diverse points of view without having those points of view represented within the collective." This is no longer a tenable position, as witnessed by the intense struggles around inclusivity and representation in feminist periodicals and presses, and in feminist organizations such as NAC, over the last decade (on NAC, see Vickers et al., 1993).

of women means. As Jo Lazenby, writing in 'member's forum' in *Kinesis* (1975) put it: "Is it possible for us to receive justice in a structure that was framed without reference to or consideration of the needs of women or their view of society? It is possible ... that Lalonde was the best man available to take on the Status of Women portfolio. The best man available in a system that wasn't designed to include us."

These more complex questions about representing women's interests exploded throughout the 1980s and into the 1990s as the category of 'woman' became more unstable. This shift in sensibilities, combined with a different demographic and political context, makes it unlikely that a report as universal in orientation as the RCSW could be produced today.[38] For example, the Canadian Panel on Violence Against Women was widely criticized by feminists for its "lack of meaningful representation of women" (Huang, 1992b), in particular women of colour and women with disabilities. Throughout the constitutional debates, regional, linguistic, economic, and racial differences between women rendered the representation of 'women's interests,' already a political polemic, even more contentious.[39] Women, it was argued, were being forced to choose between their gender and their region, or, in the case of Québecois and First Nations women, their gender and their national allegiance. This was particularly apparent in the coverage of the Native Women's Association of Canada's (NWAC) struggle for official representation at the Constitutional talks (Brown, 1992; Burke, 1992; Cameron, 1991; Day et al., 1991; Hill, 1992; Hill and Jaffer, 1992; Huang, 1992a; Jaffer, 1992) where lit-

---

38 As Jane Arscott (1995a: 52) notes, the issues of representation and identity politics "are not solely creations of a later period," but existed in the internal dynamics of the RCSW. The universalism that the Commission adopted was a "deliberate choice" (Arscott, 1995b).

39 In many respects, the old question of 'Where are the women?' was transformed into a question of 'Where are the _____ women?' A report on a conference on women and the Constitution at UBC in 1992 noted that: "Although attempts were made to include women from grassroots women's organizations, a representative cross-section of women in BC was not achieved. Almost all of the participants were from the Lower Mainland and the majority of the working group was composed of academics and professionals. The absence of women from poverty, lesbian, single mothers, domestic workers and health groups, among others, was noticeable" (Huang, 1992a: 3).

tle attention was given to the role of women such as Rosemary Kuptana and Mary Simon,[40] because they were not at the table as women per se. Yet the presence of women such as Kuptana and Simon, and Nellie Cornoyea from the Northwest Territories, was repeatedly held out as an answer to women's concerns about lack of representation at the table (Day, 1992: 72)

Thus, the first line of critique was against the assumption that men can represent women, which, at least in its earlier manifestations, assumed that women could. Yet this fairly direct understanding of representation has collapsed into itself, as the categories that must be thus represented have proliferated, forcing multiple identities to be (impossibly) adjudicated. The shift, then, is to a critique of representation more generally, via an analysis of the historically available structures and processes that 'represent' representation. The evolving challenges to the representation of 'women's interests' are forcing important questions onto the agenda, not only about manner in which the state has (mis?)represented women, but about "a set of practices that *feminists* use to represent 'women,' practices that hold a hierarchy of privilege in place, rather than to ask for more and better representation in them" (Findlay, 1994: 220; emphasis added).

It is clear that feminists have developed a more complex and nuanced approach to the state, understanding it as non-unitary, and not necessarily rational, not just as a set of institutions, but as a social force, as the site of struggle between different interests, and as both enabling and constraining. 'The state,' as an arena of political practice, is not something feminists can choose or refuse to enter. As Anne Curthoys (1993: 34) summarizes it: "We can no longer conceive of the state as something outside us, and retain that impossible (modernist, oppositional) dream of a pure feminism, born outside of the state, contemplating entering into it to achieve its own ends." I would argue that this represents an important critique of modernist conceptions of politics. By the latter, I mean those that tend to see the state as a relatively unified set of institutions which administer the entity called the nation state, and which may be understood as acting somewhat rationally in accordance with identifiable 'interests,' and against which politically self-conscious movements can 'act.'

40　Representing the Inuit Tapirisat.

While this understanding of the state characterizes much of the theoretical reflection on feminist politics,[41] 'the state' thus conceived does not figure as a key concept in issue-oriented feminist analyses, for this is not the way that 'the state' is experienced in the course of the day-to-day struggles of feminist movements. Instead, we find reference here to 'government,' 'police,' 'welfare,' 'law,' 'courts,' 'advisory councils,' 'violence' and so on. As Briskin (1991: 39) suggests, "the map of feminist practice is not shaped within the same parameters as the map of abstract theoretical principle." Is it, then, implicitly 'post-modern,' as many have come to understand that term, in that it is so highly contextualized, particular, grounded in the local, and that it challenges, through specific and daily struggles, the 'grand narratives' of both theory and liberal democratic practice? It would seem, for example, that the textual record of feminist politics understands well Foucault's insights on governmentality:[42] the simultaneously individualizing and totalizing moments of the state, the techniques and technologies of government. These are the stuff of feminist political analysis: not the 'state' as some mysterious entity, but systems of income support, forms of administration, systems of intervention into various organizations, representations of 'expertise,' effects of policing, and localities of power. The shift in focus away from the 'state' as some unified entity which defines legitimate political activity, and the problematization of interests and their representation, locates feminist critique as integral to the critique of liberalism. At the same time, feminism remains ambiguously attached to the language of modernism and humanism, invoking equality and justice as its normative backdrop in the politicization of gender.

It is also clear that 'gender' has never existed, as an identity or political resource, outside of its location in the differently situated statuses of women — particularly in terms of class, race, ethnicity, sexual orientation, language, and region.[43] Whether explicit or not, and it is clear that

---

41 Here, I am thinking of those that, according to theoretical pedigree, identify the state as 'bourgeois' or 'patriarchal' and hence as acting according to that interest.

42 See the collection edited by Burchell, Gordon, and Miller (1991).

43 The politicization of gender, then, must also be understood historically in relation to other sorts of political projects — especially those of nationalist, ethnic,

it has often *not* been articulated, 'gender' can only be grasped in relation to these differently situated statuses, and gender politics can only be understood in relation to other grounds on which both recognition and redistribution are sought.[44] This has been a hard lesson for 'majoritarian' English-Canadian feminism, but one that continues to stimulate both its 'internal' and 'external' moments. As an oppositional public, feminism cannot replicate the exclusionary characteristics of the liberal 'bourgeois' public, where political actors enter already fully formed in their identities. Any notion of the feminist public must be based on its recognition as a site of conflict and struggle over identities and interests which can never be represented as stable and/or general — not, in other words, where representation occurs, but where its meaning is negotiated. These struggles to re-organize representation must be seen, as theorists such as Janine Brodie (1995) and Sue Findlay (1994) have argued, as part of a larger re-organization of the relationship between state and civil society, for it is in this relationship that the import of social movements lies.

The Problem of Identity Politics

The politicization of gender through feminism's constitution of 'women' as a political collectivity supplies the crucial context for understanding theoretical debates. As reviewed in the previous chapter, the feminist literature of the last decade has been rife with debates over the manner in which gender has been conceptualized, its relationship to other axes of difference, and its adequacy in grounding political identities. In this literature, there has been a discernable shift from the material to the discursive, but the important questions here have always had a double nature

---

and class flavours. For an account that locates the development of feminism in Canada in the context of the politics of a 'settler society,' see Stasiulis and Jhappan, 1995.

44 Jill Vickers illustrates this point with a question as simple as when Canadian women got the vote: "The 'official' answer is 1918, when white women got the federal franchise. Québec women might answer 1940, when they won the Québec franchise after a long struggle. Some racial minority women (Asian) suffered exclusion along with their menfolk, and aboriginal women who retained their government-assigned status under the *Indian Act* were denied the vote until 1960, first exercising it in 1961" (1993: 265).

— that is, they have recognized the continued salience of gender, while simultaneously critiquing the practices and discourses by which gendered statuses and identities are produced. The complexities of mobilizing women *qua* women, while recognizing the fragility of 'women' as a coherent category, encapsulates the interrelationship of the material and the discursive that has characterized recent scholarship on social movements.

In the significant body of literature that has emerged around the rubric of 'new social movements,' a shift in theoretical emphasis from the material to the cultural is often signaled by the replacement of 'socialism' with 'radical democracy' as the reference point for emancipatory political movements.[45] To be sure, the impetus to abandon socialism as a reference point was in large part related to the failure of "actually existing socialism" in fostering democratic conditions, or even securing basic human rights. The collapse of communism in Eastern Europe also seriously undermined the legitimacy of socialism as a viable critique of capitalism. But such a shift was also demanded by the increasing importance of political voices such as feminism, gay and lesbian movements, and anti-racist movements, whose claims-making could not be adequately accounted by reference to class position. But, as the diversity of feminist political struggles shows, the 'turn to culture' hardly renders a concern with materiality redundant, nor are any of the movements generally referred to under this rubric really 'new.' What seems to be 'new' is the attention given to questions of recognition, not the questions themselves. The cultural turn is exemplified by the extent to which questions of identity, difference and representation have become central axes of debate.

The insights we can derive from the debates about gender, identity, and difference are numerous — and irreversible. As Fraser (1996: 207) has argued: "The shift from 'gender difference' to 'differences among women' to 'multiple intersecting differences' remains an unsurpassable gain." This shift is encapsulated by the debates about identity politics.

---

45 'New social movements,' as a moniker, gained currency in the 1980s through the work of a number of theorists, such as Cohen (1983, 1985), Habermas (1981), Laclau and Mouffe (1985), Melucci (1980), and Touraine (1985). While the 'old' social movements were concerned with the economics of distribution, 'new' social movements shifted the focus to culture and identity. As Habermas put it, "they concern the grammar of forms of life" (1981: 33). On 'radical democracy,' see Trend (ed.), 1996.

While 'identity politics' is hardly a new idea (historically, groups have always constructed political identities which claim some common interest), it has been associated, over the last few decades, with the politicization of particular identities as the basis for claims-making, against the general framing of 'equality of opportunity' which did little to dismantle social hierarchies of, for example, gender, race/ethnicity, and sexual orientation. As identity-based claims came up against the supposedly universal juridical subject — the classic 'modern' citizen of liberalism — the decidedly particular character of that subject was revealed — especially its maleness, whiteness, and heterosexuality. In this sense, identity politics has been most productive.[46] At the same time, however, the very possibility of constructing and deploying categorical identities has come under attack, both theoretically and politically.

As Calhoun (1996: 215) notes, the general framing of 'new social movements' functioning as a loose grouping together of "attractive movements," "vaguely on the left," has obscured the greater significance of identity politics. Left off the list are other contemporary movements, such as the religious right, anti-feminism, various versions of nationalism, and so on, which are also manifestations of identity politics. While such "new social movements" may be more identity- than class-based, we cannot assume their progressiveness.[47] I want to explore this, in the next chapter, through an analysis of the way that 'gender' — as a concept and as the basis for identity — has been taken up as a pejorative in some recent critiques of feminism.

---

46 Debates about 'identity politics' *within* feminism have tended to understand it in a relatively specific way, involving the extent to which one's political insight is organically linked to one's identity, and the extent to which a resulting 'hierarchy of oppressions' potentially splinters feminist politics. For a good account, see Adams (1989). I am using the term in a broader, though related sense, to refer to the manner in which social locations can be politicized — that is, the extent to which 'identity' can be called on as a political resource.

47 This is not to say that class is not relevant to identity formation within these movements — this is particularly the case for some versions of 'libertarian feminism' reviewed in the next chapter.

FOUR

De-legitimating Gender

Gender feminist theory is an example of intellectual fraudulence and is a theory based on phylogeny, tribadism[1] and misandry. This theory currently stalks the social and political life of this country. It is predatory and seeks to dominate and terrorize. It is a personality disorder in the body politic of the nation.

— Hon. Anne C. Cools in the Canadian Senate,
November 29, 1995[2]

I'll admit to being puzzled the first time I heard the term "gender feminist." Having been a feminist for as long as I can remember, and having spent most of my academic career working in the sociology of gender, it seemed to me that feminism was, by definition, about gender.[3] The term "gender feminist" originated in American philosopher Christina Hoff Sommers' book *Who Stole Feminism? How Women Have Betrayed Women* (1994), and has since gained fairly wide circulation as a descriptor of what

---

1 When I first read this, I thought perhaps she meant 'tribalism,' but I have since learned that 'tribadism' is slang for lesbianism. So, perhaps it's not a misprint after all.

2 Sen. Cools originally prepared this speech for a debate in Senate on Bill C-68 (gun control). She was unable to deliver it during that debate, but was permitted to have it read into the Senate record.

3 It was, in fact, when I first started hearing "gender" used in this pejorative sense that I started to think about writing this book.

is supposedly wrong with contemporary feminism. According to various commentators, "gender feminists" are elitist, dishonest, dogmatic, authoritarian, self-serving careerists, who seek to vilify men, cast women as passive victims, destroy the family, abandon children, and prohibit sexual pleasure. They have taken over our universities, our governments, and even the United Nations! As one of the critics puts it, there is "one word which expresses in a nutshell the idea of these feminists. That word is gender" (de Casco, 1995: 15). That's a lot of weight to put on one concept, but perhaps it is not misplaced. As Oakley (1997: 41) suggests: "Because gender as a concept was a basic building block of second-wave feminism, there is probably no better way to undermine feminism than by discrediting the very idea of gender." Recalling that the original political impetus for the feminist adoption of 'gender' was in its distinction from 'sex' and its rejection of biological determination, it is not surprising to find the anti-feminist critiques premised on "returning gender to sex: making social inequalities disappear inside the body" (Oakley, 1997: 34).[4]

The critique of the concept of "gender" has functioned in recent critiques of feminism in two distinct ways, which I will outline in turn. Despite their very different premises, these two versions of gender critiques converge in some important ways. I will explore this convergence with the intent of drawing out both the insights provided about 'gender' as a categorical identity and what can be gleaned about the strength of "gender" as an analytic and political concept. I'm just enough of a cynic to think that anti-feminists wouldn't be so exercised about "gender" if it didn't have some radical potential.

Gender in Brackets: The Fundamentalist Critique

One line of critique is that of the explicitly conservative, anti-feminist forces, particularly those associated with fundamentalist "pro-family,"

---

4 Anti-feminism, of course, has a history which long predates the debates of the last few years that I am concerned with here. Walby (1997) provides some comparison of earlier and later forms of anti-feminism, as does Steuter (1992). Garland Publishing has recently compiled a three-volume set of readings from oppositional literature in the U.S., covering the years 1848–1994 (Howard and Tarrant, 1998).

"pro-life" moral projects. The fundamentalist attack on "gender" and "gender feminists" gained a good deal of steam in the preparations leading up to, and the activities at, the United Nations Fourth World Conference on Women, held in Beijing in the fall of 1995. The most complete account of the fundamentalist critique of the focus on "gender" in the preparations leading up to Beijing is contained in a deceptively titled book, *Empowering Women: Critical Views on the Beijing Conference*, published by a small Australian press, which came out just prior to the conference. In the introduction, Martha Lorena de Casco, the official delegate from Honduras, asks "How could the United Nations organisers have possibly been unaware of the origin and implications of this controversial concept?" (1995, 16). The 'origin' of gender, de Casco notes, citing Judith Butler, was to "dispute the biology-is-destiny formulation." The implications? According to de Casco, "gender" means the "stark rejection of all our assumptions about what it means to be human (that men and women are not defined by their sex, but by culturally imposed norms)," and the result can only be "a new and sexless world," "the elimination of the biological family," and the destruction of "the legal, moral, financial and social support all societies have always given to the institutions of marriage and the family" (14–16). According to another contributor, "it is hard to escape the conclusion that the UN is promoting "gender analysis," not to promote women's rights, but as part of a long-run strategy to slow birth rates" (Garcia-Robles, 1995: 56). Several of the contributors recount the debates about the definition of gender that emerged in the preparatory committee meetings, culminating in the attempt by de Casco (backed by a number of conservative delegations) to have "gender" bracketed throughout the text of the draft platform for action. While they were not successful, an "informal contact group on gender" was struck at this final meeting of the preparatory committee, which was mandated to "seek agreement on the commonly understood meaning of 'gender' in the context of the Platform for Action and to report directly to the conference in Beijing" (United Nations, 1995a: 1). They reported as follows:

> Having considered the issue thoroughly, the contact group noted that: (1) the word "gender" had been commonly used and understood in its ordinary, generally accepted usage in numerous other United Nations forums and conferences;

> (2) there was no indication that any new meaning or conno-
> tation of the term, different from accepted prior usage, was
> intended in the Platform for Action. (ibid.: 2)

That "generally accepted usage" is evident in the manner in which gender was provisionally defined in the preparatory committee meetings and
used throughout the Platform for Action. It recognizes that human beings exist as male and female, and that the manifest differences in their
roles and status are not determined by their biological makeup, but are
socially constructed. That is, it reflects the most basic distinction between 'sex' and 'gender.' For example, the Platform for Action notes that
although the last few decades have witnessed both a growth in knowledge about the status of women and men, and changes in their roles
and relationships, "in many countries, the differences between women's
and men's achievements and activities are still not recognized as the consequences of socially constructed gender roles rather than immutable
biological differences" (United Nations, 1995b: Para. 28). It is precisely
the basic distinction between 'sex' and 'gender,' then, that is at the heart
of the fundamentalist critique. Any "new meaning or connotation" mentioned by the working group is an oblique reference to the insistence of
some delegates that 'gender' has a 'hidden agenda,' and really means
"something other than just men and women.... It covers a whole range
of meanings, including homosexuality, lesbianism, bisexuality, whatever
you want" (Sudanese delegate Khadiga Karar, cited in Garcia-Robles,
1995: 55). As Baden and Goetz suggest in their analysis of the debates
over 'gender' at Beijing:

> factors explaining the conservative fixation on gender may
> include the perceived greater influence and presence of femi-
> nist NGO's [non-governmental organizations], the greater vis-
> ibility of lesbians in NGO's, and inclusion, for the first time
> in UN conferences on women, of very open language on sexual
> and reproductive rights. (1997: 12)

The fundamentalist attack on 'gender' is, at heart, an attack on social
constructionism. The failure of the conservative delegations to deflect
this understanding of gender as framing the Platform for Action before
the conference did not prevent it from remaining an issue at the conference itself. Sharon Hayes, a Reform MP and member of the Canadian

delegation, left the conference early in protest over what she called the dominance of "gender equity" on the conference agenda (Mickleburgh, 1995: A8). As one report summarized it: "Ms Hayes found that discussions about equality were inextricably linked to 'gender' and she soon realized the word was regarded as an assertion that human behaviour is socially constructed and that the differences between males and females result exclusively from social arrangements" (Brunet, 1995: 32). The most detailed fundamentalist critique of 'gender' at the conference came from a paper written by Dale O'Leary, an American Catholic conservative. This document, "Gender: the Deconstruction of Women" (1995), was widely circulated at the NGO forum in Beijing. As Baden and Goetz suggest, O'Leary's paper is worthy of some attention in that "of all the conservative documents available at the NGO forum, it is the only one … which engages directly with feminist theory, and thus directly outlines some ways in which conservatives are politicizing gender in reaction to feminism" (1997: 13). O'Leary begins with Christina Hoff Sommers' definition of 'gender feminists,' and proceeds to elaborate on what she sees as its philosophical roots, its presuppositions, and its dangerous implications. Through a spotty, and generally out of context, review of some feminist theories,[5] O'Leary seeks to expose the "ideology behind the public statements made by Gender Feminists," the "true nature of the Gender Feminists' agenda" and the "hidden objectives behind seemingly innocent proposals." These objectives, while numerous, include, first and foremost, those related to reproductive choice and sexual orientation (which can hardly be considered "hidden" objectives). O'Leary energetically attacks the social constructionism that underlies the concept of gender, suggesting that it does not advance the "real" interests of women, as it denies them their 'nature.' Once we loosen the link between sex and gender, hell is but a short handcart ride away — the family will lie in tatters, one would be able to change one's sexual identity at will, the population will fail to replace itself ("Obviously, more

---

5 For example, explaining that this is a textbook used in Women's Studies Programs, O'Leary cites Alison Jagger's *Feminist Politics and Human Nature* on radical feminism in such a way as to present Jagger's review of radical feminist theory as uncontested orthodoxy, when in fact it is part of a larger review *and critical commentary on* a number of different strands of feminist thought.

homosexuality, more women working outside the home, and less women seeing motherhood as natural would decrease the population" [1995: 15]). The Gender Feminists' "war against 'socially constructed roles' is a war against the natural relationships between women and their children, between women and men, and between women and their own feminine nature" (28). It is repeatedly implied throughout the conservative literature that 'gender' is but a covert means of promoting homosexuality, abortion, and even the existence of more than two sexes.[6] Not surprisingly, these concerns were also expressed in the "reservations and interpretive statements" which were annexed to the Platform for Action endorsed by the conference. Almost all the delegations appending reservations did so with specific reference to language on sexual and reproductive rights, and several specifically proffered restrictive interpretations of 'gender.' The Vatican, for example, asserted the following:

> The term "gender" is understood by the Holy See as grounded in biological sexual identity, male or female. Furthermore, the Platform for Action itself clearly uses the term "both genders." The Holy See thus excludes dubious interpretations based on world views which assert that sexual identity can be adapted indefinitely to suit new and different purposes. (United Nations, 1995b: Chapter V, Para. 11)

Guatemala, as well, explicitly "interprets the concept of gender solely as female and male gender in reference to women and men" (ibid., Para. 10). O'Leary herself notes that as long as it could be assumed that 'gender' was "simply a polite way of saying 'sex' to avoid the secondary meaning which sex has in English and that 'gender' referred to male and female human beings," there was little basis for disagreement (1995: 4). Their resistance to 'gender,' then, reflects their (correct) perception that it means much more than this.

---

6 O'Leary makes explicit reference here to the circulation of Anne Fausto-Sterling's (1993) paper at the preparatory committee meetings, which some delegates perceived as legitimating a 'right' to determine one's sexual identity.

The 'Gender-Feminist' Takeover: The Libertarian[7] Critique

While O'Leary makes specific reference to "gender feminists," her fundamentalist critique of gender differs quite substantially from the libertarian version in which the term originates. Christina Hoff Sommers coined the term "gender feminism," in opposition to "equity feminism," to describe what she saw as 'bad' and 'good' feminism. Gender feminists "believe that our society is best described as a patriarchy, a 'male hegemony,' a 'sex-gender system' in which the dominant gender works to keep women cowering and submissive" (1994: 16). Equity feminism, on the other hand, asks for nothing more than formal legal equality of individuals before the law — something we already have, so presumably it is obsolete. The libertarian critique of 'gender feminism' has crystallized around a set of texts,[8] issues,[9] and organizations;[10] key

---

7 I use the term 'libertarian' to describe this version of gender-critique, for lack of a better alternative. Some of the most frequently cited proponents (e.g., Sommers, Paglia, and McElroy) explicitly self-identify as 'libertarian,' and their work (particularly that of Sommers and Paglia) is invoked and endorsed with regularity by others writing in this vein (such as Fekete, LaFramboise, and Patai).

8 Key texts include Fekete (1994), Fox-Genovese (1996), Patai and Koertge (1994), Laframboise (1996), McElroy (1996), and Roiphe (1993).

9 These include critiques of women's studies programs and feminism in the academy more generally, and critiques of labour market initiatives such as affirmative action and employment equity, but the issues to attract the most sustained attention are those involving sexuality — especially feminist work on sexual harassment, rape, and violence against women.

10 In the U.S., the Independent Women's Forum and the Women's Freedom Network are significant in that they implicitly invoke gender consciousness (i.e., these are women's organizations) while criticizing the very notion of feminism — but it is a gender consciousness rooted in class privilege. On this, see Kaminer (1996). In Canada, the libertarian critics of feminism are more likely to organize alongside like-minded men in organizations like the Association for Academic Freedom and Scholarship or the Alberta-based MERGE (Movement for the Establishment of Real Gender Equality), which publishes the on-line magazine *Balance* (www.taiga.ca/~balance). The *Backlash* (www.backlash.com) is another online magazine which provides numerous links to 'dissident feminist,' anti-feminist, and men's rights organizations.

representatives of this view include both academics and journalists, many of whom are women. Almost all of the libertarians claim some sort of allegiance to feminism in an earlier, purer, form.[11] Many trot out their credentials as former members of feminist organizations, or their participation in political action around issues associated with feminist activism (such as abortion rights). But for all there was some turning point, and this is frequently expressed as a pendulum swinging too far, or a scale out of balance. This is a useful metaphor for understanding the antipathy toward 'gender.' The balance metaphor calls up an image of two categories of individuals, male and female, on either side of the fulcrum, with rights accorded each category according to where the scale rests or the pendulum swings. Thus, the metaphor is not disturbed by 'additive' or compensatory work — whether that work is academic (such as research on women) or political (including formal legal rights for women). At first glance, it accommodates the fair-minded inclusion of women, as long as too much does not get added to their side, which would throw things out of kilter again.[12] At a more fundamental level, such a metaphor cannot accommodate a conception of gender which is relational, processual, and not a mere descriptor of sexed individuals — gender, understood in this way, displaces the very fulcrum, or centre-point, on which an unproblematic weighing of the proper balance rests. This conceptual problem aside, the 'balance' is the metaphor of choice for the libertarian critique, and is implicit in most of the charges laid at the feet of 'gender feminism' — an inordinate focus on women-as-a-group, male-bashing, misrepresenting the extent to which the 'balance'

---

11 "First wave" feminism, particularly in its U.S. manifestations, is the model frequently held up as epitomizing "good" feminism. Sommers, in particular, holds up the Seneca Falls conference in 1848 as exemplary (1994: 33–35). For a good account of how such a reading is misrepresentative, and underestimates both its complexity and its radical dimensions, see Walby (1997), especially Chapter 7.

12 Yet even on this level it becomes problematic — for example, should we add some of the benefit of a putatively woman-favouring policy such as equal pay legislation to the man's side of the balance, given that many women add their income to a family unit that includes men? Is constitutional protection against sex discrimination added to the male or female side of the balance, given that the majority of the cases taken to the Supreme Court since its enactment in Canada have been pressed by men?

has swung in favour of women, and the promotion of victimology, just to name a few.

"Gender feminism" has, on this account, taken over (in Sommers' words, "stolen"[13]) mainstream feminism, severing it from its (proper) liberal roots, and rejecting the "enlightenment principles of individual justice" (Sommers, 1994: 22). Politicizing gender is an outrage to liberal individualism, and Sommers is particularly disturbed at the gender-feminist 'takeover' of the academy:

> when future historians go back to find out what happened to American universities at the end of the twentieth century that so weakened them, politicized them, and rendered them illiberal, anti-intellectual, and humourless places, they will find that among the principal causes of the decline was the failure of intelligent, powerful and well-intentioned officials to distinguish between the reasonable and just cause of equity feminism and its unreasonable, unjust, ideological sister — gender feminism. (52–53)

Sommers encapsulates here the wrong side of the binaries that gender feminism falls on: it is illiberal, anti-intellectual, unreasonable, unjust, ideological. The 'right' side of the binaries — the high ground claimed by libertarians — includes liberal, intellectual, reasonable, just and truthful.

The term 'gender feminist' is picked up by Wendy McElroy in her 1996 book, *Sexual Correctness: The Gender Feminist Attack on Women*, where she defines 'gender feminism' as:

> the ideology that views men and women as separate and antagonistic classes. Men oppress women. They do so through the twin evils of the patriarchal state and the free-market system. The goal is not equality: it is gender (class) justice for women. (ix)

Here, McElroy explicitly links 'gender feminism' with Marxism (via their common framework of 'class analysis'), and defends instead an 'individualist feminism' which sees government as the "greatest threat to women's

---

13 Her terminology here is extremely problematic, implying that there was some rightful "ownership" of feminism (by whom is unclear) that could be violated, and casting "gender feminists" as outlaws.

freedom." Individual rights, best secured through a free market (economic or intellectual), are again the bedrock.

"Gender-feminism" becomes, in the hands of Canadian cultural theorist John Fekete, "bio-feminism." Fekete, citing Sommers approvingly, notes that her alternative, 'equity feminism,' doesn't work in Canada, because "equity is one of the code words around which gender-obsessed biofeminists organize" (1994: 351). Biofeminism (and its offspring, biopolitics) is charged with regressing into "dark mythologies of race and gender" (12) and "fixated in gender thinking" (22). According to Fekete:

> biopolitics is anti-politics; a regression *from* politics to a new primitivism which promotes self-identification through groups defined by categories like race or sex. Biopolitics has no time for humankind; nor does it care about individuals. In fact, even its concern for individual members of its own ingroup depends on the extent to which they behave and express themselves in accordance with the stipulated essence of the group, with the features by which the group is *identifiable*, with *collective* identity. The concern is to promote the group, and to advance the group's cause *against* its enemies. (22; emphasis in the original)

"Gender," for the libertarian critics, is a "codeword" or "mantra," which, along with race, is central to the aims of feminist social engineers who have hijacked the noble cause of human rights in order to advance an authoritarian program. The politicization of gender is, here, an affront to reason, and to the 'grammar of liberalism.' The grammar of liberalism assumes a single standard of rationality, of 'reasonableness' to which all right-thinking people subscribe. "Those who fail to act in accordance with accepted models of rational behaviour do so ... because they either lack reason or are consciously flouting it..." (S.Young, 1997: 4). "Gender-feminists," apparently, are guilty on both counts, in their suggestion that prevailing "regimes of rationality" (D. Smith, 1992) may, in fact, be irrational from the perspective of those not at the centre of its making. "Gender feminists" are tarred with adjectives that are the polar opposite of those associated with "rationality" — intolerant, shrill, emotional, close-minded — and feminist scholarship is charged with violating all standards of "reasonableness": manipulating evidence, lacking in conceptual rigour, ideologically driven.[14] The wonderful thing about 'reason,' of course, when pitted against 'ideology,' is that it always wins out. Sommers can confidently predict that "once their ideology becomes unfashionable, many a gender feminist will quietly divest herself of the sex/gender lens through which she now views social reality and join the equity feminist mainstream" (1994: 275).[15]

Much Ado about 'Gender'

While, for the conservatives, 'gender' has under-emphasized, through its insistence on social construction, the 'natural' differences between men and women, the libertarian critique charges 'gender' with privileging group membership over the individual, and as promoting a biologically-linked essentialism that over-emphasizes the differences between men and women Yet as different as these accounts are, they share some fundamental similarities. Both perceive a gender-feminist conspiracy and target 'gender analysis' as an authoritarian program, and both frame their rejection of 'gender,' 'gender equity,' a 'gender perspective,' or 'gender analysis' in terms of a defence of individualism.

---

14 I am more interested in drawing out the assumptions underlying the libertarian critique of 'gender' than in documenting the many shortcomings in *their* scholarship. See, though, fn.17 regarding Daphne Patai's project later in this chapter, as well as Ehrenreich (1994), Flanders (1994), Godard (1998), and Minnich (1998) for suggestions that similar charges might apply to various writers in this genre.

15 Despite her (and others) claims to having the 'reasonable' view, Sommers is remarkably silent on what the "social reality" with respect to women might be. Wendy Kaminer (who Sommers cites approvingly as one of her fellow dissident travellers — 1994: 275) recounts the following exchange with her:

> "Are there still structural barriers to equality?" I once asked Christina Hoff Sommers after she delivered a speech excoriating "gender feminists" for portraying women as victims. It was impossible to know, she replied, because feminists have falsified statistics, exaggerating the obstacles to women's advancement. "So use your common sense," I suggested ... "You've been around for over 40 years. What does your common sense tell you about the persistence of institutionalized discrimination?" She had no response, nor could she articulate a vision of sexual justice. (Kaminer, 1996: 52)

That gender feminism is considered to be a conspiracy is evident throughout both the libertarian and fundamentalist critiques: There are 'codewords' and 'hidden agendas'; women's studies programs are indoctrination centres, thinly disguised as education, where dissent is not tolerated. What is patently clear are the presumed motives for the gender-feminist conspiracy — no, not revolutionary idealism, but sheer self-interest. The implication that feminists are tenaciously insisting on gender analysis out of self-interest and careerism is peppered throughout the critical literature:

> "the deconstruction of existing gender roles won't come easily" and will create a "veritable gender-feminist make work program" — "we'll need gender experts to define the gender perspective, gender police to enforce the gender quotas, and gender educators to mold our children." (Dykxhoorn, in Woodard, 1995)

> As improvements have occurred in women's status in this country, those committed to feminist activism find themselves in danger of losing their *raison d'être*. Ultimate success, after all, would make "feminism" superfluous. The search to uncover grave and previously undiagnosed discrimination against women thus becomes imperative. Exaggeration, scare statistics, concept-stretching and raging rhetoric all contribute to the continued existence of an institutionalized feminism with a vested interest to protect. (Patai, 1998: 254)

> Large numbers of professionals with job titles like 'sex equity expert,' 'gender bias officer' and 'harassment facilitator' are remuneratively engaged in finding, monitoring, and eradicating endless manifestations of gender bias. (Sommers, 1994: 274)

> [Many women's studies programs] have been conducted as autocratic fiefdoms, insulated from critique on their own campuses and connected to each other nationally by a network of self-interested operatives who control hiring, grants, and publications. (Paglia, 1997)

The assumption that self-interest is a prime motivator of the 'gender-feminist' conspiracy — that it is an 'industry'[16] rather than a concern with broader issues of social justice — is one common ground between the libertarian and fundamentalist critique. I will return to this problem a bit later. The other common ground between the libertarians and the fundamentalists is the premising of their critiques of gender on a defence of individualism, which becomes, in both cases, a defence of *masculine* individualism.

The fundamentalist critique is premised on a defence of natural individual difference based on biological sex. The concept of gender as socially constructed poses a threat to individualism because it challenges this conception of natural difference. This conception of individualism is implicit in the continual conflation of "gender" and "the family" in the fundamentalist analysis. De-constructing gender is equivalent to destroying the family — the latter defined as the nuclear, hetero-patriarchal family. "Gender feminists," on this account, want men and women "to be the same" (O'Leary, 1995: 9), seek to "turn women into little men by day and sexual service stations by night" (Dalzell, 1995: 47). It is a futile attempt to "redefine human nature" (Joseph, 1995: 94). The defence of individuality here is the defence of the masculine individual — produced through a rigid separation of public and private, the latter constructed around the patriarchal family. On O'Leary's account, it is only the patriarchal family that can civilize men, tie them to the future, and convince them to "take up the hard work of building society" (1995: 22). If women abdicate their natural role as defined by the patriarchal family, "society will deteriorate into anarchy" (ibid.).

The libertarian critique, on the other hand, explicitly wants to defend an abstract individual who is, on first reading, ontologically ungendered. Repeatedly, the politicization of gender (and sexuality) is criticized, generally via the assertion that gender feminism has polarized men and women in an overly antagonistic fashion, creating difference through the insistence on social construction. Consider here Fekete's charge

---

16 A number of authors refer to feminism as an "industry." Fekete (1994) for example talks about the "violence against women industry," Patai (1998) targets what she calls the "Sexual Harassment Industry," and Sommers (1994) invokes the more general "gender-bias industry."

that feminism has created a "panic culture of group antagonisms," and his closing plea that "individuals have to be able to escape from groups" (1994: 336). Donna LaFramboise calls on us "to end the accusations, the finger-pointing and the mud-slinging between men and women, to declare an armistice, if you will.... (O)ur sojourn on this earth is too brief to permit it to become twisted by feminist theories that appear to have far less to do with living, breathing human beings than with stereotype and caricature" (1996: 321–322). Daphne Patai (1996) even invents a new word to describe this supposed overpoliticization: "heterophobia": "a real, visceral and frightening antagonism toward men and a consequent intolerance toward women who insist on associating with them" (583).[17] Similarly Fekete characterizes "biofeminism" as a "backlash against heterosexual pleasure" (1994: 56). That the critique of gender hierarchies is confused with an attack on men and heterosexuality is not coincidental. As Oakley has noted: "Antifeminist attacks on gender continually conflate sex and gender, particularly in their critiques of male-bashing: critiques of mas-

---

17 Patai's work is particularly disturbing in its characterization of contemporary feminism as "heterophobic." In May 1996, she posted a notice on WMST-L (a women's studies Internet discussion list) describing her project. A large number of responses raised, in an extremely constructive fashion, problems with the manner in which she had conceptualized "heterophobia," in particular her conflation of the supposed "turn against men" and the "turn against heterosexuality." The majority of posters on this thread (including a number of men involved in women's studies) suggested that this characterization did not reflect their experience, and that when there were instances that might be characterized as such, they were fairly isolated and generally related to some specific context that needed to be taken into account. These posts were collected into a file by the WMST-L listowner that, when loaded into my wordprocessor, totalled 58 pages. Here's how Patai summarized them: "scores of hostile replies poured in, by women telling me my project was dangerous and ill-conceived, and that either there was no such thing as heterophobia within feminism or it was justified by men's behaviour. Many of the respondents, furthermore, cast aspersions on my motives in pursuing this subject, and criticized my 'methodology' for inviting anecdotal evidence to confirm what they considered to be an invalid and ideologically biassed project (a most interesting criticism, coming from feminists)" (1996: 593). Apparently Patai is convinced that "heterophobia" is a real problem, and is willing to dismiss, or use as evidence of the conspiracy she is trying to demonstrate, the "scores of responses" that told her otherwise.

culinity on the level of gender are presumed to be an attack on sex itself" (1997: 37). It is precisely on this supposed antagonism toward *hetero-sexual* men that gender feminism has created, that the libertarian and fundamentalist critiques find their common ground. The fundamentalists, as we've seen, are explicit about this, confidently citing the naturalness of heterosexuality and the neat lining-up of sex differences to support it. Although the libertarians are careful to avoid the assertions of 'natural'[18] or 'authentic' sex that pepper the fundamentalist critiques, many make a curious attempt to depoliticize gender as an identity while attempting to simultaneously reassert the legitimacy of certain types of gendered identities — particularly the masculine. This is evident from a number of themes that recur in the literature: anxiety over lack of attention to men *qua* men, pique at the inattention to the special trials of masculinity, and the supposed emasculation of men by feminism — both voluntary (in the case of those men who support feminism) and involuntary. These arguments all rely on a (sometimes explicit, but often implicit) heterosexual framing of feminine/masculine opposition and complementarity. According to Fekete's reading of feminism:

> Men should be invisible: firemen, policemen, garbagemen, mailmen, seamen, lumberjacks, and all the other men (who do indispensable daily tasks and often selfless, heroic deeds for women, for children, for other men) should disappear into gender-neutral employment categories. Men should only be identified when they can be accused by women ... Women should be identified as women at all times, lest they be marginalized and silenced. Women should be constantly noticed, appreciated, celebrated and rewarded. Men are disposable. (1994: 333)

---

18 A number of the libertarian critiques, however, endorse certain types of biological essentialism. Paglia, for example, repeatedly invokes biology and essential differences between men and women (with the latter coming up quite short in her assessment!). Critiques focussing on discrediting feminist work on sexual harassment and rape often accept as fact controversial assertions from evolutionary psychology such as those that suggest that "gender-specific differences in mating behaviour ... are the evolutionary result of the disparity between males and females in obligatory physiological investment in offspring" (La Cerra, 1998: 151).

Similarly, Donna LaFramboise argues that:

> [T]he women's movement is often silent about the hundreds
> of volunteer firemen who regularly put their brawn and their
> courage at the service of the community, about the men who've
> gone out of their way to mentor female employees, and about
> the male doctors who often still live with great personal risk
> because they perform abortions. When such men are acknowl-
> edged by feminists, they get credit for being good human be-
> ings, not good *men*. (1996: 317; emphasis in the original)[19]

Thus, it seems that much of the criticism of feminism's "gender perspective"
reflects umbrage at the eclipsing of a *male-centred* gender perspective.[20]
There is little tolerance for those men who endorse such a project. They tend
to be dismissed as "wanna-be-sensitive university men who uncritically ac-
quiesce in the most ludicrous of feminist demands" (Patai and Koertge,
1994: 209)[21] or irretrievably feminized. Paglia, for example, tells us:

---

19 LaFramboise can't seem to decide whether she wants to endorse a more general
    humanism or a 'different-but-equal' gender order. She criticizes feminists for
    viewing everything though a gender-differentiated lens, suggesting that "*Hu-
    man* suffering is the issue ...Which set of reproductive organs — or which race/
    religion/nationality/sexual orientation, etc. is associated with the person experi-
    encing the agony is, in the final analysis, beside the point" (12). Then, she criti-
    cizes International Women's Day events in Toronto for focussing on issues of
    racism and nationalism: "while these were worthy causes, they shouldn't be domi-
    nating a *women's* event" (146), criticizes the women's movement more generally
    for not giving men credit as MEN (not human beings) for allowing "women to
    travel this far" (1997: D1). Furthermore, she asks:

    > Why is it so difficult for feminism to admit that men have their own,
    > perfectly legitimate, perspective on the world? That, just as no man —
    > however hard he studies and watches — will ever completely under-
    > stand the process of giving birth, women will never fully appreciate the
    > pressures and demands involved in growing up male? (1996: 200)

20 As I was nearing completion of this chapter, a coalition of men's rights/father's
    rights groups announced their intention to develop a class-action suit against
    the Canadian federal government, charging gender bias under the Charter of
    Rights and Freedoms, as a means of protesting the federal funding provided to
    feminist groups under the Women's Program of the Secretary of State.

21 One of the cases used by Fekete to "demonstrate" the bio-feminist takeover is
    that of a professor who, after concerns were raised by students about a particu-

I have intensely disliked the tendency of many feminists to want men to be remade in a kind of shy, sensitive form to become, in essence, new kinds of women, contemporary eunuchs which is less inconvenient to women. I think this is not in the interests of the human race. We want masculine vigour, and I'm afraid that in order to get men macho again, we may have to endure a certain amount of instability in sexual relations.... So what would my advice be to the sexes at the end of the century? I would say to men: get it up![22] And to women I would say: deal with it. (1994: 15–16)

John Leo, writing in *U.S. News and World Report,* lauds a book edited by Jack Kammer (*Good Will Toward Men* [1994]) as heralding a 'de-escalation' in the 'gender war' (the latter a product of the 'gender industry,' 'gender ideologues,' 'gender obsessed'): "It's a collection of conversations with 22 outspoken women, most of them feminists, who reject male bashing and want to refocus discussion on partnership between the sexes" (1994: 24). This is contrasted with two of the many other books on gender that "pour across" his desk, Judith Lorber's *Paradoxes of Gender* (1994) and Shari Thurer's *The Myths of Motherhood,* of which he only reads the cover blurbs. Those are enough, he suggests, to "warn sensible readers to scurry away." Why? Because unlike Kammer's collection, they have not broken "the hold of victim feminism and an agenda wholly centred on women" (ibid.). These two charges run through the libertarian critiques. 'Victim feminism' is reviled, because 'victims' require 'victimizers' — if women are the former, then supposedly men are the latter, and hence the charge of 'male-bashing.' Being 'wholly centred on women' means *not* being centred on men. Given that much of the impetus for the adoption of gender as the analytic category

---

lar assignment, apparently "changed his teaching practices," and wrote a newspaper opinion piece entitled "A counter-attack in defense of political correctness" (Devlin, 1993), in which he criticized those who had used his case to argue against anti-sexist educational reforms. Fekete refuses to accept the veracity of his account, concluding instead that "having found true religion — with a little help from the threat of discipline — Devlin is not ready to recant again" (Fekete, 1994: 212).

22 For Paglia, getting it up is important. See her views on Viagra in fn.25.

of interest was to shift attention from 'women' to 'women in relation to men,' and to shift the analytic level from the individual as a player-of-roles to individuals as enmeshed in broader cultural and structural configurations of gender, critiques such as Leo's seem misplaced.

Clinging to the balance metaphor leads some of the critics to veer perilously close to a new victimology themselves.[23] Summarizing the issues here, Fekete (1994) notes that "men are the overwhelming victims not only of violence in Canada, but also of homelessness, suicide, and incarceration" (104). He elaborates on this in a rich footnote, suggesting that "some men appear to have less control than women over their quality of life (greater stress, shorter life expectancy), their socio-economic position (slaves to family obligation and women's dependency, alienated labour, hazardous work, risks to life and limb in military service), or their sex roles (chauvinist, instrumental, sexually and emotionally dependent, technophilic, 'disposable')." Here, he cites Warren Farrell and Camille Paglia as path-breakers[24] in reminding us of these "things we used to know and talk about collectively as a culture and a civilization, before two decades of biofeminism succeeded in infecting our

---

23 The new male victimology fuels many of the 'men's rights' and 'father's rights' agendas. Here's a sample from the "Male Manifesto" posted on the UK Men and Father's Rights Homepage:

> The epidemic rate of malicious false sexual harassment and other charges clearly demonstrate that men need the right to 'safe havens.' Nowhere is safe for a man at present, especially with record levels of sexual harassment charges at work. Some men may experience constant day long verbal abuse in the home from their partners and with record male unemployment the traditional safe havens such as bars and working men's clubs may be unavailable to them. (www. coeffic.demon.co.uk)

24 The libertarian critics are fond of citing one another as voices of "reason" and "rationality" (thus charging feminists with being unreasonable and irrational). In a bizarre piece of self-referentiality, Louis Marinoff's (1998) review of Fekete's *Moral Panic* places it among the few "voices in the wilderness of reasoned outrage" that appeared in 1994. Here he includes Sommer's *Who Stole Feminism*, Patai and Koertge's *Professing Feminism*, Levitt and Gross's *Higher Superstition*, and "Lou Tafler's *Fair New World*." The latter is an anti-feminist dystopian novel, intended as a political satire and cautionary tale of the dangers of feminism. Lou Tafler *is* Louis Marinoff!

thoughts and feelings with the viral cancer of half truths and the emotional tyranny of false appeals" (ibid.). We?

The convergence of the fundamentalist and libertarian conceptions of a crisis in masculinity, wrought by feminism, is illustrated as well in the mainstream media coverage of the Promise Keepers mass rally in Washington. In the *Globe and Mail*'s editorial coverage, this organization, with its $117 million budget, which is committed to a literal and fundamentalist interpretation of the Bible, is anti-gay and anti-choice, and tells men to "take back" their leadership role in the family, was portrayed as part and parcel of "a search to define a role for once-dominant men and husbands in a world of gender equality, anti-macho values and broken marriages" (*Globe and Mail*, October 7, 1997). Margaret Wente, then business editor of the *Globe*, suggested that it is "no surprise ... that so many men should find the movement so appealing. What does it mean to be a manly man in our culture? In an age when men have been repeatedly told that they're toxic in the home, and disposable in the workplace, the answer is elusive. Promise Keepers offers an anchor for men who have none, in a culture where millions have lost their moorings" (Wente, 1997: D7).[25] In other words, the same forces that decry 'gender' as legitimate grounds for political identity for women promote it as a legitimate 'anchor' for men.

---

25 While the supposed emasculation of men in feminism is a complex issue which is beyond the purview of this paper, some of the reactions to the Viagra pill recently expressed in the *Time* magazine cover story of May 4, 1998 are worth citing here. Viagra works on the physiological, not psychological, causes of impotence, by overriding an enzyme that can interfere with blood flow to the erectile tissues. Nonetheless, Bob Guccione, the publisher of *Penthouse*, attributes the demand for Viagra to — you guessed it — feminism: "Feminism has emasculated the American male, and that emasculation has led to physical problems. This pill will take the pressure off men. It will lead to new relationships between men and women and undercut the feminist agenda." Camille Paglia expands on why this is so important: "The erection is the last gasp of modern manhood. If men can't produce erections, they're going to evolve themselves right out of the human species. I want men to re-examine, really re-examine why they need this pill. Because they do need it, they need it right now. They need it to bolster themselves. They need it to stiffen their erections. It's like the steel that they would get if they were at war" (44–45).

The New Politics of Gender:
The Universalism/Particularism Dilemma Revisited

In this final section, I'd like to suggest that the extent to which this particular reading of 'gender' has been politicized in critiques of feminism is indicative of a broader shift in political discourse. Cindy Patton has contributed a novel reading of the 'reconfiguring' of social space, in which she argues that conservatives may be seen as the inheritors of the civil-rights tradition — fighting "identity with identity." On her account, the liberal pluralist tradition, which grounded the association of identity with rights in the civil rights tradition, viewed civil society as "infinitely partitionable and infinitely expandable.... (C)ivil rights was no longer a compensatory, temporary conduit designed to incorporate a class of bodies viewed as historically always present but excluded as subjects, but as an open door that permitted new bodies to make different claims to subject status" (1995: 203). The conservative move into identity politics placed, at least initially, progressive and anti-progressive forces in contention within the same space. This 'identity versus identity' positioning characterizes the debates, for example, about 'reverse discrimination.' The more recent trend, however, has been a 'respacialization' of public space in which the claim to identity and difference has been severed from the claim to rights. Social space is now the locus of consensus, not of proliferating difference, "the always already space of rights set against the fleeting fashions of special privileges" (Patton, 1995: 241). For Patton, the difficulty with identity politics is "not so much that we mistakenly believed in our self-namings, but that we believed in the promise of inalienable rights, rights which would accrue once our status as political subjects was secured" (ibid.: 241). This promise was substantially contingent on a concept and practice of space which has now been reconfigured. This is a reconfiguration which has occurred both culturally and materially, and one premised on the delegitimization of particularity as politically relevant. In other words, the only legitimate political identity is that of 'citizen' narrowly defined in terms of some 'general interest.' Although Patton's insights were forged through an examination of the solidification of the conservative cultural consensus in the U.S., it is not irrelevant to the Canadian context. For one thing, the American framing of "political correctness" as the "new McCarthyism" was quickly imported by the

Canadian media in the early 1990s.[26] Largely centred around countering feminist and anti-racist initiatives on university campuses, the panic over "political correctness" was epitomized by the cover of *Maclean's* magazine in May 1991, which depicted two young scholars — one male, one female, both white, wearing gowns and mortarboards — with gags tied around their mouths. A few years later, the back cover of Fekete's *Moral Panic* shouts "what's wrong with being politically correct?" and calls on "men and women who care about the future of democratic culture to resist the rising tide of puritanism and authoritarianism masquerading behind benevolent slogans, and to reject the mutation of 'human rights' into a control code for attacking freedom of expression, due process and equality." The language of "political correctness" has now spread far beyond the university campus, and is used to characterize any attempt to speak of gender, race, sexual orientation, bilingualism, multiculturalism, diversity, equity — any invocation of identity as having political currency. I do not wish to recount here the history of the "political correctness debates"[27] in Canada, or engage in a detailed rebuttal of their premises, as there are now several excellent sources which do just that (see, for example, Richer and Welr, 1995; Williams, 1995, Wilson, 1995). What is of interest here is the manner in which the cultural shifts embodied by the "political correctness debates" reveal a politics of identity which seeks to reassert an impossible "we" against the fracturing forces of the politically correct. Who is this "we"? In sum, it is rational individuals who claim no connection to social categories of gender, race, ethnicity, or sexual

---

26 Allan Bloom's *The Closing of the American Mind: How Higher Education has Failed Democracy and Impoverished the Souls of Today's Students* (1987) was one of the seminal (and I use that term deliberately!) texts in fuelling the PC debates in education, even though he did not use the term "politically correct." In a nutshell, here's his argument: "Liberal education flourished when it prepared the way for the discussion of a unified view of nature and man's place in it, which the best minds debated on the highest level. It decayed when what lay beyond it were only specialties, the premises of which do not lead to any such vision" (1987: 346–347).

27 As one commentator from the U.S. notes, 'debate' is something of a misnomer, in that "the political right took control of the terminology and the rhetoric of this discussion so early in the process that it cannot realistically be called a debate" (Jones, 1994: 384).

orientation — who display no particularity. Only those who check their particularity at the door are permitted to enter the public, the political, to engage in debate about the common good. *But* (and this is a big but!) there is an underlying implication that certain 'marked' identities are *incapable* of checking their particularity, and hence of thinking beyond the self to the greater public good. This is related to the charge, in both the libertarian and fundamentalist critiques, that self-interest and careerism motivate the 'gender-feminist' conspiracy. But the argument here goes beyond simple selfishness to imply an essential *inability* to transcend self-interest. A few examples:

- The new cardinal, conservative archbishop of Toronto, Aloysius Ambosius, argues against the ordination of women on the grounds that women who seek the priesthood have been tainted by feminism, and would simply be seeking power, not following a vocation (*Globe and Mail*, January 19, 1998).

- Alvin J. Schmidt, in his book *The Menace of Multiculturalism* (1997), suggests that the fatal flaw in Keynesian economics was John Maynard Keynes' sexual orientation: "why should a confirmed homosexual be concerned about deficit financing and its long-term effects? He will not have offspring who will someday have to bear the burden of his country's national deficit" (186–187).

- Barry Dank, a sociologist at California State University, in an article defending student-professor romances, suggests that feminist academics who disapprove of such liaisons are motivated by jealousy, and attempts to regulate such relationships reflect the resentment of middle-aged academic women of "the power that young women have to attract their eligibles" (Dank and Fulda, 1998: 125–126).

Like the "Charter Canadians" who appeared in Chapter Three, the weight of identity hangs heavy around the necks of those who would take it as politically relevant, and they are exiled from 'public' deliberations on matters of the 'common good.'[28] There are some common denominators in the identity politics being played out here: it is "us" (the general interest) vs. "them" (the special interests). The latter are victimizing and threat-

---

28 On this, see Linda Trimble's (1998) analysis of Canadian women and the constitutional deliberations, which is an excellent critique of assumptions about the limited interests of "Charter Canadians."

ening the former, and the line between public and private must be re-drawn so as to protect and nurture the cultural consensus. Couched in democratic rhetoric, this line of thought is profoundly anti-democratic. It appeals to a nostalgia for some non-existent past when public institutions (such as government agencies and universities) were untainted by undesirable 'group effects,' presumably before certain 'outsiders' imposed this on them. As Dorothy Smith (1997: 278) reminds us, universities (and other institutions) are by their very nature examples of the "historically sedimented local organization of race and gender." The unmarked, the normative, have never had to declare their identity.

> Members of the minorities or of non-hegemonic majorities, be they featured according to gender, race or ethnicity, are those who are summoned to state their identity. Members of the majority, embodying the norm, may quietly forget their own particularisms to play the part of the correct, cool referee. (de Sève, 1997: 112)

Thus, where the identity claims of feminists, anti-racist activists, or gay activists *are* recognized, it is only to delegitimate them as political identities — to *sever* their claims to rights. Both the moral-conservative and libertarian critiques, then, are inherently about the relationship between permissible public identities and political rights, and the coding they use provides emotional force to the neo-liberal discourse of citizenship. They trade in abstractions about 'the individual' and 'his' public independence, and draw the line around that individual so as to re-privatize and depoliticize any relations of dependence and interdependence that are necessary to produce the autonomous citizen (i.e., 'the family'). The realm of the 'political' has been drastically narrowed, permitting entry only to those 'unmarked' by particularity.

Conclusion

What can be gained from this review of the delegitimization of gender as an analytic category in feminism by its critics? Can the manner in which 'gender' has become a lightning rod for anti-feminist critiques be taken, alongside the reservations about the term expressed within feminism, as a signal that it has outlived its usefulness? Alternatively, should we just ignore the anti-feminist critiques as ill-informed and irrelevant to our tasks?[29] Obviously, I would not have devoted a whole chapter to this line of critique if I thought that was the case. On the contrary, I think that the critiques of 'gender,' in both their fundamentalist and libertarian guises, crystallize a number of important issues for feminists. As Baden and Goetz (1997: 12–13) suggest:

> The conservative challenge to the use of the concept of gender raises issues central to feminist epistemology and politics. How is the body constituted in gendered identity formation? What is the relation between gender identities and political subjectivities? Does sensitivity to gender reveal a concern for equality or a celebration of difference?

In addition to these important epistemological questions, I want to raise some other issues that the critiques of 'gender' suggest.

First, the extraordinary focus of both the fundamentalist and libertarian critiques on sexuality brings into sharp relief the heterosexual matrix of gender, and hence the threat to normalized heterosexuality that a thorough deconstruction of gender poses. This is particularly evident in the conservative anxiety over 'gender' in the UN program as opening the door to a proliferation of sexual identities and 'lifestyles,' the libertarian panic over 'heterophobia,' and the obsession with sexual harassment policies. Heterosexuality becomes, for the libertarians, a stand-in for 'family' as it appears in the fundamentalist critique: that which is natural, desirable, and defensible as an ideal, and the ultimate location of immutable gender differences.[30]

Second, the extent to which the centring of 'gender' in feminist analyses has problematized men, and has disrupted the notion of some stable,

---

29 This was, in fact, the response of one audience member to a presentation that I gave on some of this material at a recent conference, who suggested that by paying attention to what anti-feminists were saying I was serving only *their* agenda.

30 This is not to equate the move to recentre heterosexuality as simply overt homophobia. Paglia, for example, has made her own sexual preferences well known. However, even homoerotic desire is read through a rigidly hetero-gendered frame, which allows her to, for example, see gay men as "guardians of the masculine impulse" (1992: 24), having most cleanly severed their "humiliating" dependence on women (as mothers or wives).

essential masculinity which has been unjustly diluted or deformed by feminism, reinforces the importance of insisting on 'gender' as a relational concept. Both the fundamentalists and the libertarians would rather that feminists talked about 'women' than 'gender,' because such a framing makes it easier to see women as the authors of their own oppression.

Third, the manner in which 'gender' and 'race' and/or 'ethnicity'[31] are linked together, especially in the libertarian critiques, is instructive. Framed as a 'mantra,' standing in for all differences that threaten universality, this should act as a clear signal of the importance of linking the analysis and politicization of gender with those other axes of difference.

Finally, the critiques of 'gender' underscore the ambiguous relationship of feminism to debates about modernity/postmodernity. The trumpeting of one form of 'reason' and 'rationality' as the standard against which a focus on gender is measured and found lacking is a signal characteristic of the Enlightenment heritage. So, too, is the conflation of feminism and poststructuralism in the academy, with the intent of condemning both as anti-modern.[32] More crucially for political projects, these debates about 'gender' position feminism as central to debates about democracy, liberal individualism, and the presumed world-historical triumph of a particular form of liberal-democratic capitalism. 'Gender'[33] refuses to disappear into bland proclamations of universal values and disembodied 'persons.'

---

31 And, to a lesser extent, sexual orientation. Particularly in the U.S., 'multiculturalism' has become the portmanteau for challenges to the universal, and often includes feminism within its rubric. Critics such as Schmidt use it to include any perspective that challenges the authority of Christianity (feminist, gay, aboriginal, Afrocentric). In a speech at Montclair College, Elizabeth Fox-Genovese (also well known for her criticisms of feminism) argues that "If multiculturalism were only a plea for good manners, civility or perhaps what used to be called comparative studies, it would be difficult to generate much debate over it" (www.shss.montclair.edu/english/classes/stuelhler/engl105/genov1.html). In other words, just as 'gender' would be acceptable if we didn't insist on talking about sexism, so too would multiculturalism, if that pesky talk about racism didn't keep popping up.

32 The charge of *anti*-modernism is particularly underscored by Fekete's blanket term "bio-politics" to encompass the politics of race, gender, and ethnicity, and the related assertion that this is a 'new primitivism.'

33 Along with its companion terms in the "mantra."

FIVE

Restructuring Gender

> The sense that things 'can never be the same again,' that new possibilities have opened and old patterns closed off, is exactly what the historicity of gender relations is all about.
>
> — R.W. Connell (1987: 143)

For critics such as Christina Hoff Sommers, the location of feminism's ultimate truth in its classical liberal moment, asking only for a 'fair field and no favours' (1994: 51), allows the framing of gender only in individual terms. Given a 'fair playing field,' presumably achieved through the removal of formal legal barriers to equality, differences in outcome — the empirically observable difference in status of men and women — must then be attributed to primarily individual factors. The latter may be conceived of as failure (inability to assert one's individualism over stereotypical socialization, lack of motivation, personality defects), as choice (rationally weighing the options, and 'choosing' motherhood, dependency, typically feminine roles, and so on) or as the result of natural difference (biological predispositions). Each of these conceptions hypostatizes gender as pre-modern and as a difference which has, at least socially, been overcome through the formal inclusion of women as individuals in the liberal polity. Those differences that remain are not constituted as sociopolitical, but as particularities which have no substantive significance within the discourse of liberal modernity, the latter based on a progressive eclipsing of particularism by universalism.[1] Such an understanding

---

1 This, too, is the logic underlying Darby and Emberley's understanding of the

125

of gender is faulty on a number of counts, but none more so than in its failure to grasp the manner in which gender is continually produced in different ways and in different contexts. Far from being a relic of less-enlightened times, gender difference (and inequality) is constantly con-structed, reconstructed, and given varying degrees of political significance, and not always in predictable ways. As Sylvia Walby asserts, patterns of inequality between men and women have changed, "but in complex ways, not simply for better or worse" (1997: 1). That complexity appears, on the surface, paradoxical, in that there seem to be patterns indicating a simultaneous convergence and polarization, or as Donna Haraway (1991) has termed it, a simultaneous erosion and intensification of gender. But it appears paradoxical only to the extent that we hold gender to be a rela-tively static and homogeneous categorization. For example, the increase in opportunities for women-as-a-group in most industrialized nations, as measured by such standard indicators as their educational opportunities and labour market success, needs to be read alongside increased disparity between women in their access to the resources that would allow them to take advantage of a changing opportunity structure, if such measures were agreed upon as defining 'success.' The simultaneous erosion and intensi-fication of gender becomes even more pronounced when we try to un-derstand shifts in patterns of gender inequality in a global context.

It is in this context that we can see the theory and politics of gender as most intricately connected. There are echoes here of many of the themes explored in the preceding chapters, particularly of the enduring power of a linear narrative of modernist 'progress,' whose central character is the robust individual unhampered by particularity. As I've argued, while femi-nism continues to challenge this narrative, it remains ambivalently tied to it if it enacts its own narrative of the wholly gendered individual. Both these narratives are disrupted by the ways in which 'gender' — in a myriad of symbolic and material guises — is used as a resource for both the pro-duction and contestation of difference.

Maxine Molyneux has argued that, internationally, gender politics has been affected by three major trends over the last decade: the growing hegemony of neo-liberal models of economic management, the collapse

---

relationship between 'nature' and 'convention' in their defence of classical lib-eral constitutionalism, discussed in Chapter Three.

of communism, and the resurgence of nationalisms and religious fundamentalisms. As she suggests:

> While each took different and specific forms in particular regions and countries, all could be found to greater or lesser degrees in the various regions of the world. These phenomena are international in character, they affect a considerable range of countries, and they involve cross-national linkages.[2]
> (1994: 289)

They are also phenomena that are inextricably bound up with organizing gender, and shape in important ways the manner in which gender can be taken up as a political point of departure.

Two very important bodies of literature form the basis of this chapter. One is that which has explored economic and political restructuring in the context of globalization. Much significant work has been done by feminists in bringing a gender perspective to bear on these analyses, asking what taking gender to the heart of the analysis can tell us about economics and politics on a global scale. My approach here is to extend these questions, to ask what global patterns of economic and political change have to tell us about gender. The second body of literature is that of international feminisms. It is now widely acknowledged by white, western feminists that "we need to listen" to women who are not. But here, too, the general tendency has been to apply our gender-knowledge to 'others.' Again, I want to take a reverse tack, asking what non-Western feminist knowledge has to tell us about gender. I will revisit some of the issues raised in Chapter Three regarding the politicization of gender in the Canadian context, but here draw them into a wider context that emphasizes the centrality of gender to national projects,[3] and how both 'women' and

---

2 While I will not go into detail here on the cross-national linkages involved, it is important to keep these in mind. Think, for example, of the ways that international migration patterns, which alter the nature of 'citizenries,' are affected by enforced structural adjustment policies, the development of trans-national trading blocs and political entities (such as the EEC), environmental degradation, and ethnic and religious conflict. Some of these may be local in origin, but others are intimately linked to consumption patterns and socio-economic policies that have their home on the other side of the globe.

3 I use the terms 'national' and 'nation' with reservation here, in full awareness of

'men' are remade in the course of the economic and political processes that inform those projects. So, my purpose here is not simply to underscore the importance of this literature for understanding the current sociopolitical landscape, although its importance in this respect is significant. My intent is to draw on this body of work to demonstrate a more theoretical point: that 'gender' does not just signify ready-made difference, but is in fact *productive* of difference — difference which is mobilized through other modalities of difference, such as nationality, ethnicity, religion, race, and class. Gender will continue to have relevance as both an analytic and a political category, as long as we do not privilege it abstractly.[4]

Globalization, Restructuring, and Gendered Citizenship in Canada

The popular concept of 'globalization' has, like 'political correctness,' taken on an aura of undisputed truth through repetition. 'Globalization'[5] generally refers to a new economic world order, linked to technological ad-

---

their fictional character. In Canada, the fact that many Québecois and aboriginal people do not accept the sovereignty of 'Canada' as nation immediately renders the term suspect. Worldwide, there are nations without states, or that cross state boundaries (the Palestinians, the Kurds, the Six Nations, for example). As Nira Yuval-Davis notes, despite its obviously problematic nature given these cases, the fiction of 'nation' is still "at the basis of nationalist ideologies" (1997: 11).

4   In the summer of 1998, as I was working on this manuscript, I had the good fortune to attend a four-day meeting of feminist sociologists from around the globe, organized by the Women in Society Research Committee (RC-32) of the International Sociological Association, just prior to the World Congress of Sociology held in Montreal. I am indebted to many of the participants in that meeting for reminding me, through their varied research projects, that the tendency of Western/Northern feminists to *a priori* privilege gender often acts to blind us to a host of other social relations that are critical in shaping the lives of women — and in shaping the very meaning of 'gender' — in different contexts.

5   There is now a considerable sociological literature on globalization which distinguishes itself from the manner in which the term has been taken up in popular discourse. For a recent critique of the manner in which a 'discourse of globalization' has flourished, see Robertson and Khondker (1998).

vances, where trade barriers have been torn down, goods and services flow freely between nations, and democracy has spread like topsy as free markets have triumphed over political dictatorships and centralized economic planning. In a fairly representative bit of hyperbole, Thomas D'Aquino, President of the Business Council on National Issues, calls globalization:

> the most extraordinary phenomenon of our time … not since the invention of the steam engine and the onset of the Industrial Revolution in the mid-18th and early-19th centuries, followed by the spread of electric power, mass production and democracy, have we witnessed such a transformation. (1996: 17)

Linking economic, political, and social transformations, D'Aquino is confident that "at no time in history have the prospects for social progress, democratic development and human rights on a global basis been so favourable" (ibid.: 18). He recognizes that some countries are "still" saddled with economic problems, that it has been a "painful transition" to the new order for others, and that there are some countries that have modernized economically, but have "not yet responded" with political modernization. The overall picture is one of the progressive evolution of liberal democratic capitalism, whose birth pangs and glitches can be overcome. Yet despite this optimism, D'Aquino warns of the potential for economic disparities, protectionism, and political instability "fanned by ethnic and religious conflict" to deflect, or even reverse, the triumph so rosily described. Thus, he utters a "powerful and urgent message" that "we must work overtime … to give broad and sustained credibility to the new economic order that is emerging" (ibid.: 21). Here, we have a concise formulation of the 'globalization' phenomenon as it has come to be understood as an essential part of Western modernity, which despite its seemingly unstoppable force as part of the latter's evolution still requires a sustained effort to legitimate it. Paradoxically, the forces of globalization are seen as somehow above human action, but also dependent on the *correct* form of action.

Part and parcel of the transformation associated with globalization is the pressure on individual nation-states and their economies to 'restructure,' to meet the global 'competitive challenge.' In many nations, including Canada, this has become a 'national project' of the first order — a thorough remaking of the nation's personality. Restructuring initiatives aimed at fulfilling the requirements of a fully-functioning player in the global economic game have resulted in cuts to social spending, privatization and deregulation of services, transformations in labour markets, and a general retreat of the welfare state. The post-war welfare state in Canada (and in many other industrial nations) was premised on the legitimacy of state intervention into the market and on the responsibility of governments for the well-being of the citizenry. Social policy was seen as a potentially progressive force, and the realignment of the boundaries between state, market, and family opened up new spaces for political claims-making. Unemployment insurance, the family allowance, and the Canada Pension Plan were key innovations, and along with increased public investment in housing, job training, and post-secondary education demonstrated the importance of the idea of *social* citizenship in the welfare state. That is, citizenship comprised more than just formal political rights, but included the right to make more substantive social claims on the state. The social policy configuration of this welfare state was, to be sure, premised on particular assumptions about family forms and gendered statuses. "It presumed a stable working/middle-class nuclear family supported by a male breadwinner, containing a dependent wife and children, and resting on women's unpaid labour" (Brodie, 1996: 129). Feminist critiques of the welfare state have exposed the effects and limitations of 'public patriarchy,' and demonstrated the ways in which differently situated women were either excluded from social citizenship or were reinforced in dependent statuses through the manner in which policies operated. These critiques were based not on a rejection of the welfare state or the principles of social citizenship, but were aimed at extending its meaning to be more inclusive and productive of substantive equality. Significant political space was opened up for making claims about social citizenship, and this influenced the way in which the relationship between progressive movements (such as feminism) and the state were to develop.[6] However, world-wide economic troubles in the 1970s were taken to indicate that the limits of the welfare state had been reached:

> Sometime in the late 1970's and early 1980's, discussion of
> the "recession" metamorphosed into discussion of "economic

---

6 For the most detailed elaboration of this in the Canadian context, see Brodie (1995). Marian Sawer (1994) has analyzed a similar process in Australia.

restructuring." This was not just a change of rhetoric. It was, rather, a shorthand for some enduring changes in our way of life in Canada. Recession had implied that we were living through a temporary hiccup in an otherwise sound economy. Restructuring implies something more fundamental: a change in people's relationship to wage work and the concomitant alteration of a pattern of life centred on full employment of men in permanent jobs supported by women's dual roles. (Suzanne Mackenzie, cited in Cohen, 1995: 274)

The Royal Commission on the Economic Union and Development Prospects for Canada (the Macdonald Commission), which travelled the country in the fall of 1983 and reported in 1985, laid the blueprint for the course that Canadian economic and social policies were to take over the next decade. It was in the broad context of 'national' goals and strategies, all with a pro-market flavour, that such recommendations as free trade, 'flexible' labour market policies, constitutional reform, and a thorough revamping of income security programs were made. The restructuring agenda was not restricted to economic issues, but implicated significant social and political processes. Reconstructing gender relations was an integral part of this process, and a considerable body of literature now exists which documents some of the consequences.[7] Armstrong and Armstrong (1996), for example, have described a "feminization of the labour force," related to increased female- participation rates, a shift from industrial to service sectors as the source of new employment, an increase in "non-standard"[8] work and a move by some men into traditionally female areas of employment. They argue that many signs of women's "progress" in the labour force reflect a decline in the relative position of men, as what used to be "good jobs" for them "aren't so good anymore" (52). An increasing polarization of "good jobs" and "bad jobs" has also drawn attention to differences of class, race, and age within gender categories. Deficit-reduction policies, as an integral part of governments putting their financial houses in order, have also had unevenly gendered effects. Particularly hard-hit have been health and social service sectors, where women are concentrated as public sector work-

---

7 The collection edited by Isabella Bakker (1996) is a particularly good starting point.

8 This is econo-speak for work which is not full-time or full-year.

ers (Connelly and MacDonald, 1995). The privatization and 'down-load-ing' of formerly public services also represent a re-entrenchment of a clear line between public and private responsibilities for reproductive labour related to children, the elderly, or the ill. The varying conditions under which individual persons or households can respond to these shifts also highlight sharp differences within gender categories, particularly by class and race.[9] The Federal Social Security Review, undertaken in 1993–95, was largely gender-blind, despite the differential impact that such changes as eligibility requirements for unemployment insurance and revamped "employment development services" (training programs) were to have on differently situated men and women.[10]

The restructuring of gender relations that has occurred as part of these labour market and policy shifts is not, as some have suggested, a turning back of the clock. While some of the more conservative commentary betrays a misplaced nostalgia for a return to a golden domestic age that never existed — complete with a family wage for Dad and an apron for Mom[11] — this reflects neither 'popular' nor 'official' discourses on gender.[12] What has occurred is a wholesale reconstruction of the rights and obligations of 'economic subjects' more generally. As Fraser and Gordon (1994) demonstrate in their genealogy of 'dependency,' the good post-industrial citizen eschews public dependency as a pathology. Dependency is individualized,

---

9   The conditions under which well-off Canadians can 'solve' their reproductive crises by importing labour are, of course, closely related to the effects of structural-adjustment policies on developing nations, which influence the conditions under which women from these nations are compelled to "emigrate abroad to take up positions as nannies and maids in First World households" (Bakan and Stasiulis, 1996: 217), often leaving their *own* children and families behind.

10   On this, see the collection edited by Pulkingham and Ternowetsky (1996).

11   It is important to remember that ideological notions of the 'family wage,' and the 'proper' domestic role for women are precisely that — ideological notions. They have only ever been articulated in specific historical contexts, and in profoundly class- and race-bound ways. As numerous scholars have demonstrated, woman as a "domestic angel" is an icon which has *never* applied to working-class or racialized women.

12   Livingstone and Luxton's (1989) study of steelworkers and their spouses provides an interesting case study in the "modification of the male breadwinner norm."

and seen as a problem amenable to individual solutions. Where women were once viewed as legitimately entitled to *public* support for their roles as mothers, full-time mothering now has no legitimacy "outside the context of the self-financing hetero-patriarchal family form." For example, while Social Asistance reform in Ontario certainly seeks to reprivatize dependence, it is not an explicit pushing of women back into the home, nor a valorization of some maternal ideal.[13] Redrawing the line between public and private, while gendered in its effects, is not simply drawing a line between the genders.[14] That women have interests and identities outside of the domestic sphere is now a given.[15] But the broad sweep of restructuring does reflect redefinition of what constitute publicly legitimate identities, and relevant matters for political recognition and/or intervention.

In the two Canadian provinces that have elected governments that most closely aspire to the minimal, neo-liberal model — Alberta and Ontario — these aspects become clear. If you visit the Ontario government's website, you will be hailed, not as a citizen, but as a 'taxpayer.'[16] Bakker (1996: 4) summarizes the premises underlying the neo-liberal

---

13 Single parents are deemed employable as soon as their youngest child is old enough for whatever publicly available care is available. For example, if junior kindergarten is available locally, children can start as young as $3\frac{1}{2}$ years of age, depending on their birthdate, and the expectation is that while the child is in school, the parent is available for work. Where there are two parents in the home, they are both deemed employable as early as when the youngest is three months old. In this case, the same parental leave provisions that the federal Employment Insurance program provides apply, and when the leave is up, you're labour-market ready.

14 The conceptual error of conflating the division of public and private with a gendered division of labour is something I have written on at length (Marshall, 1994). Briefly, they are related contingently, not organically.

15 See for example Everitt (1998), who tracks shifts in public support for feminism and equality in Canada since the early 1970s. Her analysis suggests that both men and women have demonstrated growing support for women's public presence.

16 The Government of Ontario website is at www.gov.on.ca, and underneath the provincial logo is the banner "Open for Business." Navigate through to the Premier's page, where you can find the "progress" report, identified as "report to Ontario's taxpayers."

philosophy: "that institutions such as the state and the market should reflect the motivation of individual self-interest, that states provide a minimum of public goods ... and that the most efficient allocation of resources and maximization of utility occurs through markets." We're open for business, as certain politicians are wont to say.

As the market becomes the standard for evaluating needs, both economic and social, political agency appears to be removed from the picture. So much for the 'moral economy' of the welfare state described by Cloward and Piven in the early 1980s, where they suggested that: "The market, with its mysterious and autonomous laws, has receded. In its place there are political leaders who are causing things to be the way they are" (1981: 230). Fast forward to the '90s, where political leaders can throw up their hands and say "It's not our fault, it's the global economy"[17] — the triumph of the self-legitimacy of the market. As Marjorie Cohen summarizes it:

> Both globalization and restructuring are terms which imply a kind of inevitability to the policy changes which are occurring, changes beyond the control of people. In this sense, restructuring appears apolitical and outside the purview of social analyses dealing with gender, class and racial issues. (1997: 30)

The claim that it's all about economics is, as a number of analysts have shown, patently false. Whether through the federal government's massive renovations of the social security system, or provincial 'revolutions' — such as the 'Common Sense' revolution in Ontario, or the "new normal'[18] in Alberta, states have been active players in re-forming the citizenry. Denis (1995a, 1995b), analyzing the legislative record and media coverage of the first eighteen months of the Klein government[19]

---

17 Linda McQuaig (1998) has called this the 'cult of impotence' — a demasculinizing metaphor which sits uneasily beside the implicit masculinism of the new neo-liberal state.

18 This is Alberta treasurer Jim Dinning's phrase, cited in Denis (1995b) and Helmer (1995).

19 The election of Ralph Klein's Conservatives in 1993 was widely hailed as a political watershed in the move to the right. He has been looked to as epitomizing neo-liberal governance, both from admirers (such as Mike Harris in Ontario, who sought to emulate him) and critics.

in Alberta, argues that, far from seeing a decreased role for government, Klein's administration was "very busy carrying out its task of redefining the relationship between government and society" (1995a: 375). The message communicated to the population, both through legislation and public relations, was one of self-discipline: don't look to government to coddle or support you; take responsibility for yourself. "Alberta is being disciplined for a new age of capitalism" (Denis, 1995b: 98). Massive cuts to the public service, health, and education were indicative of the new attitude. All disproportionately affected women, many of whom lost their jobs in the public service, and were expected to "pick up the slack" on the home front, as previously public services were eliminated or severely curtailed (Dacks, Green, and Trimble, 1995: 277). Similarly, the economic turn to the right in Ontario must be seen as part of a broader political shift, which is redefining the very meaning of social citizenship as we have come to understand it. As Ian Morrison (1997) argues, the Harris regime in Ontario has hollowed out the substance of citizenship in a number of ways: socially, politically, and legally. Significant here is the granting of extensive 'regulation-making power' to the cabinet, thereby centralizing and removing from political contestation much of the power to rule. Far from signalling a decreased role for government, made impotent by global economic forces, the Harris government has continually flexed its muscles in disciplining the population: "good neo-liberal citizens are defined by their distance from claims on the state and absence of claims rooted in personal identity" (Morrison, 1997: 77). One of Harris's first initiatives was to dismantle existing employment equity and pay equity measures, which provided specific grounds for identity-based claims. The poor — a group within which women are disproportionately represented — have been singled out for disciplinary measures. Cuts in social assistance rates and the introduction of workfare programs are integral to the agenda of moral regulation that seeks to remake the citizenry as independent, self-interested, and self-supporting actors. The reintroduction of the 'spouse-in-the-house' rule,[20] which makes someone ineligible for welfare if they are

---

20 This was reintroduced in 1995 as part of the Conservatives' overhaul of the welfare system in Ontario. On August 14, 1998, the Social Assistance Review Board released its decision on a constitutional challenge to the definition of

found to be cohabiting with an unrelated person of the opposite sex, is clearly aimed at sole-support mothers, and explicitly reinforces private dependence for women (Kitchen, 1997). The introduction of welfare 'snitch lines' — where one can report, for example, that the woman on welfare next door has what appears to be men's clothing hanging on the line[21] — extends the disciplinary regime from self-discipline to the policing of one's neighbours, all in the name of the public interest. Those boundaries between public and private, which have always served as shifting mechanisms of political legitimation — of the inclusion or exclusion of certain particularities — are redrawn in such a way as to de-politicize them and prevent their contestation. That they are fluid boundaries is underscored by the extent to which the supposed retreat of the state from intervention in the 'private' is never evenly applied, but is usually accompanied by increased intervention and surveillance with respect to certain 'deviant' populations, such as welfare recipients.

At the federal level, Janine Brodie's careful analyses of restructuring initiatives shows how the discourse of globalization and restructuring has resulted in a wizened space for political negotiation, and eroded the grounds on which rights can be claimed on behalf of women.[22] At the centre instead is the beleaguered 'ordinary Canadian': women no longer have political legitimacy as a collective subject, but simultaneously "individual women are redefined as members of specially disadvantaged groups which require targeting to address their shortcomings so that they can become 'ordinary' degendered citizens" (Brodie, 1996: 137) The extent to which these are disciplinary, 'normalizing' initiatives should not be underestimated. As Brodie (1997a) elaborates, the "meso-discourse of

---

'spouse' used to apply this rule, brought by four women on social assistance. The Board held that it was, in fact, a violation of the equality provisions of the Charter, and ordered the women's benefits reinstated. It remains to be seen whether the Ontario government will appeal this decision.

21 This 'hypothetical' example is based on an incident in my community. The clothing was, in fact, her teenage daughter's, who just happened to favour black jeans and t-shirts!

22 On this, Sylvia Bashevkin (1998b) asks, "how is it that new conservatives manage to thump their tubs day and night about individual rights for men, but never for women?"

performativity[23] ... explicitly rejects the relevance of gender.... Within this barren and phantasmic discursive terrain, performativity sees only one social agent — only one good citizen — the atomized market player" (237).

Once again, we are drawn into the universalism/particularism dilemma. The new moral ethic of the market seeks to reassert the free-play of market forces as the only grounds upon which individual liberty and democracy can rest. Particularity is antithetical to the market, and women *qua* women, according to its rules, are particular. The universal subject of neoliberal economics is male, and women are admitted so long as they mimic this subject. But this puts them in a bind. Not only will they be disciplined if they fail to disguise their particularity (in any number of ways, from sexual harassment to relegation to the 'mommy track'), but they must also play their part in the *creation* of the autonomous, self-reliant, independent citizen. As Jessica Benjamin (1988: 201) noted more than a decade ago: "The moment women take advantage of the logic of universality ... the advocates of autonomy trot out the hidden gender clause. The unspoken assumption is that women, by upholding the private sphere and creating a nurturing environment, create the framework for the autonomous individuality of men," and that any feminist attempt to restructure this relationship is "transformed into a nightmare vision of raising children like Purdue chickens" (206).[24] With the shift to a self-legitimating market, the thrust for individual success *appears* to allow women a central place, but the apparent gender neutrality leaves fundamental social relations unchallenged.

The veneer of gender neutrality is also disrupted by the extent to which gender continues to function as a symbolic resource in political culture.

---

23 Brodie uses the terms 'meso-discourse' and 'meso-narrative' to get at "the discursive space between Lyotard's meta-narratives of modernity and the specific public policies, the micro-technologies of power and the politics of the everyday.... Meso-narratives are an historical consensus about what is understood to be rational, progress, emancipation, justice and so on" (1997a: 227). She suggests that the meso-narrative of performativity, which characterizes the neo-liberal state, has five critical moments: privatization, commodification, familialization, decentralization, and criminalization.

24 See, for example, the series of editorials on daycare in the *Globe and Mail* in January of 1998 (Peyton, 1998; Thorsell, 1998; Zyla, 1998).

Not only is a distinctly gendered identity for the 'ordinary' citizen normalized, but so too is the identity of the state. The new neo-liberal state is a lean, mean, deficit-fighting machine. It is competitive, rational (not emotional), and makes the tough choices.[25] It oozes strength and muscularity — in other words, masculinity. It is no coincidence that this masculine, minimalist state is seen to foster the "masculine virtue of self-reliance in its citizens" (Sawer, 1996: 122). The welfare state, on the other hand, has been metaphorically feminized — as Marian Sawer has argued, this is encapsulated in images such as the 'nanny state' and the 'public tit' from which citizens must be 'weaned.' As a recent book published under the auspices of the Fraser Institute[26] summarizes it, social assistance is "the overprotective mother supporting and nurturing her brood, embracing her dependents with loving arms while keeping them firmly fastened to her apron-strings" (Sabatini, 1996: 256). It's time, we're told, for those aspiring to legitimacy as 'citizens' to cut the apron-strings, to be self-reliant and independent — in other words, to be manly once more.

It is clear that the transition from the Keynesian welfare state to the neo-liberal state represents not just a shift in welfare regimes, but also in citizenship regimes more broadly conceived. Citizenship regimes may be understood as concrete manifestations of abstract constructions of citizenship, as they exist within particular nation-states (Jenson and Phillips, 1996). The post-war citizenship regime in Canada was characterized by a particular set of assumptions about inclusion, access, and representation. These included a strong presumption of "pan-Canadian" identity, with institutions and programs developed to promote a sense of "belongingness"[27] and national standards for access to services and programs.

---

25 According to the *Alberta Report*, Alberta is paradigmatic of this sort of governing identity, and "Albertans enjoy a thriving business climate arising from private, competitive enterprises and individual freedom, initiative and responsibility." In contrast, their neighbours in Saskatchewan are "drowning in social justice" (Byfield, 1996).

26 The Fraser Institute is a (very!) conservative think-tank and research institute located in Vancouver.

27 Here, Jenson and Phillips note the development of multiculturalism policies, the Official Languages Act, and the strengthening of the citizenship branch of the Secretary of State (1996: 116–117).

There was also an acceptance of "equity and social justice discourse" and a willingness to support extra-state organizations as legitimate representatives of collective interests. As Jenson and Phillips summarize it: "Achieving social justice and equity were legitimate goals, and therefore groups which made claims, and programs which responded to such claims, were in the political mainstream" (ibid.: 118–119). Significant in this citizenship regime was the creation of spaces *within* the state for the representation of particular collective interests — exemplified by the creation of the 'women's state' described in Chapter Three. Thus it is no surprise that the dismantling of such institutions is integral to the shift to a new citizenship regime — one which sees the state withdrawing from a commitment to fostering equality. State funding to feminist organizations was drastically cut,[28] and official state programs to represent women's interests were either dismantled, scaled down, or relocated to other departments (Bashevkin, 1998a; Jenson and Phillips, 1996). Thus, as women are disproportionately affected by restructuring and cuts to social spending, they have fewer resources or points of entry for advocacy or collective protest.[29] The shrinking of public space for the articulation of collective interests is epitomized by the extent to which those making group claims are cast as particularistic 'special interests' who "violate the new norms of citizenship" (Brodie, 1994: 57). That this shift in citizen-

---

28 Both LEAF (Women's Legal Education and Action Fund) and NAC (National Action Committee on the Status of Women) were particularly hard hit by funding cuts to advocacy groups.

29 It is not just women's groups whose legitimacy is being eroded. As Jenson and Phillips note, there is a general undermining of collective representations in policy-making discussions in favour of individual contributions. For example, they note the 1990 Citizen's Forum on Canada's Future which "used the opportunity of a national consultation exercise to hear individuals as *individuals*, not as members of interest groups and which judged its success by the number of participants involved, no matter how minimally these individuals participated: a phone call to a 1-800 number was sufficient" (1996: 126). Marjorie Cohen notes that it is "probably not politically insignificant" that movements seeking to make claims on behalf of collectives, such as feminism and labour movements, are referred to as "special interest groups," while business is commonly referred to as a "community" (1995: 293).

ship purports to be gender-neutral belies the extent to which it both draws on and shapes anew gender as a key axis of social differentiation.

A reconstruction of gender has been central to the process of realigning the relationship of 'states' to 'societies' in the shift to neo-liberal governance and neo-conservative economic policies in the industrialized West. But 'globalization' has not only effected restructuring in the West — the imposition of Structural Adjustment Programs on other nations and the formation of transnational trading blocs have realigned the state/society relationship in ways to facilitate the market. And, as noted in the introduction to this section, part of the popular understanding of the 'globalization' phenomenon is the spread of democracy as integral to the spread of 'free' markets. The reconfiguration of the relationship between gender and citizenship that has occurred with the decline of the welfare state in our own backyard is not a complete story.

Gender and Citizenship in Post-Soviet Europe

One of the most interesting illustrations of the manner in which gender is organized in relation to shifting conceptions of citizenship is in post-Communist Eastern Europe, where the fluidity of nations and states themselves is evident. Writ large here is the reorganization of the relationship between the public and private in the formation of new citizenship regimes. As Gal (1994) argues, significant historical transformations[30] can have profoundly different interpretations when gender is brought into view. A number of scholars have demonstrated the gendered dimensions of the break-up of the Soviet bloc and the decline of state socialism. Although there are significant differences between specific national struggles,[31] each mobilizes gender in some way as it is reorganized as part of

---

30 The list of relevant sources here would be lengthy, but noteworthy are Kelly-Gadol (1984) on the Italian Renaissance and Landes (1988) on the French Revolution.

31 Different national histories, religious influences, and ethnic diversity are all important, and are best grasped at the level of individual countries. See, for example, the collection edited by Funk and Mueller (1993), which includes contributions on Bulgaria, Romania, the Czech and Slovak Republics, the former Yugoslavia, the former GDR, Hungary, Poland and the former USSR. Two

reconfigured national identities. Commonly noted aspects of the dismantling of state socialism include a dramatic decline in the representation of
women in newly democratic parliaments, a disproportionate number of
women becoming unemployed or employed in low-wage, low-status work,
and curtailment of reproductive rights, particularly access to abortion,[32]
and in general an "intensification of gender segregation in the economy
and society as a whole" (Molyneux, 1994: 293). Also noted is a marked
antipathy to "feminism" in many Eastern European countries. Alena
Heitlinger (1996), writing on the Czech Republic, suggests that Western
feminism[33] has little resonance with Czechs, as its utopian, emancipatory rhetoric, the accompanying concepts such as "women's equality," and
its focus on collective action all have a negative association with the now-
defunct socialist state. Western feminism is also perceived as failing to
recognize the positive valuation of motherhood and family, and is perceived as anti-male.

> Western feminist discourse emphasizes women's oppression by
> patriarchy and capitalism, while interpretations of grievance
> among Czechs focus on communist forms of oppression. Capi-
> talism is seen as a positive goal to strive for, while men are
> regarded as co-victims of communism and as partners in the
> difficult transition to a market economy and democracy.
> (Heitlinger, 1996: 86)

Joanna Goven (1993), writing on Hungary, suggests that antifeminism
there is more than just part of a backlash against communism, but engen-
ders a "critique of state socialism as having contravened nature, a critique
based on the notion that the bedrock of a healthy society is sexual essentialism" (227). In the literature she examines, it is repeatedly alleged that

---

special issues of *Social Politics* (v.2[1] in 1995 and v.3[2] in 1996) have also
been devoted to exploring the relationship between gender, citizenship and political transitions in Eastern Europe. There are also relevant articles in special
issues of *Feminist Review* (#39, 1991), *Women's Studies International Forum*
(v.19[1/2], 1996) and *Canadian Woman Studies* (Winter, 1995).

32 There are individual exceptions to each of these trends.

33 Heitlinger is clear in her argument that it is a particular perception of Western
feminism that is key here, not the actual content, in all its diversity, of Western
feminism.

the 'emancipation' of women under state socialism resulted in a woman-state alliance that emasculated men and weakened the development of a democratic political culture, suggesting that women who leave the private sphere of home and family are "socially dangerous" (236). In this sense, the communist regime was a crime against nature. The quest for an 'authentic' national culture, as against the perceived alien and artificial totalitarianism of state socialism, has nurtured discourses of the 'natural' — which contain distinct conceptions of 'real women' and 'real men' (Molyneux, 1994: 308). Of course the 'naturalness' of this assertion of sexual difference is belied by the ways both public and private authorities are engaged in actively constructing and regulating this 'authentic' womanhood.

Peggy Watson, however, suggests that it is a mistake to understand the reorganization of gender in post-communist Eastern Europe as "explicable almost exclusively in terms of the experience of communism" (1997: 144). In other words, she argues that to attribute the lack of full democratization, reflected in a loss of rights for women and the entrenchment of gender difference, as a legacy of communism, is to "sustain the illusion of modernity in the West" (153). Instead, she argues, it is democratization itself that "allows gender the opportunity to become a politically exclusionary/inclusionary social characteristic, and an important principle for the patterning of precisely the social/political power under which communism had been eradicated" (145): it is democratization itself that "engages and mobilizes difference in the construction of political identities" (156). Precisely how this is played out will be affected by a myriad of factors, including differing ways in which religious, ethnic, and national interests are mobilized. Democracy is not just mapped onto ready-made gender identities, but gender is actively constructed and invoked in the translation of the abstract rights of democracy into the concrete rights of embodied persons. As an example, she suggests that the claim to rule of men in the transition to parliamentary power in Poland could not be made on the grounds of experience, as the procedures were new, nor on qualifications, as women, as a group, were as educated as men, so "deep differences of gender" were invoked. Watson's argument is a compelling one, as it highlights the ease with which majoritarian feminists in the West tend to bracket our own critiques of the supposed universalism of democratic citizenship. Rather, "the dramatic changes in gender relations in Eastern Europe give a visible measure of the masculinism at the heart of Western democracy, which here too — until recently — was the subject of systematic silence" (Watson, 1993: 485). Certainly, the resonance with the tactic of collapsing gender into sex deployed by both the fundamentalist and libertarian critiques of feminism in the West, reviewed in the previous chapter, should caution us against any modernist arrogance that makes assumptions about the inherently inclusionary potential of democratization. It is only the explicit politicization of gender, which always occurs in specific contexts,[34] that puts gender equality on the political agenda and makes it a priority (or not). In the same way that feminists criticized the early 'women and development' approaches, which assumed that modernization would, eventually, just by its logic, bestow its bounty on women, so too must we exercise caution in assuming that the transition to more ostensibly democratic forms carries with it an inherently progressive form of gender regime. If the articulation of gendered interests as the basis for political action is to occur, it will happen because gender is given new relevance in the spaces opened through democratization, not as an organic component of democratization itself. It cannot be determined in advance.[35] Nor should we assume that the manner in which gender may be politicized in other nations will eventually come to resemble what we are familiar with as gender politics in the West.

---

34 This may occur, in some contexts, through external pressure on particular nation-states, rather than primarily through internal pressure by feminists. For example, formal gender equity measures will be imposed on countries in the former Soviet bloc that aspire to membership in the European Economic Community.

35 Watson is, however, optimistic with respect to Poland, arguing that "the development of feminism is a product of the experience of the masculinism inherent in civil society; it depends crucially on the creation of social distance between men and women, on a perceived imbalance of social power and sense of worth. In these terms, the development of feminism in Eastern Europe is simply a matter of time" (1993: 82). I think her undue faith in convergence, and attribution of 'inherent' masculinism to civil society undermines an otherwise sharp analysis.

Alena Heitlinger has also suggested to me, in personal communication, that an important factor that now needs to be considered is age. In the last decade, a generation of Czechs who have formed their experience of work/family outside of the communist regime has 'come of age,' and this may have significant implications for how struggles about gender and citizenship develop.

Gender Travels:
Lessons from International Feminisms

As feminism itself becomes more internationalized, the charge that Western feminists have overprioritized gender has become more common, and needs to be taken seriously. Alexander and Mohanty, for example, suggest a "convergence between the way gender emerged as a primary category of analysis and the social, demographic and class composition of those who actually theorize gender in the U.S. academy" (1995: xvii). There is now a rich and varied literature of feminist work written from standpoints other than that of the 'originary' conception of gender.[36] In particular, writings by 'Third World'[37] feminists have been notable in their success at 'disaggregating' (Afshar, 1996) gender, demonstrating its constitution through race, ethnicity and class, and drawing out the ways in which diverse political contexts — and how women have been constituted as political actors — actively shape and reshape gender relations. The import of this work goes far beyond its "filling in the gaps," or "summoning Third-World feminism in the service of (white) Western feminism's intellectual and political projects" (Alexander and Mohanty, 1995: xx). It has, I think, important implications for rethinking gender as an analytic category, which goes beyond seeing 'difference' as either anomalous or as providing colourful examples of some general principle.[38] I

---

36 See, for example, Afshar (1996), Anthias and Yuval-Davis (1989), Alexander and Mohanty (1995), Jayawardena (1986), Moghadam (1994), Mohanty, Russo, and Torres (1991), Waylen (1996), and Yuval-Davis (1997).

37 I use the term 'Third World' here only because it is still common currency in the literature to which I am referring, even though that literature goes a long way toward problematizing it. Mohanty (1991) presents a comprehensive review in this respect. Angela Miles (1996: 159) has used the term 'Two-Thirds World' to remind us of "the South's predominance in both population and land mass." In general, 'Third World' signifies Africa, Asia and Latin America, while 'First World' or 'Western' signifies Europe and North America. Increasingly 'North' and 'South' are used to signify the difference between economically unequal parts of the world. All of these terms, of course, overly homogenize whatever population they refer to, obscuring internal diversities and inequalities.

38 For an insightful critique and discussion of some of the ways 'modern' social theory has tried to deal with difference, see Seidman (1997), especially Chap-

read this literature here, then, not so much for what it tells me about 'Third World' women and their experience of gender as a means of filling in gaps (although that, too, is a significant contribution), but for what it can say about the *consequences* of those gaps for thinking about 'gender' in any context. To see only 'other' feminisms as constructed in and through national and ethnic struggles, is to see Western feminisms, and their centering of gender, as somehow innocent of these messy and complicating factors.[39] There are a number of questions that underscore the relevance of looking at gender in a more global context: How is gender related to national and ethnic projects? To what extent can we speak of 'gender interests'? Are the different ways in which gender is politicized comparable to the point of being able to speak about feminism as a 'global movement,' or is such an understanding of feminism a Western imposition, an extension of imperialism and colonialism?

Anthias and Yuval-Davis (1989: 7) have outlined five major ways in which women are implicated in ethnic and national processes: as biological reproducers of the members of ethnic groups, as reproducers of the

---

ter 5. As he frames the important question: "What would it mean to acknowledge difference without surrendering its otherness? It would be a difference that refuses assimilation, that resists surrendering its 'alien' status, an otherness that cannot be erased by being rendered a mere variation, instance, phase, or inferior subordinate moment" (99).

39 This is not, of course, an original insight. Vickers (1993, 1994) and Ng (1993), among others, have explored Canadian feminism in relationship to nationalism. A useful contribution to the unpacking of some of these issues over a range of national contexts is the collection *Unsettling Settler Societies*, edited by Daiva Stasiulis and Nira Yuval-Davis (1995). The point I wish to make here is more related to the tendency to accord such analyses supplementary status when thinking about gender, except in 'other' contexts. Sinith Sittirak captures this well when speaking of her experience as a graduate student from a 'developing' nation studying in Canada, watching her Canadian classmates preparing to go off to do fieldwork overseas: "Officially, there are no regulations to prevent me from exploring Canadian or any other ethnic groups. However, like many other 'international students' who received scholarships from development projects, it implicitly seemed that we 'should' focus on our own issues in our own homes.... Canadian students had much more academic privilege and freedom to study and speak about women's issues in any continent from around the world" (1998: 119).

boundaries of ethnic or national groups, as transmitters of the culture of the group, as signifiers of group difference, particularly in ideological constructions of ethnic and national categories, and as participants in ethnic or national struggles, including economic, political, and military struggles. Vickers (1994) emphasizes, in a similar manner, the need to understand reproduction (including its biological aspects) as integral to grasping the gendered nature of state and international politics. Recognizing that reproduction will be of different significance for "women and men located in secure, dominant cultures" than it will be for "those located in minority or threatened communities" is crucial to understanding differences among feminists on reproductive issues (190). The production of sexualized bodies, the bio-politics of populations, the cultural and discursive practices that position women and men as symbols and/or agents of the collectivity — all are constitutive of, and given meaning by, a system of gender relations in which the ideological and material are inseparable, and which is neither freely chosen nor unilaterally imposed.

In a later elaboration, Anthias and Yuval-Davis (1992) have added a sixth dimension — the positioning of women in a gendered and racially segregated labour market, including the particular locations of migrant women. Migrant labour, as a component element of the global economy, is a constituent of shifting gender relations in both the immigrant and emigrant contexts. Migration patterns, both prompted and constrained by international economic and political practices, can be contradictory in their gendered effects. Women migrants, for example, may experience new freedoms and increased independence in the country of destination, but may also experience intensified workloads (as kin-based networks contract), discrimination and harassment in workplaces, and isolation as they are cast as 'dependents' of male migrants. Women left behind by male migrants experience equally contradictory effects. Women also migrate without men — both as workers and/or refugees, independently or as part of a family economy (Morokvasic, 1991; Pettman, 1996; Zlotnik, 1990). They, too, are remaking gender in a myriad of ways.

The interrelationships of gender with national and ethnic projects is complex, involving bodily and reproductive practices, cultural reproduction, labour, and political struggle. Through all of these processes, nationalisms and nation-building are bound up with racialized conceptions of 'manhood' and 'womanhood' — Canada and other 'developed nations' are no exceptions here (Stasiulis and Jhappan, 1995; Vickers, 1994).[40] Given this complex set of gendered processes, can we speak of 'women's interests,' in a political sense, at all?

A widely used framework for analyzing the various ways in which 'women's interests' have been politicized is Maxine Molyneux's (1985) distinction between strategic gender interests and practical gender interests. "Women's interests," she argues, are better understood as "gender interests," to avoid positing a "false homogeneity," recognizing that the interests women may have as a group are "shaped in complex and sometimes contradictory ways" (232). Gender interests "are those that women (or men, for that matter) may develop by virtue of their social positioning through gender attributes" (ibid.). These may develop as either practical gender interests — those which arise in response to an immediate need — or strategic gender interests — those which demand alternative social arrangements, and which are generally those identified as 'feminist.' Thus, women's positioning within a gendered division of labour as those responsible for the well-being of their families may lead them to politicize practical interests around food, water, or health care, without demanding the strategic goal of gender equality that would transform that division of labour. While this is a useful way of understanding the variety of 'interests' which may be considered gendered, and recognizing that these will be constructed in complex ways, the distinction has been criticized for privileging Western feminism's understanding of gender-consciousness and such goals as 'gender equality.' In different contexts, this can mean a privileging of middle-class and elite women's organizations, which articulate these strategic interests, as 'feminist.' Jasbir Puar, elaborating on this problem, argues that such a distinction obscures the extent to which practical gender interests may feed into, complement, contradict, or challenge strategic gender interests (1996: 77). In responding to such criticisms, Molyneux (1998) reminds us that the distinction was never meant as a rigid dichotomy, but continues to be useful in a heuristic way to raise questions about the politics involved in the relationship between practical and strategic gender interests. Whether or not struggles around practical interests lead to demands that challenge larger struc-

---

40 See also the special issue of *Gender and History* on Gender, Nationalism and National Identities (v.5, summer 1993).

tures of gender inequality "is to a large degree contingent on political and discursive interventions which help to bring about the transformation of these struggles" (78).

This contingency is illustrated by the varying ways that struggles for strategic gender interests are portrayed as related to nationalist struggles. The ambivalent and often antagonistic stance of Third-World nationalisms to Western modernity has rendered feminism vulnerable to being characterized as an imperialistic imposition of Western notions of gender equality. However, as Jayawardena's (1986) important historical study demonstrates, although imperialism and the influence of Western thought were among contributing elements, the development of feminist movements in the late nineteenth and early twentieth centuries in Asia and the Middle East could not be reduced to this. Feminist politics emerged alongside nationalist struggles — rather than being imposed from "outside," they grew from the same soil. The association of feminism with Western-style modernity continues to be deployed in a variety of ways. Canada's REAL Women,[41] a conservative anti-feminist women's group, issued a series of press releases at the Beijing Conference on Women calling the Platform for Action a racist and imperialist document, asserting that it "attempts to override the culture and religious values of developing countries. It would impose western cultural values on these nations" (REAL Women, 1995). While in some contexts 'feminism' is associated with imperialism and 'the West' in this negative sense, in others, the language of Western-style progress has been appropriated by some states to cast local women's movements as anti-modern and anti-progressive. Gopika Solanki (1998), for example, has explored this sort of rhetoric in relation to women's resistance to state imposition of some forms of contraceptive promotion in India.[42]

The contingent relationship between practical and strategic gender interests is also demonstrated by the manner in which 'traditional' at-

---

41   REAL stand for Realistic, Active and Equal for Life, indicating their origin (and continuing emphasis) in anti-choice politics.

42   Solanki suggests that state promotion of long-term contraceptives, such as injectable hormones, takes control of reproduction out of women's hands, and that women's interests are subordinated to the "good of the nation."

tributes of gender may be taken up as political resources. In a wide range of contexts and issues, women "have invented political practices that redefine and redesign not only the structure of the fields of knowledge, but also the meaning and spaces of politics" (Melchiori, 1998: 91). One of the ways that women have done this is to claim public space and political legitimacy for identities generally consigned to the private. The Mothers of the Plaza de Mayo and Women in Black[43] are two examples which stand out here as politicizing traditional gender identities to advance struggles that extend far beyond the accustomed boundaries of those identities. Significant, too, are the claims for public hearings and public redress of conventionally private wrongs, particularly with respect to sexual violence. As Melchiori notes, these have taken many forms — the public apology demanded by the Japanese army's 'comfort women,' demands for recognition of rape as a war crime, and efforts to revise the criteria for refugee status and political asylum to take the specific forms in which violence is enacted on women into account. "Women's Rights are Human Rights,"[44] the slogan adopted at the 1993 UN Conference on Human Rights in Vienna, and the motif of the 1995 UN Conference on Women in Beijing, is a malleable assertion, and one which, in that malleability, encapsulates the ambivalent relationship of feminism to the Enlightenment project of emancipation.

Putting Gender in its Place

Read against the sharpness with which a diversity of feminisms have drawn out the contexts in which gender is produced and regulated, the remaking of gender in the shifting economic and political context of late-twen-

---

43 The Mothers of the Plaza de Mayo started in Argentina in 1977, as a group of mothers protesting the 'disappearing' of their family members under the military dictatorship. The most comprehensive account is Bouvard (1994). Women in Black originated in Jerusalem, as a silent protest of the Israeli occupation, adopting the traditional garb of a mother in mourning as their symbol. There is also a Women in Black group in the former Yugoslavia, protesting ethnic violence there. See Helman and Rapoport (1997) and Korać (1996).

44 Compare this to REAL Women's slogan: "Women's rights, not at the expense of human rights." A revealing juxtaposition, indeed.

tieth-century Canada can be seen as illustrative of gender's historicity. It seems that you not only cannot go home again, but that there was never an unproblematic home in the first place. There is no originary status for gender, no stable vantage point from which to engage the world. We need to be able to construct a "history of the present" that puts gender in place, the latter understood not only as presence, but also as location. An emphasis on location, perhaps, will encourage "the development of a politics grounded in affinities and coalitions, rather than some pristine, coherent consciousness" (Bondi, 1993: 98). The mainstreaming of gender in sociology, and its privileging as a concept in feminism have accorded it presence, but its location requires far more substance and far less fixity.

It is worth reminding ourselves at this point that gender's historicity, and embeddedness in a host of other social relations, makes and remakes 'men' as well as 'women.' There is little point in theorizing 'women' as a fluid and shifting category if we retain an ahistorical and universalized understanding of 'men.' Masculinity, too, is constructed through national and ethnic projects, and is bound up with bodily and reproductive practices, cultural reproduction, labour and political struggles. Men, too, differ by their particular social locations in the extent to which they benefit from hetero-patriarchal gender regimes, the form and contents of which are never fixed. If we are correct in pushing for an understanding of such concepts as 'nation,' 'state,' 'economy' and 'citizenship' as *gendered*, then we cannot limit our investigations to women. As Nagel (1998: 243) suggests, such a strategy misses "perhaps the major way in which gender shapes politics — through men and their interests, their notions of manliness, and masculine micro and macro cultures." In other words, gender-blind analyses do not only render women invisible, but men *qua*men invisible as well.

The continual remaking of gender in always shifting circumstances illustrates the need to be more careful in our deployment of abstract concepts. Both the abstract concepts that feminists have shown to be gendered in their assumptions and effects, and the abstract concept of 'gender' itself, can only be apprehended adequately through their concrete embodiments. Here, I am thinking of work like that of Zillah Eisenstein (1994), who has interrogated American democracy from the standpoint of the pregnant woman of colour, Cynthia Enloe (1993), who asks what the militarism of the Gulf War means to a Filipina domestic working in Kuwait, and Sinith Sittirak (1998), who critically analyzes development models by asking what 'development' means to her mother, a Thai woman with a particular biography. Relevant, too, is R.W. Connell's (1995) exploration of 'masculinity' via ethnographic inquiry with differently situated men. I highlight these not to argue for any privileged epistemic standpoint from which 'reality' may be more fully apprehended, but simply to suggest that 'gender' is taken up very differently once we move from the abstract to the concrete.[45] Like the turn of a kaleidoscope, as different pieces reconfigure, the picture changes. But neither do I wish to suggest that 'gender,' conceptualized at a higher level of abstraction, can serve no useful analytic or strategic purpose. Here, I think Sylvia Walby is correct to argue that "we need to have concepts at different levels of abstraction" (1997: 5), and that to foreswear macro-level and comparative analysis of larger patterns of gender inequality, in the name of recognizing the importance of local contexts, would be a mistake. That the patterns and issues are so recognizable — poverty, violence, sexual autonomy, reproductive choice — is not insignificant. The question remains, however, as to whether or not 'gender,' as a concept, is up to the task.

---

45 I am indebted to Derek Sayer's (1987, 1988) elaboration of Marx's method in taking this up as an integral characteristic of adequate analysis. Moving from the concrete (the world as experienced) to the abstract (the concepts which allow description) yields 'simple abstractions.' A complete analysis also requires going from the abstract to the concrete, in that "it is only through the particular and the concrete that the general and abstract has any real existence" (1988: 5).

CONCLUSIONS

Re-Configuring Gender?

> That life is complicated is a fact of great analytic importance....
> Such acknowledgment complicates the supposed purity of
> gender, race, voice, boundary: it allows us to acknowledge the
> utility of such categorizations for certain purposes and the
> necessity of their breakdown on other occasions. It compli-
> cates definitions in its shift, in its expansion and contraction
> according to circumstance, in its room for the possibility of
> creatively mated taxonomies and their wildly unpredictable
> offspring.
>
> — Patricia J. Williams[1]

I'm tempted to let this quote from Patricia Williams stand on its own as
the conclusion to this book, as it so cogently summarizes what I have
taken all these pages to say — or at least, what I hope you have heard me
say. But a few more words are in order. You will know already that I think
gender has some merit both as an analytic concept and as a political resource, but that it requires some rethinking that attends to its logic-in-
use. We need to constantly ask *what it is saying* (or not saying, or allowing
to be said, or preventing to be said...), not only in the work of others,
but in our own inquiries as well.[2]

---

1 *Alchemy of Race and Rights*, 1991: 10–11.

2 It seems that every scholarly work worth its salt has a quote from Wittgenstein
somewhere in it, so here's mine: "The way you use the word 'God' does not
show *whom* you mean — but, rather, *what* you mean" (1946/1980:50e).

The emergence of gender as a central category of social analysis is in no small part the result of feminist politics, whose development was/is closely related to broader patterns of social and economic change. Similarly, the fracturing of gender as a unified category is largely the result of other sorts of political movements, which have also emerged in relation to social and economic change. Once we try to analyze gender as a social category it is already bound up with a whole range of social relations that will shape its experience, representation, effects, and the ways in which it is politicized. This is the essence of its historicity.

There is certainly the possibility that a focus on gender may dilute its feminist intent. As is far too often the case in mainstream scholarship, research that invokes gender does not necessarily concern itself with the fundamental asymmetries and inequalities that feminist analyses of gender have taken to be central. The too-frequent synonymy of 'gender' with 'women' may lead to the problematization of women rather than of gendering as a social process. An over-reliance on 'gender' as an explanatory device can render it over-determining and unable to illuminate the complexities of the construction of gender categories, and the diversity within and between those categories. There are problems, too, in the way in which gender has developed, particularly in its relationship to that thing called 'sex,' which has led it to be understood as having cultural dimensions (identity, status, inequality) that can be 'discovered.' This misses the point about both gender and sex as "created and recreated when practised and discussed" (Yuval-Davis, 1997: 119). On this, perhaps it is the moral conservatives who have best grasped gender's radical impulse — its denaturalizing of sex as well. None of the problems raised through these critiques, however, are problems organically linked to gender as a concept. They are problems which are concerned with the tactical uses of 'gender' in its variable role as a theoretical construct and as a political category. As I have attempted to show, the theory and politics of gender are intimately related, and it is through understanding this relationship that we can begin to sort through some of its complexities.

I want to suggest that the recent remappings of identity, difference, and rights that I have explored throughout the book reflect both the theoretical and political crises of categorical identities, of which gender might be taken as an exemplary case. With respect to the theoretical crises, there is no question that the force of 'gender' as a stable ontological category has been undermined. One of the primary objections to the dissolution of identity categories suggested by the postmodern critique has been the fear that once we have deconstructed gender, we have deconstructed 'women,' and hence there will be no secure grounds for political action. Without a clearly articulated 'subject,' whither feminist politics? But "the dissolution of the category 'woman' as an epistemological referent is not the same as arguing that gender is not a category of oppression" (Ashenden, 1997: 55).

Grasping both the discursive and the material is essential to any transformative politics, and is crucial to developing an understanding of 'identity politics' that neither invokes the name of a manifest empirical category, nor rejects attention to social structure as necessarily reifying. Categories, such as those of gender, sexuality, and race, are formed and reformed in different contexts and through processes of struggle over meaning, recognition, and distribution. As Pettman (1991) has argued with respect to race and ethnicity, as categories they are both discursive and systematic — that is, they exist in and through languages, images, and ideological practices, but at the same time they produce and reproduce unequally structured social relations which have material consequences for living, breathing persons. As Pettman's analysis suggests, the use of categories for *analytic* or for *political* purposes invokes different strategies: "Some may seek to deconstruct and demystify categories, to reveal the politics behind their makings and remakings. Others, *or else the same people in different contexts*, may seek to use the category as a resource" (1991: 192; emphasis added).

Gender *is* discursive, ideological, a fiction, a construction. But it also has very practical and material consequences for both women and men. As Ann Oakley argues, "femininities and masculinities are created and sustained as ideational representations linked in systematic ways to institutionalized forms of power" (1998: 134–135). The recognition of gender's material configurations, however, does not require that we reconstitute gender as a unifying basis for politics, as Oakley's subsequent argument against postmodernism implies. While Oakley is sensitive to the contributions of deconstructive feminisms to unravelling the complexities of sex, gender, and their interrelationship, and in countering essentialist formulations, she fears the loss of second-wave feminism's unifying 'subjecthood,' and hence its practical import. "Postmodern feminism," she charges, "is wrapped up in its own wordy academic debates, and is failing to address the relationship between feminist scholarship and women's studies and the situation of women out there in a world that does definitely exist, and that remains obdurately structured by a dualistic, power-driven gender system" (1998: 143). In large measure, I share her concerns, and have made a very similar argument in my previous work (Marshall, 1994: 108–111). I am now less sanguine about the potential of a strategy which accepts, even for reasons of political expediency, a 'subjecthood' for 'women' as its basis. How can we struggle against that obdurately structured gender dualism if we take it, no matter how reluctantly, as our ontological foundation? Once we do so, it is difficult to sustain the focus on gender as 'out there,' and explanations invariably turn to 'in here' — to gender as a characteristic of individuals. This *accepts,* rather than refuses, the terms of the discourse so energetically exercised by the critics of feminism. The attacks on the social construction of gender, in both its moral conservative and libertarian cloaks, are, as I have demonstrated, premised on reasserting the existence of a pre-social individual, either one tied to biology, or one who can cast off the mantle of 'gender victim' (if you happen to be a woman) if you just have sufficient fortitude. In any case, the underlying logic shores up the dualism of gender. It doesn't matter how strenuously we argue about its origins or its future, it is the *binary* that becomes overdetermining, both in terms of description and explanation.

A more productive point of departure is the theorization of gender categories not as binary constructions, but as 'series.' Iris Marion Young (1994) appropriates Sartre's concept of seriality to understand women as "a way of thinking about women as a social collective without requiring that all women have common attributes or a common situation. Gender as seriality, moreover, does not rely on identity or self-identity for understanding the social production and meaning of membership in collectives" (1994: 723). Seriality — as a provisional collectivity — is derived from contexts which passively link individuals, from which self-consciously collective action can arise. All sorts of historically materialized products — bodies, language, artifacts — "constitute the gendered series women through structures like enforced heterosexuality and the sexual division of labour" (730). Race, class, and other 'collective structures' may be thought of in a similar way, and individuals may choose to make some or none of their serialized memberships significant in terms of identity. 'Groups,' which have self-consciousness as collective, arise on the basis of these serialized conditions: "The gendered being of women's groups arises from the serial being of women, as taking up actively and reconstituting the gendered structures that have passively unified them" (736). For this reason, "feminist politics must always be coalition politics" (737).[3]

However, I do not think that Young goes quite far enough in emphasizing the degree of strategic action required for interests to coalesce in and around serialized identities. She uses, as a framing example, her work in an African American woman's campaign for a local school committee, where white women responded to her flyers with delight that a *woman* was running for the school committee. "This African American woman claimed to speak for women in Worcester, and some white women noticed and felt identity with her as a woman" (713). When I read this, I was reminded of this story told by Makeda Silvera:

> A couple of nights ago I was waiting for the train and this drunk guy, big redneck, came up and started shouting, 'Bitch! Bitch!' ... This white woman walks up on the platform and he starts up again. We kind of look at each other in solidarity and I feel less scared because at least there is another woman. But then, this drunk started calling out "Nigger! Nigger!" and looking directly at me. That woman, she just looked right through me and there wasn't that kind of connection, that solidarity, anymore. (in Bannerji et al., 1983: 9)

Here, the 'seriality' around gender quickly broke down as the harasser focussed on Silvera's race. If seriality has potential as a political resource, it must be capable of recognizing that which is not shared by its partici-

---

3 A related re-formulation of 'woman' which seeks to undermine binary formulations is Linda Nicholson's (1994) conception of 'woman' as an internal coalition. She draws on linguistic philosopher Ludwig Wittgenstein's concepts of 'games' and 'family relationships' to sketch out an understanding of 'woman' as "illustrating a map of intersecting similarities and differences" (101). She suggests that feminists understand well the idea of coalitions — that different groups with different interests may come together temporarily to find common ground for some purpose — but that our theorization of 'woman' itself needs to reflect such an understanding.

pants as well as that which is. Otherwise, it can replicate too closely the 'bracketing' of one's particularities in the manner of the bourgeouis public sphere.[4]

While Young is correct to argue that we need ways of conceptualizing women as a collective, or political category, in order "to maintain a point of view outside of liberal individualism," even liberal individualism, while it denies the legitimacy of 'groups' as political actors, implicitly invokes them. Every form of politics must. Categories, however unstable and provisional, are politically necessary. Anna Yeatman (1993: 230) defines politics as "the space between established policy and an emancipatory movement's claims on equality.... These claims are made through showing how policy wrongs the emancipatory subject by excluding or marginalizing the category of persons to whom this subject belongs." Here, she is drawing on Jacques Rancière, who argues that 'politics' always involves the encounter between two rather heterogenous processes: policy, or 'governance,' and emancipation. As he describes it: "the process of emancipation is the verification of the equality of any speaking being with any other speaking being. *It is always enacted in the name of a category denied either the principle or the consequences of that equality*" (1992: 59; emphasis added). This is as true for claims for equality made on behalf of "taxpayers" or "ordinary Canadians" as it is for those made on behalf of "women" or "gays and lesbians" or "divorced fathers." What are the practices that call these categories into being as political entities, and sustain them as intelligible groupings? Social relations do not just produce and govern identities, but also the practices and institutions which constitute the political. Thus politics is not so much a contest or struggle between individuals who present themselves as fully formed, as it is the struggle over the *formation* of the identities.[5] As Mouffe (1992: 30) puts it, "Politics is the constitution of the political community, not something that takes place inside the political community."

As I have argued elsewhere (Marshall, 1994), the formation of identities is a simultaneously individual and social project, always undertaken

---

4 On this, see the discussion of Habermas in Chapter Three.

5 The underlying assumption that political actors enter the public sphere already fully formed in their identities seems, to me, to be a key weakness in Habermas' recent (1996) formulation of 'deliberative democracy.'

in the context of historically available interpretations, and the latter are always the result of contestation and resistance, which permit some interpretations and suppress others. Politically, we can (and must) adopt identities strategically, without mistaking them as a representation of the 'authentic' self. Once we recognize these as socially located, then the arguments of those who would cast 'gender' as 'biopolitics' collapse. 'Gender' is only available as an identity — collective or individual — because of the social and cultural formations that make it so: that accord it identifying, differentiating, and valuating authority. Gender, in its constitution as an identity which can be claimed for political purposes, is produced through the practices that have worked to exclude or suppress it.

This is well demonstrated in the literature on citizenship. Like any category, that of 'citizenship' has no essential referent. Abstractions like citizenship, liberty, equality and justice are "like the printed words on a blank cheque," and "the way we fill in the cheque from time to time is matter of history" (Hallet Carr, cited in Kessler-Harris, 1988: 243–244). Or, as Rancière sums it up, "The universality is not enclosed in *citizen* or *human being*; it is involved in the 'what follows,' in its discursive and practical enactment" (1992: 60). It is in this enactment that 'politics' and the construction of political categories and identities — and the *exclusion* of certain identities from the realm of legitimate political actors — takes place. The exclusion of gender from the realm of political discourse has been part and parcel of the reassertion of individualism as the dominant idiom of claims-making. The logic of individualism, Scott (1992:17) argues, has conceived of group differences "categorically and not relationally, as distinct entities rather than interconnected structures or systems created through repeated processes of the enunciation of difference" and forces claims-making into the shape of claiming individual wrongs. This delegitimizes the normative claims of *groups*, which are marginalized and delegitimized as "special interests."

So, politics is necessarily identity politics. As Rancière has described genuine political participation, it is "the invention of that unpredictable subject which momentarily occupies the street," and democracy is "the continual renewal of the actors and of the forms of their actions, the ever-open possibility of the fresh emergence of this fleeting subject" (1995: 61). It does not suggest or require a foundation of authenticity with respect to those identities. Yet rejecting authenticity does not mean that we must accept an unbounded fluidity in the construction of those "fleeting subjects." The materiality of a gender order that continues to construct its subjects in terms of a fairly predictable asymmetry can only be brought to light by the *strategic* politicization of those identities it permits. We might revise, then, that stalwart assertion of early second-wave feminism to suggest that the personal *can* be political. Identities, while rooted in specific contexts, are not just enacted. They are, particularly as they become framed as oppositional identities (as 'gender' categories have functioned within feminism), strategically deployed.

That 'gender' has suffered something of a legitimacy crisis, both theoretically and politically, is clear. The manner in which the political assault on 'gender' has been coded, in both its fundamentalist and libertarian versions, and the erosion of political legitimacy attached to gender *when it applies to women* should stand as clear warnings of the dangers should feminists fail to take up some of the difficult questions involved. So, too, should the inadequacies of any originary sense of gender, which places it unproblematically in the Enlightenment discourse of rights, and for which the complaints about it from 'others' are treated as merely supplementary. In this form, 'gender' has not travelled very well.

If 'gender' is to have any theoretical or political purchase, then the tendency to conceptualize it categorically — as having some fixable referent — rather than as part of the process of constructing categories, must be resisted. The utility of any such concept is entirely pragmatic — what does it allow us to do, or say, in terms of a given purpose, in a given time and place? In the case of 'gender,' there is nothing useful to be said about it, outside of the concrete specificity of particular social relations, for it is this ensemble of historically located social relations that constitutes *any* identity. But to limit our critique to the discursive deconstruction of categories like 'gender' risks letting their material effects go unchecked, and to let the realities of women's oppression "fall between the many stools of feminist anxieties over identity" (Baden and Goetz, 1997: 19). If we resist talking about gender as a politically constituted identity, because it is unstable and untenable as a theoretical category, its significance as a social, political, and economic marker is not diminished. As Craig Calhoun has noted: "The gendered construction of social life not only reflects *but helps to produce* a discourse in which the ruling apparatus, the economy, the state, etc. appear as though they were actorless systems" (1995: 187;

emphasis added). Or, to paraphrase one of the great critics of liberal individualism, "The political suppression of (gender)[6] not only does not abolish (gender); it actually presupposes its existence" (Marx, 1843: 33).

Gender *can*, I think, permit us to develop the kind of carefully contextualized and situated research that is called for. If 'gender' does not assume a pre-constituted or homogeneous category, but focusses instead on relational and thoroughly social processes, it should be expected that it will be constituted differently across historical and political contexts. But neither does it make 'women' (or 'men') disappear, for it is impossible to talk about gender in the abstract — it can only have meaning through its concrete appearances in specific bodies.[7] To simultaneously recognize the fiction of gender while treating it as concrete is not, as one critic of feminism charges, "epistemological schizophrenia."[8] It is what feminism has historically always been about: in Denise Riley's (1988: 112) much-cited words, accepting that "'women' don't exist — while maintaining a politics of 'as if they existed' — since the world behaves as if they unambiguously did." Jeffrey Weeks has outlined a similar tack in conceptualizing sexual identities as "necessary fictions" (1995). I'm tempted to suggest that we dispense with 'gender' as a noun altogether, and use it instead only adjectivally or, even better, as a verb (to 'gender,' 'gendering,' 'gendered'). To go to this length, though, would be to obscure the way that we tend to experience gendered relations and identities. To reinforce the material dimensions of these 'fictional' identities, that which is experienced most immediately and insistently, I think we need to capture more forcefully the *apparent* concreteness of gender — to treat it as a 'virtual reality,' if you will. At the same time, it is imperative to avoid reifying gender as an overdetermining product of socialization, which can only consign it to the ahistorical and descriptive level. As a social relation, grasping its historicity is essential. E.P. Thompson said

---

6   The original text reads 'private property' here.

7   Let us not forget that in those 'concrete appearances,' gender is not always experienced as oppressive, but may be a source of pleasure and, sometimes, eroticism.

8   This is John Fekete's diagnosis. As he describes it, on the one hand "biofeminism" is "objectivist" about identity, but on the other hand "constructivist" about its prospects (1994: 334).

the following about 'class,' and it is no less true of 'gender': "Like any other relationship, it is a fluency which evades analysis if we attempt to stop it dead at any given moment and anatomize its structure" (1969: 9). We can, however, observe how it is taken up, regularized, institutionalized, resisted, contested, transformed. Historicity and contingency as guiding principles don't infer unintelligibility. What is required is a willingness to work with gender as a construct existing at various levels of abstraction, always understanding that we are 'freezing' a complex and fluid set of social relationships through its usage. Also required is an openness to relinquishing gender's hegemony as a *starting point* for analysis, looking instead to if and how it emerges as significant in particular circumstances. For example, Siltanen (1999) suggests that instead of beginning with a general pattern of male/female difference and then asking how other factors such as race and class might modify this general pattern, we might try "looking through the other end of the telescope" (14). Such a strategy would aim at producing "limited generalizations" which are capable of "respecting diversity when gendered experience is unique, while at the same time identifying common gendered experience across diversity groupings" (15).

If there is one lesson to be learned from the trials of this vexed concept, it is that how gender comes into focus is, always, already bound up with its constitution in and through a complex set of social relationships that are simultaneously historical, political, cultural, structural, and biographical. To end on a personal note, it means that my understanding of gender, as a member of the dominant culture,[9] is *no* less exempt from that complexity than that of those who are differently located. That recognition doesn't limit me to writing or thinking about gender in purely autobiographical terms. On the contrary, it provides me with a renewed critical interest in asking some very big questions, and a willingness to work with the uncertainty and complexity that will inevitably ensue.

---

9 The list of descriptors I could use to position myself here would be a long one, and inexhaustible: white, heterosexual, able-bodied, middle-aged, economically and educationally privileged, anglo-Canadian feminist academic mother living near the close of the twentieth century.... The specific adjectives and nouns are less important than the general point that there is no politically innocent ground for theoretical concepts like gender, no matter where we happen to stand.

References

Abbott, Pamela. 1991. Feminist perspectives in sociology. In J. Aaron and S. Walby, eds., *Out of the Margins: Women's Studies in the Nineties*. London: Falmer.

Acker, Joan. 1989. The problem with patriarchy. *Sociology* 23, 235–240.

Adams, Mary Louise. 1989. There's no place like home: On the place of identity in feminist politics. *Feminist Review* 31: 22–33.

Adamson, Nancy, Linda Briskin, and Margaret McPhail. 1988. *Feminist Organizing for Change: The Contemporary Women's Movement in Canada*. Toronto: Oxford University Press.

Afshar, Haleh. 1996. Introduction (1–6). In Haleh Afshar, ed., *Women and Politics in the Third World*. London: Routledge.

Agger, Ben. 1991. Critical theory, poststructuralism, postmodernism. *Annual Review of Sociology* 17, 105–131.

Alcoff, Linda. 1988. Cultural feminism versus post-structuralism: The identity crisis in feminist theory. *Signs* 13(3): 405–436.

Alexander, M. Jacqui, and Chandra Talpade Mohanty. 1995. Introduction: Genealogies, legacies, movements (xiii–xliii). In M. Jacqui Alexander and Chandra Talpade Mohanty, eds., *Feminist Genealogies, Colonial Legacies, Democratic Futures*. London: Routledge.

Allen, Tim. 1994. *Don't Stand Too Close to a Naked Man*. New York: Hyperion.

Alway, Joan. 1995. The trouble with gender: Tales of the still-missing feminist revolution in sociological theory. *Sociological Theory* 13(3): 209–228.

Amiel, Barbara. 1995. The madness of the unisex experiment. *Macleans* (August 28): 13.

Anderson, Benedict. 1983. *Imagined Communities*. New York: Verso.

Anderson, Karen L. 1996. *Sociology: A Critical Introduction*. Toronto: Nelson.

Anthias, Floya. 1990. Race and class revisited: Conceptualizing race and racisms. *Sociological Review* 38(1): 19–42.

Anthias, Floya, and Nira Yuval-Davis, eds. 1989. *Woman-Nation-State*. London: Macmillan.

—— (in association with Harriet Cain). 1992. *Racialized Boundaries: Race, Nation, Gender, Colour and Class and the Anti-Racist Struggle*. London: Routledge.

Aptheker, Bettina. 1989. *Tapestries of Life: Women's Work, Women's Consciousness and the Meaning of Daily Experience.* Amherst: University of Massachusetts Press.

Arat-Koç, Sedef. 1989. In the privacy of our own home: Foreign domestic workers as solution to the crisis in the domestic sphere in Canada. *Studies in Political Economy* 28: 33–58.

Arat-Koç, Sedef, and Winona Giles. 1994. Introduction. In Winona Giles and Sedef Arat-Koç, eds., *Maid in the Market: Women's Paid Domestic Labour* (1–12). Halifax: Fernwood Publishing.

Armstrong, Pat. 1997. Pay equity: Not just a matter of money. In Caroline Andrew and Sandra Rodgers, eds., *Women and the Canadian State* (122–137). Montreal: McGill-Queens University Press.

Armstrong, Pat, and Hugh Armstrong. 1978. *The Double Ghetto.* Toronto: McClelland and Stewart.

———. 1996. The feminization of the labour force: Harmonizing down in a global economy. In Isabella Bakker, ed., *Rethinking Restructuring: Gender and Change in Canada* (29–54). Toronto: University of Toronto Press.

Arni, Caroline, and Charlotte Müller. 1997. Feminist classics meet the classical mainstream: Harriet Martineau and Jenny P. d'Héricourt. Paper presented at the European Sociological Association Conference, Essex, U.K., April 1997.

Arscott, Jane. 1995a. Twenty-five years and sixty-five minutes after the Royal Commission on the Status of Women. *International Journal of Canadian Studies* 11, 33–58.

———. 1995b. The deliberate choice of false universalism: The Royal Commission on the Status of Women on race and ethnicity. Paper presented at the 'Race, Gender and the Construction of Canada' Conference, University of British Columbia, October 19–21.

Ashenden, Samantha. 1997. Feminism, postmodernism, and the sociology of gender. In David Owen, ed., *Sociology After Postmodernism* (40–64). Thousand Oaks, CA: Sage.

Backhouse, Constance, and David H. Flaherty, eds. 1992. *Challenging Times: The Women's Movement in Canada and the United States.* Montreal: McGill-Queens University Press.

Baden, Sally, and Anne Marie Goetz. 1997. Who needs [sex] when you can have [gender]? Conflicting discourses on gender at Beijing. *Feminist Review* 56: 3–25.

Bakan, Abigail B., and Daiva K. Stasiulis. 1996. Structural adjustment, citizenship and foreign domestic labour: The Canadian case. In Isabella Bakker, ed., *Rethinking Restructuring: Gender and Change in Canada* (217–242). Toronto: University of Toronto Press.

Bakker, Isabella, ed. 1996. *Rethinking Restructuring: Gender and Change in Canada.* Toronto: University of Toronto Press.

Bannerji, Himani. 1995. *Thinking Through: Essays on Feminism, Marxism and Anti-Racism*. London, Toronto: Women's Press.

Bannerji, Himani, Dionne Brand, Prabha Khosla, and Makeda Silvera. 1983. We appear silent to those who are deaf to what we say. *Fireweed* 16: 8–15.

Baron, Ava. 1998. Romancing the field: The marriage of feminism and historical sociology. *Social Politics* (Spring): 17–37.

Barrett, Michele. 1992. Words and things: Materialism and method in contemporary feminist analysis. In Michele Barrett and Anne Phillips, eds., *Destabilizing Theory* (210–219). Cambridge: Polity Press.

Barrett, Michele, and Anne Phillips. 1992. Introduction. In Michele Barrett and Anne Phillips, eds., *Destabilizing Theory* (1–9). Cambridge: Polity Press.

Bashevkin, Sylvia. 1989. Free trade and Canadian feminism: The case of the National Action Committee on the Status of Women. *Canadian Public Policy* 15(4): 363–375.

———. 1996. Losing common ground: Feminists, conservatives and public policy in Canada during the Mulroney years. *Canadian Journal of Political Science* 29(2): 211–242.

———. 1998a. *Women on the Defensive: Living Through Conservative Times*. Toronto: University of Toronto Press.

———. 1998b. Letter to the editor. The *Globe and Mail*. January 21.

Beechey, Veronica. 1979. On patriarchy. *Feminist Review* 3. 66 83.

Begin, Monique. 1992. The Royal Commission on the Status of Women in Canada: Twenty years later. In Constance Backhouse and David Flaherty, eds., *Challenging Times* (21–38). Montreal: McGill-Queens University Press.

Bell, Diane, and Renate Klein, eds. 1996. *Radically Speaking: Feminism Reclaimed*. London: ZED Books.

Benhabib, Seyla. 1989. On contemporary feminist theory. *Dissent* 36: 366–370.

———. 1990. Epistemologies of postmodernism: A rejoinder to Jean-François Lyotard. In Linda Nicholson, ed., *Feminism/Postmodernism* (107–130). London: Routledge.

Benjamin, Jessica. 1988. *The Bonds of Love*. New York: Pantheon.

Bernard, Jessie. 1971. *Women and the Public Interest*. Chicago: Aldine.

———. 1973. My four revolutions: An autobiographical history of the ASA. *American Journal of Sociology* 78: 773–801.

Bloom, Allan. 1987. *The Closing of the American Mind: How Higher Education has Failed Democracy and Impoverished the Souls of Today's Students*. New York: Simon and Schuster.

Bondi, Liz. 1993. Locating identity politics. In Michael Keith and Steve Pile, eds., *Place and the Politics of Identity* (84–101). London: Routledge.

Booth, Barbara, and Michael Blair. 1989. *Thesaurus of Sociological Indexing Terms*. San Diego: Sociological Abstracts.

Bordo, Susan. 1990. Feminism, postmodernism and gender-scepticism. In Linda Nicholson, ed., *Feminism/Postmodernism* (133–156). London: Routledge.

Bottero, Wendy. 1998. Clinging to the wreckage? Gender and the legacy of class. *Sociology* 32(2): 469–490.

Bouvard, Marguerite Guzman. 1994. *Revolutionizing Motherhood: The Mothers of the Plaza de Mayo*. Wilmington, DE: Scholarly Resources Inc.

Bradley, Harriet. 1996. *Fractured Identities: Changing Patterns of Inequality*. Cambridge: Polity Press.

Braidotti, Rosa. 1994. Feminism by any other name (interviewed by Judith Butler). *differences: a journal of feminist cultural studies* 6(2/3): 27–61.

Breaking the Silence. 1984. Inside feminist organizations, part 1. *Breaking the Silence* 2(4): 7–14.

Briskin, Linda. 1991. Feminist practice: A new approach to evaluating feminist strategy. In Jeri Dawn Wine and Janice L. Ristock, eds., *Women and Social Change: Feminist Action in Canada* (24–40). Toronto: James Lorimer.

Brodie, Janine. 1994. Shifting the boundaries: gender and the politics of restructuring. In Isabella Bakker, ed., *The Strategic Silence: Gender and Economic Policy* (46–60). London: ZED Books.

———. 1995. *Politics on the Margins: Restructuring and the Canadian Women's Movement*. Halifax: Fernwood.

———. 1996. Restructuring and the new citizenship. In Isabella Bakker, ed., *Rethinking Restructuring* (126–140). Toronto: University of Toronto Press.

———. 1997a. Meso-discourses, state forms and the gendering of liberal-democratic citizenship. *Citizenship Studies* 1(2): 223–242.

———. 1997b. The politics of abortion in Canada. In Caroline Andrew and Sandra Rodgers, eds., *Women and the Canadian State* (291–305). Montreal: McGill-Queens University Press.

Brown, Jackie. 1992. BC women say 'no way'. *Kinesis* (October).

Brunet, Robin. 1995. The other side of the Beijing story. *Alberta Report* (September 25): 32.

Brym, Robert J. 1986. Anglo-Canadian sociology. *Current Sociology* 34(1): 1–152.

———, ed. 1998. *New Society: Sociology for the 21st Century*, 2nd edition. Toronto: Harcourt Brace.

Brym, Robert J., with Bonnie Fox. 1989. *From Culture to Power*. Toronto: Oxford University Press.

Buist, Margaret. 1987. One foot in the door. *Broadside* 9(1): 4–5.

Burchell, Graham, Colin Gordon, and Peter Miller, eds. 1991. *The Foucault Effect: Studies in Governmentality*. Chicago: University of Chicago Press.

Burke, Catherine. 1992. Looking at the latest con job. *Kinesis* (February): 9.

Burt, Sandra. 1986. Women's issues and the women's movement in Canada. In Alan Cairns and Cynthia Williams, eds., *The Politics of Gender, Ethnicity and Language in Canada* (111–169). Toronto: University of Toronto Press.

———. 1995. The several worlds of policy analysis: Traditional approaches and feminist critiques. In Sandra Burt and Lorraine Code, eds., *Changing Methods: Feminists Transforming Practice* (357–378). Peterborough: Broadview Press.

Busque, Ginette. 1991. Quebec's largest women's group speaks (interview with Germaine Vaillancourt, president of FFQ). *The Womanist* (Summer): 37.

Butler, Judith. 1990. *Gender Trouble.* London: Routledge.

Byfield, Ted. 1996. Saskatchewan drowns in social justice. *Western Report* 11(33): 20–21.

Cairns, Alan. 1988. Citizens (outsiders) and government (insiders) in constitution making. *Canadian Public Policy* 14: S121–145.

Calhoun, Craig. 1995. *Critical Social Theory.* Oxford: Blackwell.

———, ed. 1992. *Habermas and the Public Sphere.* Cambridge, MA: MIT Press.

Cameron, Barbara. 1991. Towards a feminist constitutional agenda. *The Womanist* (Summer): 40.

Carty, Linda, ed. 1994. *And Still We Rise: Feminist Political Mobilizing in Contemporary Canada.* Toronto: Women's Press.

Carver, Terrell. 1998. A political theory of gender. In Vicky Randall and Georgina Waylen, eds., *Gender, Politics and the State* (18–28). London: Routledge.

Cealey, Harrison W., and J. Hood-Williams. 1998. More varieties than Heinz: Social categories and sociality in Humphries, Hammersley and beyond. *Sociological Research Online* 3(1): http:// www.socresonline.org.uk/socresonline/3/1/8.html.

Cecill, Bet. 1998. TG discussion needs compassion (letter to the editor). *Kinesis* (June): 20.

Christiansen-Ruffman, Linda. 1998. Developing feminist sociological knowledge: processes of discovery. In Linda Christiansen-Ruffman, ed., *The Global Feminist Enlightenment: Women and Social Knowledge* (13–36). Madrid: International Sociological Association.

Cloward, Roger, and Frances Fox Piven. 1981. Moral economy and the welfare state. In David Robbins, ed., *Rethinking Social Inequality* (213–240). London: Gower.

Cohen, Jean. 1983. Rethinking social movements. *Berkeley Journal of Sociology* 28: 97–114.

———. 1985. Strategy or identity? New theoretical paradigms and contemporary social movements. *Social Research* 52(4): 663–716.

Cohen, Marjorie. 1993. The Canadian women's movement. In Ruth Roach Pierson, Marjorie Griffin Cohen, Paula Bourne, and Philinda Masters, eds., *Canadian Women's Issues, Volume 1: Strong Voices* (1–31). Toronto: James Lorimer.

———. 1995. Feminism's effect on economic policy. In Ruth Roach Pierson and Marjorie Griffin Cohen, *Canadian Women's Issues, Volume II: Bold Visions* (263–298). Toronto: James Lorimer.

———. 1997. From welfare state to vampire capitalism. In Patricia M. Evans and Gerda R. Wekerle, eds., *Women and the Canadian Welfare State* (28–67). Toronto: University of Toronto Press.

Cole, Susan. 1987. Meech Lake: Troubled waters. *Broadside* 9(2): 3.

Connell, R.W. 1985. Theorising gender. *Sociology* 19(May): 260–72.

———. 1987. *Gender and Power*. Cambridge: Polity Press.

———. 1990. The state, gender and sexual politics: Theory and appraisal. *Theory and Society* 19: 507–544.

———. 1995. *Masculinities*. Berkeley: University of California Press.

———. 1996. New directions in gender theory, masculinity research and gender politics. *Ethnos* 61(3/4): 157–176.

Connelly, M. Patricia, and Martha MacDonald. 1995. The labour market, the state, and the reorganizing of workers. In Isabella Bakker, ed., *Rethinking Restructuring: Gender and Change in Canada* (82–91). Toronto: University of Toronto Press.

Cook, Judith, and Mary Margaret Fonow. 1990. Knowledge and women's interests: Issues of epistemology and methodology in feminist social research. In Joyce McCarl Neilson, ed., *Feminist Research Methods* (69–93). Boulder: Westview Press.

Cook, Michael. 1995. Not a motherhood statement: A UN master plan for women. In Michael Cook, ed., *Empowering Women: Critical Views on the Beijing Conference* (19–24). Crows Nest, NSW, Australia: Little Hills Press.

Coole, Diana. 1988. *Women in Political Theory*. Brighton: Harvester/Wheatsheaf.

———. 1994. Whither feminisms? *Political Studies* 42: 128–134.

Cooper, Anna Julia. 1993. The coloured woman's office [1892]. In Charles Lemert, ed., *Social Theory: The Multicultural and Classic Readings* (194–199). Boulder: Westview Press.

Creese, Gillian, and Daiva Stasiulis. 1996. Introduction: Intersections of gender, race, class and sexuality. *Studies in Political Economy* 51: 5–14.

Crenshaw, Kimberlee. 1991. Demarginalizing the intersection of race and sex: A black feminist critique of antidiscrimination doctrine, feminist theory and antiracist politics. In Katharine T. Bartlett and Rosanne Kennedy, eds., *Feminist Legal Theory: Readings in Law and Gender* (57–80). Boulder: Westview Press.

———. 1995. Mapping the margins: Intersectionality, identity politics, and violence against women. In Dan Denielsen and Karen Eagle, eds., *After Identity: A Reader in Law and Culture* (332–354). London: Routledge.

Crittenden, Danielle. 1990. Let's junk the feminist slogans: The war's over. *Chatelaine* (August): 37–39, 62.

Curthoys, Ann. 1993. Feminism, citizenship and national identity. *Feminist Review* 44: 19–38.

Dacks, Gurston, Joyce Green, and Linda Trimble. 1995. Road kill: Women in Alberta's drive toward deficit elimination. In Gordon Laxer and Trevor Harrison, eds., *The Trojan Horse: Alberta and the Future of Canada* (270–285). Montreal: Black Rose Books.

Dalzell, Catherine. 1995. The bracket brigade at work: The UN's vision of utopia. In Michael Cook, ed., *Empowering Women: Critical Views on the Beijing Conference* (25–47). Crows Nest, NSW, Australia: Little Hills Press.

Dank, Barry M., and Joseph S. Fulda. 1998. Forbidden love: Student-professor romances. In Barry M. Dank and Roberto Refinetti, eds., *Sexual Harassment and Sexual Consent* (Sexuality and Culture, V.1) (107–130). New Brunswick, NJ: Transaction Publishers.

D'Aquino, Thomas. 1996. Reconciling globalization and human rights (speech to the Academy of International Business). *Canadian Speeches* 10(7): 16–21.

Darby, Tom, and Peter C. Emberley. 1996. 'Political correctness' and the constitution. In Anthony A. Peacock, ed., *Rethinking the Constitution: Perspectives on Canadian Constitutional Reform, Interpretation and Theory* (233–248). Oxford: Oxford University Press.

Day, Shelagh. 1992. Speaking for ourselves. In Kenneth McRoberts and Patrick Monahan, eds., *The Charlottetown Accord, the Referendum and the Future of Canada* (58–72). Toronto: University of Toronto Press.

Day, Shelagh, Gloria Nicholson, and Judy Rebick. 1991. The constitutional debate: What's at stake for women. *Kinesis* (April): 11–13.

de Beauvoir, Simone. 1949/1961. *The Second Sex*. New York: Bantam Books.

de Casco, Martha Lorena. 1995. The battle at Beijing. In Michael Cook, ed., *Empowering Women: Critical Views on the Beijing Conference* (19–17). Crows Nest, NSW, Australia: Little Hills Press.

de Lauretis, Teresa. 1991. Queer theory and lesbian and gay sexualities: An introduction. *differences: A Journal of Feminist Cultural Studies* 3: iii–xviii.

Delphy, Christine. 1993. Rethinking sex and gender. *Women's Studies International Forum* 16(1):1–9.

Denis, Claude. 1993. Quebec-as-distinct society as conventional wisdom: The consitutional silence of anglo-Canadian sociologists. *Canadian Journal of Sociology* 18(3): 251–269.

———. 1995a. 'Government can do whatever it wants': Moral regulation in Ralph Klein's Alberta. *Canadian Review of Sociology and Anthropology* 32(3): 365–383.

———. 1995b. The new normal: Capitalist discipline in Alberta in the 1990's. In Gordon Laxer and Trevor Harrison, eds., *The Trojan Horse: Alberta and the Future of Canada* (86–100). Montreal: Black Rose Books.

———. 1997. *We Are Not You: First Nations and Canadian Modernity*. Peterborough: Broadview Press.

de Sève, Micheline. 1992. The perspectives of Quebec feminists. In Constance Backhouse and David H. Flaherty, eds., *Challenging Times* (110–116). Montreal: McGill-Queens University Press.

———. 1997. Gendered feelings about our national issue(s). *Atlantis* 21(2): 111–117.

Devlin, Richard. 1993. A counter-attack in defense of political correctness. *Toronto Star* (March 8): A15.

Drainie, Bronwyn. 1986. Meet the post-feminist women. *Chatelaine* (September): 58–59, 95.

du Cille, Ann. 1994. The occult of true black womanhood: Critical demeanor and black feminist studies. *Signs* 19(3): 591–629.

Durkheim, Emile. 1897/1951. *Suicide.* New York: Free Press.

Ehrenreich, Barbara. 1994. A feminist on the outs. *Time* (August 1).

Eichler, Margrit. 1980. *The Double Standard: A Feminist Critique of Feminist Social Science.* New York: St. Martin's Press.

———. 1985. And the work never ends: Feminist contributions. *Canadian Review of Sociology and Anthropology* 22(5): 619–644.

———. 1988. *Non-sexist Research Methods.* Wellington: Unwin Hyman.

———. 1992. The unfinished transformation: Women and feminist approaches in sociology and anthropology. In William Carroll, Linda Christiansen-Ruffman, Raymond F. Currie, and Deborah Harrison, eds., *Fragile Truths: 25 Years of Sociology and Anthropology in Canada* (71–101). Ottawa: Carleton University Press.

Eisenstein, Zillah R. 1994. *The Color of Gender.* Berkeley: University of California Press.

Emberley, Peter C. 1996. *Zero Tolerance: Hot Button Politics in Canada's Universities.* Toronto: Penguin.

Enloe, Cynthia. 1993. *The Morning After: Sexual Politics at the End of the Cold War.* Berkeley: University of California Press.

Epstein, Barbara. 1995. Why post-strucuralism is a dead end for progressive thought. *Socialist Review* 25(2): 83–119.

Everitt, Joanna. 1998. Public opinion and social movements: The women's movement and the gender gap in Canada. *Canadian Journal of Political Science* 31(4): 743–765.

Farganis, Sondra. 1986. Social theory and feminist theory: The need for dialogue. *Sociological Inquiry* 56(1): 50–68.

Fausto-Sterling, Anne. 1993. The five sexes: Why male and female are not enough. *The Sciences* (March/April): 20–24.

Featherstone, Mike. 1991. Georg Simmel: An introduction. *Theory, Politics and Society* 8(3):1–16.

Fekete, John. 1994. *Moral Panic: Biopolitics Rising.* Montreal: Robert Davies Publishing.

Felski, Rita. 1989a. Feminist theory and social change. *Theory, Culture and Society* 6: 219–240.

———. 1989b. Feminism, postmodernism and the critique of modernity. *Cultural Critique* 13: 33–56.

———. 1995. *The Gender of Modernity.* Cambridge, MA: Harvard University Press.

———. 1997a. The doxa of difference. *Signs* 23(1): 1–21.

———. 1997b. Reply to Braidotti, Cornell and Ang. *Signs* 23(1): 64–69.

Ferguson, Kathy. 1993. *The Man Question: Visions of Subjectivity in Feminist Theory.* Berkeley: University of California Press.

Ferree, Myra Marx, and Elaine J. Hall. 1996. Rethinking stratification from a feminist perspective: Gender, race and class in mainstream textbooks. *American Sociological Review* 61(4): 929–950.

Findlay, Sue. 1987. Facing the state: The politics of the women's movement reconsidered. In Heather Jon Maroney and Meg Luxton, eds., *Feminism and Political Economy* (31–50). Toronto: Methuen.

———. 1994. Problematizing privilege: Another look at the representation of 'women' in feminist practice. In Linda Carty, ed., *And Still We Rise: Feminist Political Mobilizing in Contemporary Canada* (207–224). Toronto: Women's Press.

Flanders, Laura. 1994. The "stolen feminism" hoax: Anti-feminist attack based on error-filled anecdotes. *Extra!* (September/October).

Flax, Jane. 1986. Gender as a problem: In and for feminist theory. *American Studies/ Amerika Studien* 31(2): 193–213.

Fonow, Mary Margaret, and Judith A. Cook, eds. 1991. *Beyond Methodology: Feminist Scholarship as Lived Research.* Bloomington: Indiana University Press.

Foucault, Michel. 1980a. *The History of Sexuality* (Volume 1). New York: Vintage Books.

———, 1980b. Two lectures. In Colin Gordon, ed., *Power/Knowledge* (78–108). New York: Pantheon.

———. 1991. Governmentality. In Graham Burchell, Colin Gordon, and Peter Miller, eds., *The Foucault Effect: Studies in Governmentality* (87–104). Chicago: University of Chicago Press.

Fox, Bonnie. 1988. Conceptualizing 'patriarchy'. *Canadian Review of Sociology and Anthropology* 25(2): 163–182.

Fox-Genovese, Elizabeth. 1996. *Feminism Is Not the Story of My Life: How Today's Feminist Elite Has Lost Touch with the Real Concerns of Women.* Garden City: Doubleday.

Franklin, Sarah. 1996. Introduction. In Sarah Franklin, ed., *The Sociology of Gender* (ix–xivii). Brookfield, VT: Edward Elgar.

Fraser, Nancy. 1989. *Unruly Practices.* Minneapolis: University of Minnesota Press.

———. 1996. Equality, difference and radical democracy: The United States feminist debates revisited. In David Trend, ed., *Radical Democracy: Identity, Citizenship and the State* (197–208). London: Routledge.

———. 1997. *Justice Interruptus.* London: Routledge.

Fraser, Nancy, and Linda Gordon. 1994. 'Dependency' demystified: Inscriptions of power in a keyword of the welfare state. *Social Politics* 1(1): 4–31.

Fraser, Nancy, and Linda Nicholson. 1990. Social criticism without philosophy: An encounter between feminism and postmodernism. In Linda Nicholson, ed., *Feminism/Postmodernism* (19–38). London: Routledge.

Friedman, Susan Stanford. 1995. Beyond white and other: Relationality and narratives of race in feminist discourse. *Signs* 21(1): 1–49.

Frith, Hanna, and Celia Kitzinger. 1997. Talk about sexual miscommunication. *Women's Studies International Forum* 20(4): 517–528.

Funk, Nanette, and Magda Mueller, eds. 1993. *Gender Politics and Post-Communism*. New York: Routledge.

Fuss, Diana, ed. 1991. *Inside/Out: Lesbian Theories, Gay Theories*. London: Routledge.

Gal, Susan. 1994. Gender in the post-socialist transition: The abortion debate in Hungary. *East European Politics and Societies* 8(2): 256–286.

Garcia-Robles, Susana. 1995. Beijing backstage: A gender agenda. In Michael Cook, ed., *Empowering Women: Critical Views on the Beijing Conference* (49–63). Crows Nest, NSW, Australia: Little Hills Press.

Gerhard, Ute. 1995. The role of social movements for the project of civil society: The case of the women's movement. Unpublished paper given at the Second European Conference for Sociology, "European Societies: Fusion or Fission?", Budapest, 1995.

———. 1999. Über das komplizierte Verhältnis zwischen Feminismus und Soziologie. Paper presented at the Symposium on Feminism and Classical Sociological Theory, Institute for Women and Gender Studies, Frankfurt, January 1999 (translation provided).

Giddens, Anthony. 1971. *Capitalism and Modern Social Theory*. Cambridge: Cambridge University Press.

———. 1987. *Social Theory and Modern Sociology*. Cambridge: Polity Press.

Globe and Mail. 1997. Editorial: Is it wrong to keep a promise? (October 7): A18.

Godard, Barbara. 1998. Pedagogic fictions. *Topia* 1: 83–99.

Goven, Joanna. 1993. Gender politics in Hungary: Autonomy and antifeminism. In Nanette Funk and Magda Mueller, eds., *Gender Politics and Post-Communism* (224–240). London: Routledge.

Gray, Charlotte. 1989. The new F-word. *Saturday Night* 104(4): 17–20.

Gray, John. 1992. *Men are From Mars, Women are From Venus*. New York: Harper Collins.

Gross, Paul, and Norman Levitt. 1994. *Higher Superstitions: The Academic Left and its Quarrels with Science*. Baltimore: Johns Hopkins University Press.

Habermas, Jurgen. 1981. New social movements. *Telos* 49, 33–37.

———. 1989. *The Structural Transformation of the Public Sphere*. Cambridge, MA: MIT Press.

———. 1996. *Between Facts and Norms: Contributions to a Discourse Theory of Law and Democracy*. Cambridge, MA: MIT Press.

Hale, Sylvia M. 1995. *Controversies in Sociology: A Canadian Introduction*, 2nd edition. Toronto: Copp Clark.

Handy, Bruce. 1998. The Viagra craze. *Time* (May 4): 38–45.

Hansen, Karen V., and Ilene J. Philipson, eds. 1990. *Women, Class and the Feminist Imagination: A Socialist-Feminist Reader*. Philadelphia: Temple University Press.

Haraway, Donna J. 1991. *Simians, Cyborgs and Women*. London: Routledge.

Harding, Sandra. 1986. The instability of the analytical categories of feminist theory. *Signs* 11(4): 645–664.

Hausman, Bernice L. 1995. *Changing Sex: Transsexualism, Technology and the Idea of Gender*. Durham, NC: Duke University Press.

Hawkesworth, Mary. 1989. Knowers, knowing, known: Feminist theory and claims to truth. *Signs* 14(3): 533–557.

———. 1997. Confounding gender. *Signs* 22(3): 649–685.

Heitlinger, Alena. 1996. Framing feminism in post-communist Czech republic. *Communist and Post-Communist Studies* 29(1): 77–93.

Helman, Sara, and Tamar Rapoport. 1997. Women in Black: Challenging Israel's gender and socio-political orders. *British Journal of Sociology* 48(4): 681–700.

Helmer, Joanne. 1995. Redefining normal: Life in the new Alberta. In Gordon Laxer and Trevor Harrison, eds., *The Trojan Horse: Alberta and the Future of Canada* (70–83). Montreal: Black Rose Books.

Hénaut, Dorothy Todd. 1991. Passionate ambiguity. *The Womanist* (summer): 36.

Hennessy, Rosemary. 1995. Queer visibility in commodity culture. In Linda Nicholson and Steven Seidman, eds., *Social Postmodernism* (142–183). Cambridge: Cambridge University Press.

Henslin, James M., and Adie Nelson. 1996. *Sociology: A Down to Earth Approach*. Canadian edition. Scarborough: Allyn and Bacon.

Herdt, Gilbert. 1994. *Third Sex, Third Gender: Beyond Sexual Dimorphism in Culture and History*. New York: Zone Books.

Hill, Miche. 1992. Native women and the constitution: Still fighting for a seat. *Kinesis* (June).

Hill, Miche, and Jaffer, Fatima. 1992. Native women and the constitution: Doors open on talks. *Kinesis* (September).

Hoeker-Drysdale, Susan. 1992. *Harriet Martineau: First Woman Sociologist*. Oxford: Berg.

Hoff, Joan. 1994. Gender as a postmodern category of paralysis. *Women's Studies International Forum* 17(4): 443–447.

———. 1996. The pernicious effect of poststructuralism on women's history. In Diane Bell and Renate Klein, eds., *Radically Speaking: Feminism Reclaimed* (393–412). London: ZED Books.

Hood-Williams, John. 1996. Goodbye to sex and gender. *Sociological Review* 44(1): 1–16.

hooks, bell. 1990. *Yearning: Race, Gender and Cultural Politics*. Toronto: Between the Lines.

Horowitz, Irving Louis. 1993. *The Decomposition of Sociology*. Oxford: Oxford University Press.

Howard, Angela, and Sasha Ranae Adams Tarrant. 1998. *Antifeminism in America* (3 volumes). Hamden, CT: Garland Publishing.

Huang, Agnes. 1992a. Designing a constitution. *Kinesis* (June).

———. 1992b. Canadian Panel on Violence against Women: Some things never change. *Kinesis* (September).

Human Resources Development Canada. 1997a. *Gender-based Analysis Backgrounder.* Ottawa: Women's Bureau, Strategic Policy Branch.

———. 1997b. *Gender-based Analysis Guide.* Ottawa: Women's Bureau, Strategic Policy Branch.

Huyssen, Andreas. 1990. Mapping the postmodern. In Linda Nicholson, ed., *Feminism/Postmodernism* (234–277). London: Routledge.

Ingraham, Chrys. 1994. The heterosexual imaginary: Feminist sociology and theories of gender. *Sociological Theory* 12(2): 203–219.

Iyer, Nitya. 1997. Disappearing women: Racial-minority women in human rights cases. In Caroline Andrews and Sandra Rodgers, eds., *Women and the Canadian State* (241–261). Montreal: McGill-Queens University Press.

Jackel, Susan. 1991. Rethinking equality and citizenship. In David Schneiderman, ed., *Conversations Among Friends/Entre Amis: Proceedings of an Interdisciplinary Conference on Women and Constitutional Reform* (43–48). Edmonton: University of Alberta Centre for Constitutional Studies.

Jackson, Stevie, and Sue Scott. 1997. Gut reactions to matters of the heart: reflections on rationality, irrationality and sexuality. *Sociological Review* 45(4): 551–575.

Jaffer, Fatima. 1992. Referendum on Accord: What's up next? *Kinesis* (November): 3–4.

Jagger, Alison. 1983. *Feminist Politics and Human Nature.* Totowa, NJ: Rowman and Allanhold.

Jary, David, and Julia Jary, eds. 1991. *Collins Dictionary of Sociology.* New York: Harper-Collins.

Jayawardena, Kumari. 1986. *Feminism and Nationalism in the Third World.* London: ZED Books.

Jeffreys, Sheila. 1994. The queer disappearance of lesbians: Sexuality in the academy. *Women's Studies International Forum* 17(5): 459–472.

———. 1996. Return to gender: post-modernism and lesbianandgay theory. In Diane Bell and Renate Klein, eds., *Radically Speaking: Feminism Reclaimed* (359–374). London: ZED Books.

Jenson, Jane. 1987. Changing discourse, changing agendas: Political rights and reproductive policies in France. In Mary Fainson Katzenstein and Carol McClurg Mueller, eds., *The Women's Movements of the United States and Western Europe* (64–88). Philadelphia: Temple University Press.

Jenson, Jane, and Susan D. Phillips. 1996. Regime shift: New citizenship practices in Canada. *International Journal of Canadian Studies* 14 (Fall): 111–136.

Jones, Nancy Baker. 1994. Confronting the PC "debate": The politics of identity and the American image. *NWSA Journal* 6(3): 384–403.

Jordanova, Ludmilla. 1989. *Sexual Visions: Images of Gender in Science and Medicine between the Eighteenth and Twentieth Century.* Madison: University of Wisconsin Press.

Joseph, Rita. 1995. Beijing's blueprint for revolution: An experiment in social engineering. In Michael Cook, ed., *Empowering Women: Critical Views on the Beijing Conference* (81–104). Crows Nest, NSW, Australia: Little Hills Press.

Kaminer, Wendy. 1996. Will class trump gender? The new assault on feminism. *The American Prospect* 29 (Nov./Dec.): 44–52.

Kammer, Jack. 1994. *Good Will Toward Men.* New York: St. Martin's Press.

Kandiyoti, Deniz. 1998. Gender, power and contestation: Rethinking 'bargaining with patriarchy'. In Cecile Jackson and Ruth Pearson, eds., *Feminist Visions of Development: Gender, Analysis and Policy* (135–151). London: Routledge.

Kealey, Linda, Ruth Pierson, and Joan Sangster. 1992. Teaching Canadian history in the 1990's: Whose "national" history are we lamenting? *Journal of Canadian Studies* 27(Summer): 129–31.

Kelly-Gadol, Joan. 1984. *Women, History and Theory.* Chicago: University of Chicago Press.

Kendall, Diana, Jane Lothian Murray, and Rick Linden. 1997. *Sociology in Our Times.* First Canadian edition. Scarborough: Nelson.

Kessler-Harris, Alice. 1988. The just price, the free market and the value of women. *Feminist Studies* 14(2): 235–249.

Kitchen, Brigitte. 1997. "Common sense" assaults on families. In Diana S. Ralph, André Régimbald, and Nérée St. Amand, eds., *Open for Business, Closed to People: Mike Harris's Ontario* (103–112). Halifax: Fernwood.

Komarovsky, Mirra. 1946. Cultural contradictions and sex roles. *American Journal of Sociology* 52: 184–189.

Kome, Penney. 1983. *The Taking of Twenty-Eight: Canadian Women Challenge the Constitution.* Toronto: Women's Press.

Korać, Maja. 1996. Understanding ethnic-national identity. *Women's Studies International Forum* 19(1/2): 133–143.

La Cerra, Peggy. 1998. Gender-specific differences in evolved mating "strategies": The evolutionary basis of sexual conflict. In Barry Dank and Robert Refinetti, eds., *Sexual Harassment and Sexual Consent* (Sexuality and Culture, V.1) (151–174). New Brunswick, NJ: Transaction.

Laclau, Ernesto, and Chantal Mouffe. 1985. *Hegemony and Socialist Strategy.* New York, London: Verso.

LaFramboise, Donna. 1996. *The Princess at the Window: A New Gender Morality.* London, New York: Penguin Books.

———. 1997. You've come a long way, baby. And what for? *The Globe and Mail* (July 26): D1, D3.

Lamoureux, Diane. 1987. Nationalism and feminism in Quebec: An impossible attraction. In Heather Jon Maroney and Meg Luxton, eds., *Feminism and Political Economy* (51–68). Toronto: Methuen.

Landes, Joan. 1988. *Women and the Public Sphere in the Age of the French Revolution.* Ithaca: Cornell University Press.

Laqueur, Thomas. 1990. *Making Sex: Body and Gender from the Greeks to Freud.* Cambridge, MA: Harvard University Press.

Lazenby, Jo. 1975. Member's Forum. *Kinesis* (December): 17.

LeGates, Marlene. 1996. *Making Waves: A History of Feminism in Western Society.* Toronto: Copp Clark.

Lemert, Charles, ed. 1993. *Social Theory: The Multicultural and Classic Readings.* Boulder: Westview.

Leo, John. 1994. De-escalating the gender war. *U.S. News and World Report* (April 18): 24.

Lichtblau, Klaus. 1989/90. Eros and culture: Gender theory in Simmel, Tönnies and Weber. *Telos* 82: 89–110.

Lipmen-Blumen, Jean, and Ann R. Tickamyer. 1975. Sex roles in transition: A ten-year perspective. *Annual Review of Sociology* 1: 297–337.

Livingstone, D.W., and Meg Luxton. 1989. Gender consciousness at work: Modification of the male breadwinner norm among steelworkers and their spouses. *Canadian Review of Sociology and Anthropology* 26(2): 240–275.

Lopata, Helen Z., and Barrie Thorne. 1978. On the term "sex roles". *Signs* 4(3): 718–721.

Lorber, Judith. 1994. *Paradoxes of Gender.* New Haven: Yale University Press.

———. 1996. Beyond the binaries: Depolarizing the categories of sex, sexuality and gender. *Sociological Inquiry* 66(2): 143–159.

Luxton, Meg. 1980. *More Than a Labour of Love: Three Generations of Women's Work in the Home.* London, Toronto: Women's Press.

Marinoff, Louis. 1998. Review of 'Moral Panic' by J. Fekete. In Barry M. Dank and Roberto Refinetti, eds., *Sexual Harassment and Sexual Consent* (Sexuality and Culture, V.1) (293–297). New Brunswick, NJ: Transaction Publishers.

Marshall, Barbara. 1994. *Engendering Modernity: Feminism, Social Theory and Social Change.* Boston: Polity Press and Northeastern University Press.

———. 1995. Communication as politics: Feminist print media in English Canada. *Women's Studies International Forum* 18(4): 563–474.

Martin, Jane Roland. 1994. Methodological essentialism, false difference and other dangerous traps. *Signs* 19 (3): 630–657.

———. 1996. Aerial distance, esotericism and other closely related traps. *Signs* 21(3): 584–614.

Marx, Karl. 1843/1978. On the Jewish question. Reprinted in R. Tucker, ed., *The Marx-Engels Reader*, 2nd edition (26–52). New York: Norton.

Marx, Karl, and Frederick Engels. 1872/1978. The communist manifesto. Reprinted in R. Tucker, ed., *The Marx-Engels Reader*, 2nd edition (469–500). New York: Norton.

Mascia-Lees, Frances E., Patricia Sharpe, and Colleen Ballerino Cohen. 1989. The postmodernist turn in anthropology: Cautions from a feminist perspective. *Signs* 15(1): 7–33.

Maynard, Mary. 1990. The re-shaping of sociology? Trends in the study of gender. *Sociology* 24(2): 260–290.

McCarthy, E. Doyle. 1996. *Knowledge as Culture*. London: Routledge.

McDonald, Lynn. 1994. *The Women Founders of the Social Sciences*. Ottawa: Carleton University Press.

McElroy, Wendy. 1996. *Sexual Correctness: The Gender Feminist Attack on Women*. Jefferson, NC: McFarland and Co.

McLaughlin, Lisa. 1993. Feminism, the public sphere, media and democracy. *Media, Culture and Society* 15, 599–620.

McQuaig, Linda. 1998. *The Cult of Impotence: Selling the Myth of Powerlessness in the Global Economy*. Toronto: Viking.

Melchiori, Paola. 1998. Redefining political spaces and the concept of politics: Migrating practices of consciousness-raising. In Linda Christiensen-Ruffman, ed., *The Global Feminist Enlightenment: Women and Social Knowledge* (91–104). Madrid: International Sociological Association.

Melucci, Alberto. 1980. The new social movements: A theoretical approach. *Social Science Information* 19: 199–226.

Mickleburgh, Rod. 1995. Perturbed MP leaves UN meeting early. *The Globe and Mail* (September 11): A8.

Miles, Angela. 1996. *Integrative Feminisms: Building Global Visions 1960's–1990's*. London: Routledge.

Millman, Marcia, and Rosabeth Moss Kanter, eds. 1975. *Another Voice*. Anchor Books.

Minnich, Elizabeth Kamarck. 1998. Review essay: Feminist attacks on feminisms: patriarchy's prodigal daughters. *Feminist Studies* 24(1): 159–175.

Modleski, Tania. 1991. *Feminism Without Women*. London: Routledge.

Moghadam, Valentine M. 1994. *Identity Politics and Women: Cultural Reassertions and Feminisms in International Perspective*. Boulder: Westview Press.

Mohanty, Chandra Talpade. 1991. Cartographies of struggle: Third-World women and the politics of feminism. In Chandra Talpade Mohanty, Ann Russo, and Lourdes Torres, eds., *Third World Women and the Politics of Feminism* (1–47). Bloomington: Indiana University Press.

Mohanty, Chandra Talpade, Ann Russo, and Lourdes Torres, eds. 1991. *Third World Women and the Politics of Feminism*. Bloomington: Indiana University Press.

Molyneux, Maxine. 1985. Mobilisation without emancipation? Women's interests, the state and revolution in Nicaragua. *Feminist Studies* 11: 227–254.

———. 1994. Women's rights and the international context: Some reflections on the post-communist states. *Millenium* 23(2): 287–313.

———. 1998. Analysing women's movements. In Cecile Jackson and Ruth Pearson, eds., *Feminist Visions of Development: Gender, Analysis and Policy* (65–88). London: Routledge.

Money, John. 1995. *Gendermaps: Social Constructionism, Feminism, and Sexosophical History.* New York: Continuum.

Moore, Henrietta. 1994. *A Passion for Difference: Essays in Anthropology and Gender.* Bloomington: Indiana University Press.

Moore, Lorrie. 1986. *Anagrams.* New York: Warner Books.

Morokvasic, Mirjana. 1991. Fortress Europe and migrant women. *Feminist Review* 39: 69–84.

Morrison, Ian. 1997. Rights and the right: Ending social citizenship in Ontario. In Diana S. Ralph, André Régimbald, and Nérée St-Amand, eds., *Open for Business/Closed to People* (68–78). Halifax: Fernwood.

Mouffe, Chantal. 1992. Citizenship and political identity. *October* (61): 28–2.

———. 1993. *The Return of the Political.* New York, London: Verso.

Murray, Georgina. 1997. Agonize, don't organize: A critique of postfeminism. *Current Sociology* 45(2): 37–47.

Nagel, Joane. 1998. Masculinity and nationalism: Gender and sexuality in the making of nations. *Ethnic and Racial Studies* 21(2): 242–269.

Ng, Roxanna. 1993. Sexism, racism and Canadian nationalism. In Sneja Gunew and Anna Yeatman, eds., *Feminism and the Politics of Difference* (197–211). Halifax: Fernwood.

Nicholson, Linda, ed. 1990. *Feminism/Postmodernism.* London: Routledge.

———. 1994. Interpreting gender. *Signs* 20(1): 79–105.

Oakes, Guy, ed. 1984. *Georg Simmel: On Women, Sexuality and Love.* Translated and with an introduction by G. Oakes. New Haven: Yale University Press.

Oakley, Ann. 1972. *Sex, Gender and Society.* New York: Harper and Row.

———. 1974. *The Sociology of Housework.* New York: Pantheon.

———. 1989. Women's studies in British sociology: To end at our beginning? *British Journal of Sociology* 40(3): 442–470.

———. 1997. A brief history of gender. In Ann Oakley and Juliet Mitchell, eds., *Who's Afraid of Feminism? Seeing Through the Backlash.* London: Hamish Hamilton, 29–55.

———. 1998. Science, gender and women's liberation: An argument against postmodernism. *Women's Studies International Forum* 21(2): 133–146.

O'Brien, Mary. 1981. *The Politics of Reproduction.* Boston: Routledge and Kegan Paul.

OISE. 1987. Conference on Women and the State, Feb. 6–8. Conference documentation, located in the Canadian Women's Movement Archives.

O'Leary, Dale. 1995. Gender: The deconstruction of women. Unpublished paper, circulated at the NGO Forum at the United Nations Fourth World Conference on Women, Beijing.

Oudshoorn, Nellie. 1994. *Beyond the Natural Body: An Archaeology of Sex Hormones.* London, New York: Routledge.

Paglia, Camille. 1990. *Sexual Personae.* New Haven: Yale University Press.

———. 1992. *Sex, Art and American Culture.* New York: Vintage.

———. 1994. *Vamps and Tramps.* New York: Vintage.

———. 1997. Feminists must begin to fulfill their noble, animating ideal. *Chronicle of Higher Education*, reprinted in the newsgroup paglia-l (July 25, 1997): B4.

Palmer, Bryan. 1990. *Descent into Discourse: The Reification of Language and the Writing of Social History.* Philadelphia: Temple University Press.

Parsons, Talcott. 1942. Age and sex in the American social structure. *American Sociological Review* 7: 604–616.

Parsons, Talcott, and Robert Bales. 1955. *Family: Socialization and Interaction Process.* New York: Free Press.

Patai, Daphne. 1996. Heterophobia: The feminist turn against men. *Partisan Review* (Fall): 580–94.

———. 1998. The making of a social problem: Sexual harassment on campus. In Barry Dank and Roberto Refinetti, eds., *Sexual Harassment and Sexual Consent* (Sexuality and Culture, V.1) (219–236). New Brunswick, NJ: Transaction Publishers.

Patai, Daphne, and Noretta Koertge. 1994. *Professing Feminism: Cautionary Tales from the Strange World of Women's Studies.* New York: Basic Books.

Patton, Cindy. 1995. Refiguring social space. In Linda Nicholson and Steven Seidman, eds., *Social Postmodernism: Beyond Identity Politics* (216–249). Cambridge: Cambridge University Press.

Pettman, Jan Jindy. 1991. Racism, sexism and sociology. In Gill Bottomley, Marie de Lepervanche, and Jeannie Martin, eds., *Intersexions: Gender/Class/Culture/Ethnicity* (187–202). Sydney, St. Leonards NSW, Australia: Allen and Unwin.

———. 1996. *Worlding Women: A Feminist International Politics.* London, New York: Routledge.

Peyton, Andrew. 1998. The time bomb of day care. *Globe and Mail* (January 17): D6.

Pierson, Ruth Roach, Marjorie Griffin Cohen, Paula Bourne, and Philinda Masters, eds. 1993. *Canadian Women's Issues, Volume 1, Strong Voices.* Toronto: James Lorimer.

Pierson, Ruth Roach, and Marjorie Griffin Cohen, eds. 1995. *Canadian Women's Issues, Volume 2: Bold Visions.* Toronto: James Lorimer.

Pollack, Nancy. 1990. Meech, another dead lake: Exclusion and confusion. *Kinesis* (July/Aug.): 4.

———. 1993. Death of a thousand cuts. *Kinesis* (March): 3.

Pollert, Anna. 1996. Gender and class revisited: Or, the poverty of 'patriarchy'. *Sociology* 30(4): 639–659.

Porter, Marilyn. 1995. Call yourself a sociologist — and you've never even been arrested?! *Canadian Review of Sociology and Anthropology* 32(4): 415–438.

Probyn, Elspeth. 1996. *Outside Belongings*. London, New York: Routledge.

Puar, Jasbir K. 1996. Nicaraguan women and the politics of aid. In Haleh Afshar, ed., *Women and Politics in the Third World* (73–92). London, New York: Routledge.

Pulkingham, Jane, and Gordon Ternowetsky, eds. 1996. *Remaking Canadian Social Policy: Social Security in the Late 1990's*. Halifax: Fernwood.

Rancière, Jacques. 1992. Politics, identification and subjectivization. *October* 61 (Summer): 58–64.

——. 1995. *On the Shores of Politics*. New York, London: Verso.

Rand, Erica. 1995. *Barbie's Queer Accessories*. Durham, NC: Duke University Press.

Rathberger, Eva M. 1990. WID, WAD, GAD: Trends in research and practice. *Journal of Developing Areas* 24(4): 489–502.

Razack, Sherene. 1991. *Canadian Feminism and the Law: The Women's Legal Education and Action Fund and the Pursuit of Equality*. Toronto: Second Story Press.

REAL Women. 1995. Press Releases (August 28, September 11, September 13, September 15).

Rich, Adrienne. 1980. Compulsory heterosexuality and lesbian existence. *Signs* 5: 631–660.

Richardson, Diane, and Victoria Robinson. 1994. Theorizing women's studies, gender studies and masculinity: The politics of naming. *European Journal of Women's Studies* 1(1): 11–27.

Richer, Stephen, and Lorna Weir, eds. 1995. *Beyond Political Correctness*. Toronto: University of Toronto Press.

Riley, Denise. 1988. *Am I That Name? Feminism and the Category of 'Woman' in History*. Minneapolis: University of Minnesota Press.

Robertson, Roland, and Habib Haque Khondker. 1998. Discourses of globalization. *International Sociology* 13(1): 25–40.

Robinson, Victoria, and Diane Richardson. 1996. Repackaging women and feminism. In Diane Bell and Renate Klein, eds., *Radically Speaking: Feminism Reclaimed* (179–187). London: ZED Books.

Roiphe, Katie. 1993. *The Morning After: Sex, Fear and Feminism on Campus*. Boston: Little, Brown and Co.

Roseneil, Sasha. 1995. The coming of age of feminist sociology: Some issues of practice and theory for the next twenty years. *British Journal of Sociology* 46(2): 191–205.

Rowbotham, Sheila. 1981. The trouble with patriarchy. In Feminist Anthology Collective, eds., *No Turning Back: Writings from the Women's Liberation Movement* (72–78). London, Toronto: Women's Press.

Sabatini, E. (Rico) (with Sandra Nightengale). 1996. *Welfare — No Fair: A Critical Analysis of Ontario's Welfare System, 1985–1994*. Vancouver: The Fraser Institute.

Sangster, Joan. 1995. Beyond dichotomies: Re-assessing gender history and women's history in Canada. *left history* 3(1): 109–21.

Sawer, Marion. 1994. Reclaiming the state: Feminism, liberalism and social liberalism. *Australian Journal of Politics and History* 40: 159–72.

———. 1996. Gender, metaphor and the state. *Feminist Review* 52(Spring): 118–134.

Sayer, Derek. 1987. *The Violence of Abstraction*. Oxford: Basil Blackwell.

———. 1988. Karl Marx and the 'real world'. Paper presented at the Political Economy of the Margins Conference, Toronto, May, 1988.

———. 1991. *Capitalism and Modernity*. London, New York: Routledge.

Schaefer, Richard T., Robert P. Lamm, Penny Biles, and Susannah J. Wilson. 1996. *Sociology: An Introduction*. 1st Canadian edition. Toronto: McGraw-Hill.

Schmidt, Alvin J. 1997. *The Menace of Multiculturalism: Trojan Horse in America* Westport, CT: Praeger.

Scott, Joan W. 1988. *Gender and the Politics of History*. New York: Columbia University Press.

———. 1992. Multiculturalism and the politics of identity. *October* 61: 12–19.

Sedgwick, Eve Kosofsky. 1990. *Epistemology of the Closet*. Berkeley: University of California Press.

———. 1993. How to bring your kids up gay. In Michael Warner, ed., *Fear of a Queer Planet* (69–81). Minneapolis: University of Minnesota Press.

Seidman, Steven. 1994. Symposium: Queer theory/sociology: A dialogue. *Sociological Theory* 12(2): 166–177.

———. 1995. Deconstructing queer theory, or the undertheorizing of the social and ethical. In Linda Nicholson and Steven Seidman, eds., *Social Postmodernism* (116–141). Cambridge: Cambridge University Press.

———, ed. 1996. *Queer Theory/Sociology*. Oxford: Basil Blackwell.

———. 1997. *Difference Troubles: Queering Social Theory and Sexual Politics*. Cambridge: Cambridge University Press.

Shannon, Esther. 1994. Commentary on feminist journalism and *Kinesis*: Influences and inspiration. *Kinesis* (June): 18.

Shope, Janet Hinson. 1994. Separate but equal: Durkheim's response to the woman question. *Sociological Inquiry* 64(1): 23–36.

Siltanen, Janet. 1999. Connecting theory, research and policy: Issues with 'gender' in gender-based analysis. Paper presented at the Canadian Sociology and Anthropology Association Meetings, Bishop's University, Lennoxville, June 1999.

Sittirak, Sinith. 1998. *The Daughters of Development: Women in a Changing Environment*. London: ZED Books.

Smith, Dorothy. 1974. Women's perspective as a radical critique of sociology. *Sociological Inquiry* 44: 7–13.

———. 1987. *The Everyday World as Problematic.* Toronto: University of Toronto Press.

———. 1990. *The Conceptual Practices of Power.* Toronto: University of Toronto Press.

———. 1992. Remaking a life, remaking a sociology: Reflections of a feminist. In W. Carroll, L. Christiansen-Ruffman, R. Curries, and D. Harrison, eds., *Fragile Truths: Twenty-five Years of Sociology and Anthropology in Canada* (125–134). Ottawa: Carleton University Press.

———. 1997. Textual repressions: Hazards for feminists in the academy. *Canadian Journal of Women and the Law* 9(2): 269–300.

Smith, Laura C. 1996. Crocker VIII: Bakin' Betty gets her eighth facelift. *PEOPLE Daily*, Thursday, March 21 (http://www.pathfinder.com/people/daily/96back/960321.html#8).

Solanki, Gopika. 1998. Development in whose interest? An analysis of state rhetoric, development myths, and feminist challenges. Paper presented at the RC-32 Precongress of the International Sociological Association, Ste. Anne de Bellevue, Quebec, July 21–26.

Sommers, Christina Hoff. 1994. *Who Stole Feminism? How Women Have Betrayed Women.* New York: Simon and Schuster.

Spelman, Elizabeth. 1988. *Inessential Woman: Problems of Exclusion in Feminist Thought.* Boston: Beacon Press.

Spender, Dale. 1982. *Women of Ideas and What Men Have Done to Them.* London: Routledge.

Stacey, Judith, and Barrie Thorne. 1985. The missing feminist revolution in sociology. *Social Problems* 32(4): 301–316.

Stanley, Liz. 1997. Introduction: On academic borders, territories, tribes and knowledges. In Liz Stanley, ed., *Knowing Feminisms* (1–17). Thousand Oaks, CA: Sage.

Stanley, Liz, and Sue Wise. 1990. Method, methodology and epistemology in feminist research processes. In *Feminist Praxis* (20–60). London, New York: Routledge.

Stasiulis, Daiva K. 1990. Theorizing connections: Gender, race, ethnicity and class. In Peter S. Li, ed., *Race and Ethnic Relations in Canada* (269–305). Toronto: Oxford University Press.

Stasiulis, Daiva, and Radha Jhappan. 1995. The fractious politics of a settler society: Canada. In Daiva Stasiulis and Nira Yuval-Davis, eds., *Unsettling Settler Societies: Articulations of Gender, Race, Ethnicity and Class* (95–131). Thousand Oaks, CA: Sage.

Stasiulis, Daiva, and Nira Yuval-Davis, eds. 1995. *Unsettling Settler Societies: Articulations of Gender, Race, Ethnicity and Class.* Thousand Oaks, CA: Sage.

Status of Women Canada. 1995. *Setting the Stage for the Next Century: The Federal Plan for Gender Equality.* Ottawa: Status of Women Canada.

———. 1996. *Gender-based Analysis: A Guide for Policy Making.* Ottawa: Status of Women Canada.

Steuter, Erin. 1992. Women against feminism: An examination of feminist social movements and anti-feminist counter-movements. *Canadian Review of Sociology and Anthropology* 29(3): 288–306.

Stienstra, Deborah. 1996. From Mexico to Beijing: International commitments on women. *Canadian Woman Studies* 16(3): 14–17.

Stoller, Robert. 1968. *Sex and Gender: The Development of Masculinity and Feminity* (vol. 1). New York: Science House.

Sydie, R.A. 1987. *Natural Women, Cultured Men: A Feminist Perspective on Sociological Theory*. Toronto: Methuen.

——. 1994. Sex and the sociological fathers. *Canadian Review of Sociology and Anthropology* 31(2): 117–138.

Sylvester, Christine. 1994. *Feminist Theory and International Relations in a Postmodern Era*. Cambridge: Cambridge University Press.

Tafler, Lou. 1994. *Fair New World*. Vancouver: Backlash Books.

Tannen, Deborah. 1990. *You Just Don't Understand: Women and Men in Conversation*. New York: William Morrow and Company.

Taylor, Barbara. 1983. *Eve and the New Jerusalem: Socialism and Feminism in the 19th Century*. New York: Pantheon.

Thobani, Sunera. 1991. Racism: The illusion of 'unlearning'. *Kinesis* (April): 6–7.

——. 1993. The new immigration act. *Kinesis* (March): 12–13.

Thompson, E.P. 1969. *The Making of the English Working Class*. London: Penguin.

Thompson, Kenneth. 1996. *Key Quotations in Sociology*. London, New York: Routledge.

Thorsell, William. 1998. In support of the two-parent family. *The Globe and Mail* (January 17): D6.

Touraine, Alain. 1985. An introduction to the study of new social movements. *Social Research* 52, 749–88.

Trend, David, ed. 1996. *Radical Democracy: Identity, Citizenship and the State*. New York: Routledge.

Trimble, Linda. 1998. "Good enough citizens": Canadian women and representation in constitutional deliberations. *International Journal of Canadian Studies* 17(Spring): 131–56.

Unger, Rhoda. 1998. *Resisting Gender: Twenty-five Years of Feminist Psychology*. Thousand Oaks, CA: Sage.

United Nations. 1995a. Report of the informal contact group on gender, 7 July 1995. New York: United Nations.

——. 1995b. Platform for Action. Adopted at the World Conference on Women, Beijing, China, September 1995.

——. 1995c. Beijing Declaration. Adopted at the World Conference on Women, Beijing, China, September 1995.

Upstream Collective. 1980. Upstream says goodbye. *Resources for Feminist Research* 9(3): 8–9.

Valverde, Marianna. 1990. Poststructuralist gender historians: Are we those names? *Labour/Le Travail* 25: 227–236.

Vancouver Status of Women Council. 1974. Notes on the organization of the Vancouver Status of Women Council (pamphlet).

Van Vucht Tijssen, Lieteke. 1991. Women and objective culture: Georg Simmel and Marianne Weber. *Theory, Culture and Society* 8: 203–218.

Vickers, Jill. 1993. The Canadian women's movement and a changing constitutional order. *International Journal of Canadian Studies* 7/8: 261–284.

———. 1994. Notes toward a political theory of sex and power. In H. Lorraine Radtke and Hederikus J. Stam, eds., *Power/Gender: Social Relations in Theory and Practice* (174–193). Thousand Oaks, CA: Sage.

———. 1996. Difficult choices: The knowledge strategies of feminist social science and the knowledge needs of women's movements. In Uma Parameswaran, ed., *Quilting a New Canon* (221–240). Toronto: Sister Vision Press.

Vickers, Jill, Pauline Rankin, and Christine Appelle. 1993. *Politics as if Women Mattered: A Political Analysis of the National Action Committee on the Status of Women.* Toronto: University of Toronto Press.

Walby, Sylvia. 1990. *Theorizing Patriarchy.* Oxford: Blackwell.

———. 1992. Post-post-modernism? Theorizing social complexity. In Michele Barrett and Anne Phillips, eds., *Destabilizing Theory: Contemporary Feminist Debates* (31–52). Palo Alto, CA: Stanford University Press.

———. 1997. *Gender Transformations.* London, New York: Routledge.

Watson, Peggy. 1993. Eastern Europe's silent revolution: Gender. *Sociology* 27(3): 471–487.

———. 1997. (Anti)feminism after communism. In Ann Oakley and Juliet Mitchell, eds., *Who's Afraid of Feminism* (144–161). London: Hamish Hamilton.

Waylen, Georgina. 1996. Analysing women in the politics of the Third World. In Haleh Afshar, ed., *Women and Politics in the Third World* (7–24). London, New York: Routledge.

Weber, Max. 1919/1946. Science as a vocation. In Hans Gerth and C. Wright Mills, eds., *From Max Weber* (129–156). New York: Oxford University Press.

Weeks, Jeffrey. 1995. *Invented Moralities: Sexual Values in an Age of Uncertainty.* New York: Columbia University Press.

Weir, Lorna. 1987. Women and the state: A conference for feminist activists. *Feminist Review* 26: 93–103.

Wente, Margaret. 1997. Onward Promise Keepers? *Globe and Mail* (October 4): D7.

Wilkinson, Sue, and Celia Kitzinger. 1996. The queer backlash. In Diane Bell and Renate Klein, eds., *Radically Speaking: Feminism Reclaimed* (375–382). London: ZED Books.

Williams, Jeffrey, ed. 1995. *PC Wars: Politics and Theory in the Academy.* London, New York: Routledge.

Williams, Patricia J. 1991. *The Alchemy of Race and Rights.* Cambridge, MA: Harvard University Press.

Williams, Raymond. 1983. *Keywords: A Vocabulary of Culture and Society.* London: Fontana Press.

Wilson, John K. 1995. *The Myth of Political Correctness.* Durham, NC: Duke University Press.

Wine, Jeri. 1989. A fond farewell to Broadside. *The Womanist* (May/June): 8.

Wine, Jeri Dawn, and Janice L. Ristock, eds. 1991. *Women and Social Change: Feminist Activism in Canada.* Toronto: James Lorimer.

Wittgenstein, Ludwig. 1946/1980. *Culture and Value,* ed. G.H. von Wright, trans. P. Winch. Chicago: University of Chicago Press.

Wobbe, Teresa. 1998. Elective affinities: Georg Simmel and Marianne Weber on differentiation and individuation. Paper presented at the World Congress of Sociology (RC08), Montreal, July 1998.

Wollstonecraft, Mary. 1792/1997. *A Vindication of the Rights of Men and A Vindication of the Rights of Women,* eds. D.L. Macdonald and Kathleen Scherf. Peterborough: Broadview Press.

Woo, Virginia, Jeanne d'Arc, Maria N. Penn, and Clara. 1998. The struggle for women-only space: Women's organizations and the BC Human Rights Code. *Kinesis* (March): 15–16.

Woodard, Joe. 1995. A fembo agenda for gender bending. *Alberta Report* (September 11): 34–37.

Yeatman, Anna. 1986. Women, domestic life and sociology. In C. Pateman and E. Gross, eds., *Feminist Challenges: Social and Political Theory* (157–172). Sydney: Allen and Unwin.

———. 1993. Voice and representation in the politics of difference. In Sneja Gunew and Anna Yeatman, eds., *Feminism and the Politics of Difference* (228–245). Halifax: Fernwood.

Young, Iris Marion. 1994. Gender as seriality: Thinking about women as a social collective. *Signs* 19(3): 713–738.

Young, Kate. 1997. Gender and development. In N. Visvanathan, L. Duggan, L. Nisonoff, and N. Wiegersma, eds., *The Women, Gender and Development Reader* (51–54). Halifax: Fernwood.

Young, Stacey. 1997. *Changing the Wor(l)d: Discourse, Politics and the Feminist Movement.* London: Routledge.

Yuval-Davis, Nira. 1997. *Gender and Nation.* Thousand Oaks, CA: Sage.

Zeitlin, Irving. 1997. *Ideology and the Development of Sociological Theory.* 6th edition. Englewood Cliffs, NJ: Prentice-Hall.

Zlotnik, Hania. 1990. International migration policies and the status of women. *International Migration Review* 24(2): 372–81.

Zyla, Melana. 1998. Hacking away at family life. *The Globe and Mail* (January 16): A14.

Index